Developmental Regulation in Adulthood

Age-Normative and Sociostructural Constraints as Adaptive Challenges

Human behavior is very flexible, and ontogenetic potential adds to the scope of variability of developmental paths. Therefore, development in the life course needs to be regulated. Developmental regulation by the individual is scaffolded by external constraints. External constraints to development based on biological aging, institutional age grading, and internalized age norms provide an age-graded agenda for striving for developmental growth and avoiding developmental decline.

The life-span theory of control proposes that control of one's environment is the key to adaptive functioning throughout the life span. The theory identifies the evolutionary roots and the life-span developmental course of human striving to control the environment (primary control) and the self (secondary control). Primary control is directed at producing effects in the external world, while secondary control influences the internal world so as to optimize the motivational resources for primary control. A series of studies illustrate the rich repertoire of the human control system that exists to master developmental challenges in various age periods and developmental ecologies.

Jutta Heckhausen is senior research scientist at the Center for Lifespan Psychology, Max Planck Institute for Human Development. Since 1991, she has been an associate member of the MacArthur Foundation Research Network on Successful Mid-Life Development and, from 1995 to 1996, was a Fellow at the Center for Advanced Study in the Behavioral Sciences at Stanford University. She is coeditor, with Carol Dweck, of *Motivation and Self-Regulation across the Life Span*.

Developmental Regulation in Adulthood

Age-Normative and Sociostructural Constraints as Adaptive Challenges

JUTTA HECKHAUSEN

CAMBRIDGE
UNIVERSITY PRESS

PUBLISHED BY THE PRESS SYNDICATE OF THE UNIVERSITY OF CAMBRIDGE
The Pitt Building, Trumpington Street, Cambridge CB2 1RP, United Kingdom

CAMBRIDGE UNIVERSITY PRESS
The Edinburgh Building, Cambridge CB2 2RU, UK   http://www.cup.cam.ac.uk
40 West 20th Street, New York, NY 10011-4211, USA   http://www.cup.org
10 Stamford Road, Oakleigh, Melbourne 3166, Australia

First published 1999

Printed in the United States of America

Typeset in New Baskerville 10/12 pt, in Penta [RF]

A catalog record for this book is available from the British Library.

Library of Congress Cataloging-in-Publication Data
Heckhausen, Jutta (date)
Developmental regulation in adulthood : age-normative and
sociostructural constraints as adaptive challenges / Jutta
Heckhausen.
p. cm.
Includes bibliographical references and indexes.
ISBN 0-521-58144-3
1. Developmental psychology.   2. Control (Psychology).   3. Self-
control.   I. Title.
BF713.H46   1998
155 – dc21   98-6509
                                                          CIP

ISBN 0 521 58144 3 hardback

Contents

v

Acknowledgments

The theoretical and empirical work presented in this book was conducted in the most conducive context for research in life-span development, which Paul B. Baltes and his colleagues have created at the Max Planck Institute for Human Development in Berlin. The Center for Lifespan Psychology at the institute provided an intellectually rich and most stimulating ecology for a scientist to develop a research program. This includes the unique opportunity to debate and collaborate with the life-course sociologists at the Center for Sociology and the Study of the Life Course. The interdisciplinary discussions and joint empirical work with Karl Ulrich Mayer, Johannes Huinink, and Martin Diewald were a great enrichment to my research. For all this I thank my colleagues at the Max Planck Institute, and Paul B. Baltes in particular for his support and constructive criticism throughout the various stages of this research program.

Over the years the research discussed in this book involved the following colleagues, listed in chronological sequence: Paul B. Baltes, Jacqui Smith, Roger A. Dixon, Joachim Krueger, and William W. Fleeson. Advice for data analyses was given by Steven W. Cornelius, John R. Nesselroade, Bernhard Schmitz, Christiane Spiel, and Todd D. Little. The constant assistance of the following undergraduate and graduate students provided invaluable day-to-day support for the empirical studies: Bettina Hosenfeld, Jutta Hundertmark, Birgit Grabow, and Carsten Wrosch. Moreover, subject recruiting and data collection would not have been possible without the persistence and ingenuity of the following research assistants: Anita Günther, Peter Usinger, Anette Baumeister, Gaby Faust, and Annette Rentz. Finally, Ulrich Knappek and the staff at the central secretariat of the institute contributed their great secretarial and Anne Tschida her invaluable editorial expertise in completing this work. After the manuscript was submitted, two reviewers provided most thoughtful critiques and suggestions that have greatly helped me to improve the book.

The unique institutional context at the Max Planck Institute also facilitated important collaborations that reached beyond the institute. The involvement as an associate member of the MacArthur Foundation Research Network on Successful Midlife Development (director: Gilbert O. Brim) promoted interdisciplinary discourse and furnished a study on self- and other-related conceptions about midlife, which was jointly conducted with Gilbert O. Brim. A year as a Fellow at the Center for Advanced Study in the Behavioral Sciences, Stanford (John D. and Catherine T. MacArthur Foundation, grant No. 8900078) and its most conducive intellectual climate have greatly facilitated the revision of the book manuscript.

The development of this research program has immensely benefited from the collaboration with Richard Schulz (University of Pittsburgh). Over the years, Rich Schulz and I have developed a life-span theoretical conception of control-related behavior, which has already proven fruitful for interpreting empirical findings across various areas of research, and holds, as we believe, the potential to stimulate manifold empirical inquiries in the future. We are told that congenial intellectual collaboration in the social sciences is a rare event, and we continue to be amazed at how well we get on, and on to new things.

Tables and Figures

ix

Introduction

In this introductory section the conceptual rationale and structure of this book is laid out. First, it seems important to mention that the sequential structure of chapters follows a conceptual logic rather than the chronology of events. Some of the empirical work was conducted before or concurrently with the development of the life-span theory of control (J. Heckhausen & Schulz 1995) and its specification for phenomena of developmental regulation (J. Heckhausen & Schulz 1993a; Schulz & J. Heckhausen 1996). This means that the nine empirical studies presented in Chapters 2, 6, and 7 do *not* represent empirical tests of the theory in a strict sense. Instead, they serve to illustrate the usefulness and scope of the theory and provide the groundwork for future research. In my report of significant empirical results, I have made an effort to convey the gist of the findings rather than burden the reader with technical and statistical details. Readers interested in a more detailed account of specific studies are referred to the relevant journal publications (see References).

This book is about developmental regulation in adulthood. The regulation of development in the human life course is anything but a trivial matter. The human species is endowed with extensive behavioral flexibility and immense ontogenetic potential. Thus, to make life-span developmental change predictable and manageable both for the individual and the social community, regulation is required. Developmental regulation is achieved jointly by external constraints and the efforts of individuals. The external constraints are both biological (maturation, aging) and societal (age-graded institutions, age norms). This book focuses on the adaptive role external constraints play in scaffolding individual efforts to regulate their own development.

The basic proposition underlying the theory that is developed, discussed, and empirically investigated in this monograph is that individuals profit from, and are challenged by, external constraints to their developmental potential, including biological, sociostructural, and age-normative boundary conditions. These external constraints provide a scaffold for the individual in that they greatly reduce the vast complexity of potential options in human behavior and ontogenetic change. Moreover, these life-course constraints provide the individual with an age-graded agenda for striving for developmental growth and avoiding developmental decline.

The key proposition of the life-span theory of control is that individuals endeavor to control their environment throughout their life span. In doing this they adjust their behavior to changing developmental ecologies so as to optimize their potential to exert control. In other words, prompted and assisted by the external constraints to development across the life span, the individual strives to attain optimal levels of control of his/her environment throughout life.

This striving inherently involves experiences of failure and defeat, which may endanger the individual's essential motivational resources; they therefore need to be compensated for. Such experiences of failure and loss can come about as inevitable by-products of ambitious striving, as a consequence of biological aging, or as unfortunate twists of fate (non-normative events). In any event, experiences of failure and loss may undermine the individual's self-esteem, hopefulness for future success, and thus his/her motivational resources for future action. Compensatory strategies to protect internal motivational resources are therefore indispensable instruments of developmental regulation. Such compensatory control strategies can take various forms – for instance, self-protective attributions ("It was not my fault but tough luck"), downward social comparisons ("Others are much worse off than I"), or goal disengagement ("This was not the right thing for me anyway"). These internally directed compensatory strategies often are supported by external constraints, in that sociostructural or age-normative constraints help to adjust frames of reference for self-evaluation (e.g., in social comparisons, age-normative conceptions about aging-related loss).

In the first chapter, the fundamental requirements of human behavior are discussed, as they provide the basic challenges to be managed by individuals' developmental regulation. Two fundamental requirements result from the lack of predetermination and the enormous variability of human behavior: selectivity in resource investment and failure compensation. The extensive behavioral and developmental options require the individual to select appropriate goals for action and, once a choice has been made, to focus his/her resource investment on the chosen goal. With regard to failure compensation, the individual needs to protect his/her own motivational resources against the negative effects of experienced failures. Both requirements of human functioning become even more essential in the context of ontogenetic change across the life span.

The second chapter examines the life course as a context of an individual's actions directed at regulating his/her own development. Compared to other species, the human ontogenetic potential is immense. The human life span is extensive, comprising a long period of maturation and growth that overlaps with a long period of aging and decline. The long life span, along with the great flexibility and variability in developmental patterns, brings about a continuous dynamic of developmental gains and losses throughout the entire life span. However, this dynamic is not unstructured and unpredictable, although it is open to individual variation and intraindividual plasticity. Rather, the life course is composed of an age-graded structure of constraints provided by biological maturation and aging, social structure, and age-normative conceptions about life transitions and developmental change. These age-graded constraints not only restrict the scope of individual life courses but also scaffold developmental regulation across the life span. Age-normative conceptions about life-course transitions and developmental change are widely shared in a given society because they allow assessment and evaluation of the self and of other people, and thereby guide action directed at development.

A life-span theory of control is introduced in the third chapter. This theory distinguishes functionally different types of control-related behavior, primary and secondary control striving (J. Heckhausen & Schulz 1995). Primary control striving refers to behaviors directed at the external environment and involves attempts to change the world to fit the needs and desires of the individual. Secondary control striving is targeted at internal processes and serves to minimize losses in, maintain, and expand existing levels of primary control. The life-span theory of control proposes a functional primacy of primary control as a universal characteristic of human behavior. Both primary and secondary control striving ultimately serve the purpose of maximizing the individual's control over the environment. Across the life span, the potential for primary control follows an inverted U-shaped curve, with rapid increases in childhood and adolescence, a plateau in midlife, and a steady decline in old age. Accordingly, the individual needs to adjust his/her control behavior to optimize primary control across changes in control potential. This involves the need to compensate for the negative effects of aging-related losses on motivational and emotional resources. Therefore, we expect an increased employment of secondary control strategies in the second half of the life span, when primary control potential gradually wanes. Such compensatory investments in secondary control can be expected whenever primary control potential is irretrievably lost, be it due to aging-related decline, non-normative events (e.g., accidents, illnesses), or uncontrollable socioeconomic crises. The effectiveness of primary and secondary control strategies to manage challenges of control is most likely high but probably also has its limits, when in situations of excessive and irretrievable loss of control the control system collapses and the individual is exposed to emotional despair.

Chapter 4 integrates the first three chapters to construct a life-span model of developmental regulation. The model specifies how different kinds of primary and secondary control strategies are used to manage the two fundamental requirements of human behavior: selection and compensation. Four control strategies are specified: selective primary control, selective secondary control, compensatory primary control, and compensatory secondary control. These four control strategies need to be employed in a manner that reflects the specific requirements of the respective developmental ecology. For instance, investments in futile goals as well as premature disengagements from primary control must be avoided. Therefore, a higher-order regulatory process is required to orchestrate the various control strategies. Based on a discussion of criteria of adaptiveness, the functional requirements for such a higher-order process of optimization are identified. In this context, the adaptive role of external constraints to development becomes salient again, as they reduce the regulatory load on the individual's developmental optimization.

Chapter 5 discusses developmental goals as basic action units in developmental regulation. Developmental goals provide an organizing framework with an intermediate time range for the individual to structure his/her developmental regulation. The age-graded structure of opportunities and constraints across the life span provides a timetable for the pursuit of developmental goals and also sets final deadlines for the attainment of developmental goals (e.g., biological clock for maternity). When integrating modern action theory with the life-span theory of control and the concept of age-graded constraints, fruitful research paradigms – with regard to developmental deadlines, for instance – can be derived. Modern action theory ("Rubicon model of action phases," H. Heckhausen 1991) differentiates between predecisional (motivational) and postdecisional (volitional) processing, and thus allows for highly specific predictions about modes of processing in different action phases. In an analogous fashion, one can differentiate between predeadline and postdeadline processing and predict a radical shift from predeadline selective primary and secondary control to compensatory secondary control after passing the deadline without goal attainment.

Chapter 6 addresses developmental regulation in different life-course ecologies. Two developmental challenges with partly contrasting functional characteristics are juxtaposed both conceptually and empirically: aging-related decline and radical sociohistorical transformation in East Germany. Two empirical studies show how individuals adjusted their control strategies to different developmental ecologies. Primary control striving is typically directed at goals that fit the opportunities and constraints encountered at a given age period. Compensatory secondary control becomes more important at higher ages. The investigation of age/birth cohort differences in East German adults uncovered different patterns of control strategies that reflect the primary control potential available to the different cohorts. The study of East German cohorts also revealed limits of the control system, when, as is the case for one middle-aged cohort, primary control potential was severely constrained and at the same time disengagement from the respective primary control goals was impossible because of life-span timing (premature disengagement from occupational goals). Thus, the findings of the two studies reported in this chapter illustrate the substantial power and flexibility of individuals' developmental regulation, but they also indicate its limits under conditions of severe restrictions of control.

Chapter 7 focuses on social comparisons as prototypical strategies in developmental regulation. The individual can use upward, lateral, and downward social comparisons as models in striving for developmental goals, assessing his/her own developmental status and compensating for experienced developmental losses respectively. Two empirical studies show the adaptive function of age-normative conceptions as constraining frames of reference for social comparisons. In the first study, age-normative conceptions about developmental change in the generalized other ("most other people") appear to reflect the need of older individuals to compare favorably to age peers and thereby compensate for experienced losses. In the second study, social downgrading with regard to perceptions about problems in various life domains is identified in all age groups, but it is particularly pronounced as a response to personally experienced problems in older adults. A third study demonstrates that social comparisons with specific real or imagined persons are used commonly and regularly in everyday life. Social comparisons reflect the availability of social comparison targets and are adapted to the specific needs for control modeling or control-loss compensation.

Chapter 8 reviews the theory and empirical research presented in Chapters 1 through 7. In addition, prospects for future research on developmental regulation, its sociocultual variations, and evolutionary origins are discussed.

1 Selectivity and Failure Compensation as Fundamental Requirements of Human Behavior and Development

This chapter addresses the basic question of why regulation of behavior and development is needed. What are the fundamental challenges or problems that require regulatory processes? What obstacles does the individual have to overcome in order to organize his or her behavior? These questions lead to two key requirements of regulation, the management of selectivity and of compensation for failure or loss. Further chapters will consider the means by which the individual contributes to fulfilling these requirements (Chapter 3), especially in terms of regulating life-span development (Chapters 4 through 8) and the biological and societal mechanisms (Chapter 2) that constrain, support, and scaffold developmental regulation. In this first chapter, selectivity and failure/loss compensation are discussed as fundamental characteristics of any human behavior and of developmental regulation in particular (P. Baltes 1987; P. Baltes & M. Baltes 1990; J. Heckhausen & Schulz 1993a, 1995; Marsiske et al. 1995). Selectivity refers to the selection of goals and the focused investment of resources into goal attainment. An example is the selection of a field of study by a student and the subsequent investment of time, effort, and interest in this field. Compensation of failure and loss refers to efforts of an individual to make amends for the negative consequences of failing to attain a selected goal and of other circumstantial losses (e.g., losing a spouse). An example is the college student who views a subject in which he failed as unattractive ("sour grapes," Elster, 1983).

Selectivity and proneness to failure as basic challenges both result from the extensive variability and flexibility of human behavior. Other nonprimate species are far more programmed in terms of their repertoire of activities and behavioral responses to the environment, with more instinct-driven behavior and substantially more constrained behavioral options. Humans, in contrast, have evolved with the ability to adapt flexibly to a great range of environmental conditions, and in particular with the ability to generate new systems of behavior. Piaget

7

(1967) conceptualizes this process as a breakage of the instinct (German: "Zerbrechen des Instinktes"), by which genetic programs of behavior are demolished and give way to more flexible regulations of behavior and mental processes. The combination of genetic and environmental factors can thus generate an immense, albeit not infinite, universe of potential developmental pathways (Ford & Lerner 1992). This variability in behavior and development is as much a product of evolution as the more narrowly constrained behavioral systems of other species (e.g., Wilson 1980). However, the relative dearth of biologically based predetermination of behavior gives rise to a high regulatory requirement on the part of the human individual and the social system. The social and cultural system and the individual have to regulate behavior so that resources are invested in an organized and focused way, and that failure experiences lead to an improvement rather than to a deterioriation of behavioral means. It is this requirement for regulation that sets the stage for the phenomena addressed in this book.

A similar line of argument is also fundamental in theories of sociological anthropology (Berger & Luckmann 1966; Claessens, 1968; Gehlen 1958; see reviews in Esser 1993; Huinink 1993). The relatively weak biologically based predetermination in human behavior, according to this scientific tradition, constitutes fundamental anthropological universals. For Gehlen (1958) humans are "Mängelwesen" (flawed or impoverished beings) because they are phylogenetically not adapted to certain environmental conditions and because they are extremely helpless, exposed, and in need of support during their early but extended ontogenetic stages as infants, children, and adolescents. However, this insufficiency provides the basis for an openness to the world ("Weltoffenheit"), an ability to act, and a readiness to develop. At the same time, the relative lack of behavioral determination calls for a social equivalent or substitute to provide a scaffold for generating and reassuring an individual's behavior. The human species is therefore dependent on social institutions for behavioral regulation.

Claessens (1968) emphasizes the adaptive implications of the relative dearth of biological determination in human behavior. Humans have the ability to reflect, and thereby grasp, the environment without always having actually to physically engage it. In this process, language and culture become second-order tools that lend structure to the world and thereby substitute for the instinctual security of behavior. Moreover, being part of a social group releases some of the continuous pressure to adapt to environmental conditions. This way, the security of instincts is replaced by the approval of the group, and thus external social certainty furnishes internal individual certainty. Berger and Luckmann

(1966) built on these theoretical assumptions about anthropological universals and developed a sociology of knowledge that is most relevant for a theory of developmental regulation. Their sociology of knowledge will be discussed further in Chapter 2.

More recently, biologists and social scientists of the life span have argued that evolution has selectively optimized the prereproductive phase of the life span while posing little selective pressures for adaptive development in postreproductive ages (P. Baltes & Graf 1996; P. Baltes, Lindenberger, & Staudinger, 1998; Finch 1990). With increasing age, and particularly after the reproductive phase of adulthood, the evolutionary selection pressure weakens, allowing for dysfunctional characteristics in older individuals (e.g., senile dementia of the Alzheimer type), which would have been selected against in younger, reproducing adults. Paul B. Baltes and his colleagues (P. Baltes, Lindenberger, & Staudinger, 1998) have argued that, because evolutionary selection benefits decrease with age, this disadvantage needs to be balanced by a favorable endowment with cultural and social benefits. However, the culture of old age in our current societies is undeveloped and our social systems still deprive older adults of meaningful social roles (P. Baltes & Graf 1996). Thus, given the relative dearth of cultural compensation for the evolutionary disadvantages of old age, one could argue that the individual is called upon to take on the regulatory load of aging-related decline.

Selectivity

The great potential of human behavior variability, plasticity, and adaptivity is a cornerstone of life-span developmental theories (P. Baltes 1987; P. Baltes, Lindenberger, & Staudinger, 1998; Ford & Lerner 1992; Lerner 1989). Variability and a high degree of freedom of behavioral choice are, of course, great advantages in terms of adaptive potential to multiple contexts and challenges varying both interindividually and – in a developmental context even more importantly – intraindividually. This way the individual can make use of particularly favorable opportunities – for instance, in an elaborate educational system – or avoid the disadvantage of unfavorable conditions. Moreover, developmental paths, once chosen, do not set the individual in plaster, but allow for later modification, as for instance in career changes and retraining.

However, high variability and lack of constraints also raise the problem of behavioral selection. The organism can hardly rely on biologically based mechanisms for choosing appropriate behavior and remaining focused on that behavior. Instead, regulatory mechanisms on the level of society and/or on the level of the individual need to exist to guide the choice and the focused investment in the chosen behavior. Such mechanisms may be conscious-intentional or strategic, as in choosing to learn to play golf rather than tennis. They can also be automatized-unintentional, as, for example, when individuals raise their aspiration levels because the already attained levels fail to satisfy their striving for mastery. Attempting more difficult tasks and thereby improving performance is probably particularly adaptive in the long run, but it is the short-term need to feel proud and efficacious that drives behavior rather than long-term strategic considerations. Thus, behavioral modules, such as striving for mastery, guide behavior that is ultimately conducive to long-term maximization of resources and survival in general. Such modules may have been selected for in the process of human evolution in much the same way that selective caretaking for offspring and non-kin homicide as a proximal mechanism has promoted inclusive fitness as a distal goal (e.g., Wilson 1980). The role of proximal and distal mechanisms in developmental regulation will be discussed further in Chapter 4.

The necessity of behavioral selection involves two aspects: the need for choice and the need for focused investment of resources. Both aspects are essential prerequisites of adaptive behavior under conditions of numerous behavioral options. Success cannot be achieved when the individual has not selected a goal to strive for and a course of action upon which to focus his/her behavioral and motivational resources. First, the need for *choice* implies that the individual selects one behavioral option out of a range of possible options. Choices involve evaluations of goals and consequences as well as expectancies about feasibility and consequences of goal attainment. An example is a student facing the decision about what to major in, psychology or law. In making this decision, the student should take into account, for instance, the availability of graduate programs in psychology and law and the future employment prospects in each of these fields. In Chapter 4, the regulatory strategy of optimization will be discussed as fulfilling the function of guiding adaptive choices of goals.

Second, the need for *focused resource investment* refers to the fact that a behavioral choice can be successfully implemented only by focusing resources on the chosen activity. Resources encompass both strictly behavioral means, such as reaching for a desired object or persisting in a chosen action over a prolonged period of time, and motivational means, such as self-esteem, generalized optimism, expectancy of success, commitment, and the blocking out of alternative options. In terms of the example of the student: Once she has made the decision to study law, she should dedicate her time and effort to doing so as well as thinking enthusiastically about becoming a lawyer (e.g., to make a high income) while downgrading the previously considered alternative to study psychology (e.g., gloomy job prospects).

The two aspects of behavioral selection, choice and focused investment, might appear similar, but in fact address two very different phenomena. In Chapter 4, this will lead to the conceptualization of two processes in developmental regulation, optimization (choice) and selection (focused resource investment). In terms of motivational psychology, the conceptual distinction between choice and focused resource investment converges with the difference between selection and realization (Kuhl 1983, 1984) or, more recently, motivation and volition (H. Heckhausen 1991; H. Heckhausen & Kuhl 1985). During the motivational phase of action, the individual selects a goal, whereas during the volitional phase, the individual actively focuses her commitment on the chosen goal.

The need for selectivity is rendered even more salient when we also consider the dimension of ontogenetic change potential. Across the life span human behavioral variability results in a great diversity of life-course developmental tracks. People become butchers, generals, steelworkers, professors, or doctors; they marry or stay single, have children or not, divorce and remarry; develop conservative, liberal, or radical political views, and so on. Over the course of life, such developmental paths bear out multiple and, with time, increasing consequences. Thus, the long-term effects of choosing a particular life-course option are amplified with passing life time. For one thing, alternative paths move more and more out of reach as the individual exclusively invests resources in promoting the chosen life path. In the case of the law student above, once she has come of age as a lawyer, the opportunities to switch over to psychology will have dwindled away. Switching paths farther along the way will involve excessive costs in terms of lost investments. In addition, the scarce and precious resource of lifetime itself is being used up and can no longer be invested in alternative developmental options. This holds particularly true for long-term goals such as professional careers and family building, which consume an entire lifetime, and therefore are, at least in the given domain of functioning, an exclusive enterprise. Thus, selection of a particular life path also implies the foreshortening of future prospects for alternative options.

In consequence, making the right choices and selecting the most appropriate life path is essential for adaptive developmental regulation. This is emphasized in Baltes and Baltes's model of life-span developmental psychology (M. Baltes 1987; P. Baltes 1987; P. Baltes & M. Baltes

1980, 1990; Marsiske et al., 1995), along with the notion that the selection-based dynamic between gains and losses intensifies as lifetime passes.

It is important to note that the individual faces such fundamental choices for certain life-course developmental pathways infrequently and only at certain critical junctures (Geulen, 1981), such as when choosing an occupation or making a commitment to a long-term relationship. It is characteristic even for human developmental regulation that biological and sociostructural constraints reduce the number of such choice situations. Deciding to have a child is biologically feasible only during two or at maximum three decades of life; and entry in the labor market requires a certain age as well as basic education. In addition, options further along in life-course paths are typically contingent upon the individual having met a sequence of institutionalized and normative requirements. For example, it only makes sense to strive for promotion to a full professorship when one has fulfilled the career steps of undergraduate study, graduation, and the tenure track to associate professorship.

In this context, the notion of "constrained pathways" (i.e., "chreods," in Waddington's terminology; J. Heckhausen & Schulz, 1993a) in an "epigenetic landscape" (Waddington 1957) becomes relevant. It will be discussed in greater detail in regard to the selectivity aspect of focused resource investment. Suffice it to say that the epigenetic landscape model implies (among other things) that only a few developmental pathways are available, so that any set of initial states, however different they are, will lead to a very restricted set of discrete developmental outcomes.

The conditions which render life-course choices particularly consequential also bring about a need for remaining *focused* on one's investment of behavioral and motivational resources once a decision has been taken. What appears to be important for adaptive development is to make reasonably selective investments in one contingent life-course path for a given domain. Thus, it makes sense to go to school, do an apprenticeship, and then work in the respective occupation; but it is wasteful of lifetime and other resources to shift between occupational careers repeatedly. What is reasonable and can be seen as contingent is, of course, a function of the social system in which these life paths occur.

Restricted lifetime and a mounting gains–losses dynamic with increasing age prohibit diverse investments within an individual's life course.[1]

---

[1] The fact that exceptions to this general principle, such as radical career changes, receive so much public attention illustrates the validity of this assumption.

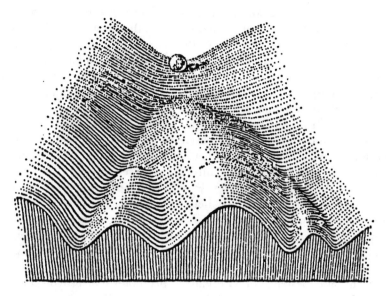

Figure 1.1. Part of an Epigenetic Landscape. The path followed by the ball, as it rolls down toward the spectator, corresponds to the developmental history of a particular part of the egg. There is first an alternative, toward the right or the left. Along the former path a second alternative is offered; along the path to the left, the main channel continues leftward, but there is an alternative path that, however, can be reached only over a threshold. (From Waddington 1957.)

Individuals fare best when investing their resources selectively so as to optimize attainment along a chosen developmental track (P. Baltes 1987; Ericsson, Krampe, & Tesch-Römer 1993). However, the regulatory load for channeling behavioral and motivational resources into certain paths does not have to be carried by the individual alone. Biological processes of maturation and aging and the social structure of the life course provide an adaptive scaffold of age-graded opportunites and constraints. These constitute "constrained pathways" (Heckhausen & Schulz 1993a) that guide individuals in their efforts to shape and regulate their own development and life course.

This "mechanism of constrained pathways" (Heckhausen & Schulz 1993a) in life-course selectivity converges with Waddington's concept of the "epigenetic landscape" (Waddington 1957). Waddington described the process by which small initial differences become amplified into very different, discrete phylogenetic or ontogenetic outcomes in terms of a landscape metaphor (see Figure 1.1). In this metaphor a sphere rolls down a sloped plane that has valleys and hills. At the beginning of its journey through the landscape the sphere might encounter almost equal opportunities to enter any valley or even change from one valley to the next. However, once the sphere gets farther along the valley, it is more and more canalized. In other words, the process is buffered against disturbances and thus runs its course with great resiliency, given the initial lack of determinedness. Such canalizations in developmental processes have been identified in the evolution of species, the development of individual organisms (Waddington 1957, 1975), limbs, cell tissues, and so on.

Phenomena of canalization are also a long-standing topic in developmental and life-course research (Featherman, 1983; Kohn & Schooler 1982; Merton 1968; Riley, Johnson, & Foner 1972; Van den Deale, 1974) and have recently attracted renewed interest (Cairns 1991; Dannefer 1987, 1988; Dannefer & Sell 1988; Gottlieb 1991; Molenaar, Boomsma, & Dolan 1993; Turkheimer & Gottesmann 1991). Gottlieb (1991) has proposed a systems perspective on canalization, according to which canalization processes not only occur at the genetic level, but at all levels of the developing organism, including genetic expression, neural activity, behavior, and experience in the environment. The typical or usual experience of an organism promotes species typical behavior and also favors species-typical over species-atypical experiences (environment, stimulation). Thus, canalization is a function of the constellation of many factors (genetic, physiological, behavioral, and environmental). Such a perspective converges with the present view on the canalization or scaffolding of individual development and aging throughout the life span by an age-graded structure of biologically and societally determined opportunities and constraints. The individual can use and is constrained by this scaffolding support in her efforts to actively shape her development and life course.

In Chapter 2, the sociostructural constraints providing the time-ordered opportunity structure for life-course choices are discussed as part of the "sociostructural scaffolding" of life-course development. Moreover, Chapter 2 also discusses the sociostructural contribution to canalization processes by way of differential allocation of social resources that becomes sequentially more pronounced over the life course.

To summarize, phenomena of human development include two related but distinct phenomena: a restricted repertoire of options constraining the *choice* and an "accumulated effect" mechanism fostering the *focusing* of resource investment. The former type of canalization refers to a select, nonarbitrary, and restricted set of socially predetermined developmental pathways, whereas the latter addresses the notion that an individual remains focused on a given pathway after having opted for it. Although mechanisms of regulation for these two aspects of selectivity, choice and focus, are interrelated, they are nevertheless distinct phenomena. For instance, life-course choices, on the one hand, involve a diversified information search and processing with regard to all available options at the given life-course decision point. Focusing the investment of resources on a given life-course track, on the other hand, requires that the individual intensify attention and processing regarding the relevant chosen track at the expense of alternatives. And while life-course choices maximize the likelihood of adjusting goals to new conditions, focused resource investment reduces it.

Failure Compensation

The extensive behavioral variability of humans is also the basis for the other fundamental characteristic of human behavior: its proneness to failure. The regulation of behavior depends greatly on the individual's effort. This holds true for both the "when" – that is, under which environmental conditions a given behavior is activated – and for the "how," that is, how a particular behavior is generated. Whereas instinct-regulated behavior is triggered by a certain array of stimuli and is predetermined in its form, most aspects of human behavior are a function of the individual's regulation of actions, although, of course, the situational affordances play an important part too. Thus, human behavior involves substantial risks for nonadaptive, inappropriate behavior, and thus failure to attain action goals. To clarify, examples from childhood, midlife, and old age might be helpful. When children learn to manipulate and construct objects, such as when building a tower, they will have experienced a great many failures before they learn how to align and balance the bricks. The midlife manager who has been promoted is likely to make mistakes with regard to tasks and roles that she previously has not had to master. And the elderly, apart from being challenged by the task of maintaining their overall functioning in spite of aging-related decline, might also experience setbacks while engaging in new free-time activities such as golf or voluntary telephone counseling.

Moreover, humans command a great potential to optimize behavior via processes of learning. Consider, for instance, processes of first and second language acquisition, learning to construct objects and write essays. However, this learning potential has the important implication of being most efficient when operating around intermediate levels of difficulty (see review in H. Heckhausen, 1991). Low levels of difficulty are not efficient in promoting acquisition because there is not much scope for improvement, whereas very high levels of difficulty do not provide processible feedback because failures are ubiquitous and thus unspecific with regard to action means. At intermediate levels of difficulty, in contrast, the individual receives a maximum of information about the contingencies of action means used and failure occurrences. Only at intermediate difficulty levels can capacities, which are not yet mastered but are already within the reach of the individual's latent competence, be realized (Brown 1982; Vygotsky 1978). Thus, humans tend to function at intermediate levels of difficulty, at which failures occur at a rate of about 50 percent. In practical terms, this means that an individual will tend to strive for goals that are just beyond his or her reach. Thus, a child will attempt a task that she has not yet managed but is just one step more difficult than the most difficult one mastered so far (H. Heckhausen 1982, 1984). An athlete will train for the competition that he has not yet been in and mastered. At the end of the life span, this principle could be transformed into: Strive for goals that were mastered yesterday but may be unattainable tomorrow. Thus, the elderly and partially disabled person will fight against giving up self-care to others every step of the way.

Given the proneness to failure of human behavior, human agents have to cope with regular and frequent failures in attaining the action goals they have set for themselves. This involves compensating for two kinds of negative emotional consequences of failure: *frustration of goal intentions* and *negative effects on the perception of self. Compensating for frustration* is important, because without it the individual would not invest persistent effort when facing difficulties. Thus, compensating for frustration protects the individual's commitment to a given goal even in the face of obstacles. Another aspect of adaptive reactions to failure involves the adjustment of action means to the feedback implied in the failure experience.

However, probably the most powerful compensatory mechanisms to combat frustration as well as attain selectivity rely on the concept of self, a capacity unique to the human mind (for detailed reviews on early developmental foundations of the interface between the self-concept and failure compensation, see J. Heckhausen 1993; J. Heckhausen & Schulz 1995). This powerful motivational resource is anticipatory self-reinforcement (see review in H. Heckhausen 1991). The individual strives for an action goal not only for the sake of its intrinsic value but also because its attainment implies positive information about the self in terms of self-ascribed competencies. For example, the high school student dedicates time and effort to studying for an exam on a beautiful summer afternoon (lots of attractive alternative activities). In so doing, she endures setbacks (e.g., forgetting half the newly acquired

French words) and motivates herself by imagining how proud she will feel when she receives an outstanding grade. Anticipatory self-reinforcement becomes a key mechanism for maintaining tolerance for the delay of gratification (Mischel, Shoda, & Rodriguez 1989) regarding long-term goals as well as persistence in the face of failures and obstacles. As a scientific construct, anticipatory self-reinforcement converges with Bandura's concept of "self-efficacy" (Bandura 1977, 1982a). The individual's perception of self-efficacy is decisive in determining the amount of effort invested and the persistence when encountering obstacles (Bandura 1986, 1988, 1992; Bandura & Cervone 1983).

However, the self-concept as a powerful motivational resource also has its perils, especially when it comes to managing the implications of failures for *negative perceptions of the self.* Failure experiences produce negative information about the self and thus may threaten self-ascribed competencies, future hope for success, and even self-esteem in general. All these consequences can endanger future motivational and emotional resources for adaptive action. For example, the graduate student who has applied unsuccesfully for forty jobs might become discouraged, start doubting his competence and imagining himself in a low-paid unqualified substitute job. To prevent such damage to motivational and emotional resources, the organism needs specifically adapted strategies to compensate for such negative implications of failure on the self. Such strategies typically are directed at the internal world rather than at the environment, and specifically target mental representations of expectations, goals, and causal attributions. In Chapter 3 these strategies will be discussed under the heading "secondary control strategies."

As is the case for selectivity, the effects of proneness to failure are enhanced in the developmental context, and therefore compensation for failure and losses is an essential process in successful development and aging (P. Baltes 1987; P. Baltes & M. Baltes 1990; Marsiske et al. 1995; Schulz & J. Heckhausen 1996). Life goals typically span extensive periods of time, across which frustrations may accumulate and thus present a substantial load for compensation. Moreover, under conditions of sequentially accumulated investments but restricted lifetime, the effects of wrong life decisions can be disastrous. An example of such a burdened situation is the musician who aims at but fails to achieve a solo career, feels unsatisfied with his job as a musician in an orchestra, but does not see any way to switch onto another career track.

Another reason for the enhanced salience of failure proneness as a challenge to the individual's management is the increasingly less favorable gains–losses ratio across the life span (P. Baltes 1987; J. Heckhausen, Dixon, & P. Baltes 1989). With advancing age, developmental decline eventually overtakes developmental growth as the predominant type of change, and it thus becomes the prevailing concern of the individual. While the young old might have enough reserve capacity to get into new activities such as travel, sports, and social services, the old old increasingly are forced to focus on maintaining everyday functioning. In addition, other types of losses also tend to concentrate during old age. Older people are more likely than younger people to have lost friends to illness and death. Such socioemotional losses are also a burden for the motivational and emotional resources available to the individual, especially when they accumulate over short periods of time. Compensating for aging failures and interpersonal losses thus becomes the hallmark of successful aging (P. Baltes, Lindenberger, & Staudinger, 1998; Schulz & J. Heckhausen, 1996).

Summary

The management of selectivity and failure compensation are discussed as fundamental requirements of human behavior in general, which result from the vast behavioral and ontogenetic potential in human behavior. Behavioral selectivity is needed for achieving successful behavior-event contingencies, and failure compensation protects the motivational resources for future successful interactions with the environment. In the context of life-span development, both requirements are enhanced in their salience and consequences. The management of selectivity comprises two aspects: the choice of behavioral options and the focusing of behavioral resources. The consequences of both choice and focus of behavior are amplified in the context of ontogenetic change across the life course. Experiences of failure and loss are inevitable and frequent in human behavior, and thus need to be compensated for. Compensation addresses two consequences of failure experiences: the frustration of goal intentions and the negative effects on self-perception in terms of competence. Positive self-perceptions are an important mechanism for allowing persistent and long-term action in pursuing a goal, and therefore they represent essential motivational resources for human action. Experiences of failure and loss have enhanced consequences in the context of development throughout the life span and become more prevalent toward the end of life. Accordingly, the need to compensate for failure and loss should be present throughout the life span but enhanced at older ages.

2 The Life Course as a Context of Action

The main purpose of this chapter is to discuss external constraints upon individuals' developmental regulation. Such external constraints include biological and sociostructural factors as well as age-normative conceptions commonly shared in a given society. The stage for a discussion of these phenomena is set by developing the conceptual framework of life-span developmental psychology. A more specific discussion of age-related constraints to developmental regulation across the life course follows in terms of a brief sketch of biological-genetic factors, a consideration of the main types of sociostructural influences, and an elaborate discussion of age-normative conceptions. In this chapter, external constraints to developmental regulation are discussed, not only as restrictive factors, but as a functional and indisposable scaffold that provides time-structured opportunities for developmental regulation across the life course.

For the human species the variability of behavior is substantial, both interindividually and intraindividually across life-course changes. This implies greatly enhanced opportunities, but it also brings about the necessity to select from the many options in terms of choosing a particular track and then staying focused on it (see Chapter 1). This selectivity requirement cannot be managed by the individual herself. The task of choosing and maintaining focus on one path from a completely unstructured pool of behavioral options would be overwhelming. Developmental regulation, therefore, relies substantially on external constraints, which provide structure to the human life course (see also Brandtstädter, 1990). Lifetime-ordered structures of constraints and opportunities serve as an adaptive scaffold for individuals' developmental regulation. These structures of constraints and opportunities are jointly provided by three sources: biology, society and its structure, and internalized age-normative conceptions. They open up select windows for personal choice and management (e.g., choice of occupation at entry in the labor market or in institutions of higher education), for which the individual has to take responsibility. However, most of the time the biological and sociostructural boundary conditions of the given life-course period (e.g., maximum age limit for fertility, minimum age limit to enter the labor market) and one's own biographical track (e.g., educational background, family composition) guide choice as well as focus in developmental regulation.

The Conceptual Framework of Life-Span Developmental Psychology

Before discussing the age-related constraints provided by biology, social structure, and particularly by age-normative conceptions, the broader conceptual framework provided by the developmental psychology of the life span will be considered.

Life-span developmental psychology views *development as a lifelong process* (P. Baltes 1987; Filipp 1987; Flammer 1988; J. Heckhausen 1994b; J. Heckhausen & Mayr, 1998; Lehr 1984; Thomae, 1959). Processes of biological change, age-graded socialization (Brim & Wheeler 1966), and personality transformation (Thomae 1970, 1988) extend beyond childhood and adolescence across adulthood and into old age. The idea of lifelong developmental change is not new, although it conflicts with widespread notions of developmental growth being restricted to childhood. This idea goes back to precursors of life-span developmental research in the last century (Carus 1808; Quetelet 1835) and even before (Tetens 1777), when development across the life span was viewed as a continuous process of self-completion and cultivation; and it goes back to the pioneers of life-span developmental theory in the early twentieth century (Erikson 1959; Hollingworth 1927; see historical reviews in P. Baltes 1983; Brandtstädter 1990; Groffmann 1970; Reinert 1979).

The inclusion of all phases of the life span, of course, calls into question unidirectional models of development that exclusively identified developmental processes with growth, a model borrowed from biology (Reese & Overton 1970). The challenge of developing a unified conception of development and aging (Thomae 1959, 1979) called for a *multidirectional* conceptualization of developmental processes that included acquisition, maintenance, transformation, and extinction – that is, growth as well as decline (P. Baltes, Reese, & Lipsitt 1980). According to this model of life-span development, different dimensions of functioning follow different age trajectories in their life span, encompassing patterns of growth and decline, each with their unique patterns of age-related timing. Thus, life-span development is viewed as multidimensional and multidirectional (P. Baltes 1983, 1987). On the whole, the *multidimensional* trajectories of functioning jointly form an inverted U-shape curve, much like popular images of the life span as a set of stairs, with negatively accelerated growth during childhood, adolescence, and early adulthood and positively accelerated decline during later adulthood and old age.

Some models of life-span developmental psychology have extended the notion of multidimensionality and multidirectionality to the conception of dynamically related developmental *gains and losses* that mutually condition each other (P. Baltes 1987; P. Baltes, Dittmann-Kohli, & Dixon 1984). According to this idea, developmental gains and losses do not occur only as types of development at different periods of the life span. Instead, they mutually produce each other, so that gains bring about losses and losses give rise to gains. Although a radical version of this claim – that is, "all gains imply losses and all losses imply gains" – seems debatable (Uttal & Perlmutter 1989), the conception of the dynamic between gains and losses is fruitful for the study of developmental regulation in view of positive and negative trade-offs (benefits versus costs) implied in developmental pathways (see Chapter 4). Life-course choices of particular pathways, for instance, preclude the pursuit of alternative pathways and thereby imply developmental losses. Similar gains–losses dynamics can be identified in various domains of functioning (P. Baltes 1987).

Another important proposition of life-span developmental psychology relates to the *intraindividual* variability of developmental processes (P. Baltes 1987; P. Baltes & M. Baltes 1980; Lerner 1984). At any given point in the life span the individual may show substantial *plasticity* in his/her behavior. In the domain of intellectual functioning, the phenomenon of plasticity has been studied in terms of developmental reserve capacity at the respective age and domain of functioning (Kliegl & P. Baltes 1987). The concept of developmental reserve capacity implies that there are constraints or limits to plasticity, which may have high diagnostic value for the developmental status of the individual (Kliegl & P. Baltes 1987; Kühl & M. Baltes 1989). In infancy and childhood, developmental reserve achievements, captured by the concept of "zone of proximal development" (Vygotsky 1978), are typically facilitated by social interaction with more able individuals and indicate upper limits of potential performance (Brown 1982). In adulthood and old age, potential and limits of plasticity have been empirically demonstrated in cognitive training research (P. Baltes, Dittman-Kohli, & Dixon 1984; P. Baltes, Dittmann-Kohli, & Kliegl 1986; P. Baltes & Schaie, 1976; Kliegl & P. Baltes 1987), and they have even been used to predict age-degenerative processes in mental functioning (Kühl & M. Baltes 1989). In the domain of personality and coping, plasticity has been addressed in terms of adaptations to aging (e.g., Brandtstädter & Renner 1990; Rudinger & Thomae 1990; Thomae 1970, 1983), resilience to developmental stress (Staudinger, Marsiske, & P. Baltes 1993), and coping with adverse events in the life course (e.g., Filipp 1981; Filipp et al. 1990; Hultsch & Plemons 1979; Thomae & Lehr 1986). The whole array of these and related phenomena are captured by the concept of developmental regulation (see conceptual Chapters 4 and 5, and empirical findings in Chapters 7 and 8). It is the degree of intraindividual variability and plasticity that sets the limits and thereby the stage for the individual to influence and manage his or her own development.

Moreover, much attention has been paid to *interindividual differences* in adaptation to aging and aging-related environmental stress in general (e.g., P. Baltes & M. Baltes 1990; Lehr & Thomae 1987). An influential theory about interindividual differences in successful aging is Thomae's "cognitive theory of adjustment to aging" (Thomae 1976, 1992). According to this theory, behavioral change is influenced more by perceptions of past, present, and future life and its changeability than by objective characteristics of the elderly's life circumstances. Moreover, these subjective perceptions are closely associated with the individual's dominant concerns and expectations ("Daseinsthematiken," Thomae 1988). According to the cognitive theory of adjustment to aging, successful adjustment to aging depends on the ability of the individual to restore a balance between cognitive and motivational structures after experiencing a threat to the homeostasis between present and desired states of the person. The compensation of threats to motivational and emotional resources is discussed in Chapter 4 as part of the model of developmental regulation. Interindividual differences in the tendency to use such compensatory strategies and their relation to preferred patterns of social comparison are empirically investigated in Study 9, Chapter 7.

A further key characteristic of life-span developmental psychology is a *contextualist* approach to developmental phenomena (P. Baltes 1987; Lerner 1989; Lerner & Kauffman 1985). The contextualist approach emphasizes the causal role of various systems of influence that are based, for instance, on historical-cultural differences (e.g., P. Baltes, Cornelius, & Nesselroade 1979), social strata (e.g., Featherman & Lerner 1985), and other characteristics of the developmental ecology. At any given point in the life span the individual's behavior is influenced by these various systems as they interact synchronically as well as diachronically with earlier or even anticipated future experiences and events (Filipp & Olbrich 1986). Baltes and his colleagues (P. Baltes, Cornelius, & Nesselroade 1979; P. Baltes, Reese, & Lipsitt 1980) have proposed to classify these contextual influences into three broad classes: age-graded influences, history-graded influences, and nonnormative influences (see also P. Baltes 1987). It is noteworthy that each of these classes of influences is also reflected in older adults' retrospective accounts of their biographies. Thomae and Lehr (1986) report that among the subjective turning points in biographical narratives of their subjects, about one-third referred to age-normative events, about one-half involved nonnormative events (personal experiences unrelated to age structure of the life course or historical events), and the bulk of the remaining turning points related to historical events (e.g., World War II).

Age-normative influences, which are of major relevance for the present research and the focus of this chapter (see sections below), comprise biological and social influences on development that bear a substantial relation to chronological age. Genetic-biological age-gradedness includes processes of maturation, aging, and age-differential evolutionary selection effects (Finch 1990). Society-related age-gradedness can be differentiated in objectified social institutions of age stratification (Hagestad 1990; Hagestad & Neugarten 1985; Riley 1985), on the one hand, and their psychological complements in age-normative conceptions as internalized and shared by the individual members of a given society (J. Heckhausen 1990a), on the other. Biological and sociostructural influences, as well as age-normative conceptions, will be discussed separately and in more detail in the following sections.

At this point, two age-graded influences that cut across the biology and social structure of the life course as well as across age-normative conceptions should be mentioned (see also review in Brandtstädter, 1990). "Developmental tasks" (Havighurst 1952, 1953; see also Oerter 1978, 1986; Thomae 1975) represent age-specific goals and developmental challenges, which result from biological changes (e.g., in fertility), transitions into new social roles (e.g., husband, see reviews in Clausen 1986; Riley 1985), and age-normative expectations about psychological change (e.g., autonomy in value judgments; see review in J. Heckhausen 1990b; J. Heckhausen & Lang 1996). The topic of age-graded developmental tasks will be taken up again in Chapter 5, where a model of developmental goals as organizers of the individual's developmental regulation is presented. The other class of potentially age-graded influences to be mentioned here consists of critical life events (Brim & Ryff 1980; Dohrenwend & Dohrenwend 1974; Filipp 1981;

Hultsch & Plemons 1979; Lowenthal, Thurnher, & Chiriboga 1977). Critical life events are major changes in an individual's developmental ecology that present a substantial stress to the individual's well-being and therefore involve major coping responses (e.g., Brim & Ryff 1980; Filipp & Gräser 1982). Critical life events may instigate life crises that present a danger to developmental regulation, but they also present the opportunity for psychological growth that would otherwise not have occurred (e.g., Olbrich 1981). Critical life events can be classified according to different components of age-normativity (Brim & Ryff 1980; see also Schulz & Rau 1985): the correlation with age, the commonness within a population, and the probability of occurrence (Brim & Ryff 1980). Prototypical age-normative critical life events, such as the first steps in childhood and retirement, are highly age-determined and happen to almost everybody with a very high probability. At the other end of the continuum are events that are nonnormative, such as the loss of a limb or winning a lottery.

Events that can be described as non-age related, happening to few and occurring with low probability (Brim & Ryff 1980), are examples of *nonnormative influences* to life-span development (P. Baltes 1987; P. Baltes, Cornelius, & Nesselroade 1979). They include positive as well as negative events (Bandura 1982b; Brim 1992). The characteristic of nonnormative influences on development is that they cannot be anticipated by the individual, that social models for coping with them are hardly available, and that social support systems are not set up to deal with them (Brandtstädter 1990; Hultsch & Plemons 1979; Schulz & Rau 1985). Because of these characteristics, nonnormative influences are particularly challenging to the individual's potential for developmental plasticity (resilience; Staudinger, Marsiske, & Baltes 1993) and can have particularly extreme effects on the individual's development.

Finally, *history-graded influences* on life-span development are associated with historical events or transitions that affect everybody alive at a given point in time. When these influences are differential for individuals at different ages, they are referred to as "cohort effects" (e.g., P. Baltes, Cornelius, & Nesselroade 1979; Ryder, 1965). History-graded influences are manifold in their characteristics and causes. They encompass sudden and hardly predictable events such as natural catastrophes, outcomes of more continuous processes such as economic crises, and nonspectacular and gradual social change or technological development (e.g., in medical treatment). History-graded influences in themselves can affect changes in the system of age-graded influences, and even in the probability and occurrence of nonnormative events (Elder 1979, 1985). Depending on how social change and historical events interact with the social and personality resources an individual brings to bear in a given situation, very different and even contrasting life-course outcomes may result (e.g., Caspi & Elder 1986; Elder 1986). Entering military service, for instance, turned many young men's life courses in a favorable direction, although, of course, it led to injury or death for many others (Elder 1986). Similarly, social hardships related to the Great Depression ultimately had a positive effect on the life satisfaction of middle-class women but a negative effect on long-range satisfaction for working-class women (Caspi & Elder 1986). The topic of history-graded influences on development will be taken up again in Chapter 6, where our own empirical research (Studies 5 and 6) about the effects of the radical sociohistorical transformation associated with German reunification on individuals' well-being and developmental regulation is reported.

Paul Baltes and colleagues (1980) have also proposed hypothetical life-course profiles reflecting the expected impact of each of the three factors of influence: age-graded, history-graded, and nonnormative. Age-graded influences are expected to be greatest in early childhood and to decline sharply thereafter, reach a minimum in young adulthood, and increase moderately again in old age. History-graded influences, in contrast, are conceptualized to peak in adolescence, when the individual, psychologically and in terms of critical life transitions, is most exposed and receptive to the broader societal context. Finally, nonnormative influences are expected to increase steadily throughout the life span, when interindividual variability fans out. The individual's degrees of freedom to actively shape her development and the need to manage the consequences of either system of influence (age-normative, history-graded, and nonnormative) depend on the interplay between these three systems of influence.

The remainder of the chapter focuses on age-graded influences on development that are characteristic of a contemporary Western industrialized society with a high division of labor. Biologically based influences are only briefly sketched. Thereafter, structures of opportunities and constraints related to the social system and its age-graded institutions are considered. And finally, age-normative conceptions about the timing of life stages, role transitions and critical life events, and psychological change are discussed in more detail.

Biological Constraints

First, biological mechanisms of maturation and aging in general and some specific, prototypical *biological constraints* are briefly considered.

Biological influences on development are typically reflected in age-related and relatively universal patterns of change, which include maturational processes as well as aging-related decline. To be sure, modern evolutionary biology and behavioral biology assert that, far from being simply determinants of change, genetic influences on development are mediated by relevant exogenous conditions for the expression of genetic programs of development (Gottlieb 1991; Plomin 1986). Genetically controlled patterns of biological development extend far beyond childhood into adulthood and old age. These create epigenetic landscapes in the sense of Waddington's model, which mold and canalize development into certain paths. However, the "canalization" of development that is based on selection for reproductive fitness (i.e., evolutionary genetic influences) weakens at ages beyond childhood (McCall 1979). This is so because reproductive fitness is essentially determined by the ability to mate, produce offspring, and rear these offspring to maturity. In the early phylogeny of humans in hunter-gatherer communities, all these reproduction-related activities were typically completed by midlife. Thus, evolutionary selection was working on the survival and optimization of reproductive activities that take place in the first three decades of the life span. The few individuals who reached old age in these early communities had little influence on the survival of offspring. In old age, evolutionary genetic influences become less functionally adapted, because at ages beyond reproduction genetically determined characteristics are less subject to evolutionary selective processes.

It is important to note that, often, canalized evolutionary processes bring about side effects that are not adaptive in and of themselves but, for reasons of anatomical structure (e.g., inherently related features in anatomy) or genetic transmission (e.g., physical linkage of genetic information), simply accompany selection processes (Gould 1977; Gould & Lewontin 1979). Such side effects of evolutionary selection may, at some later stage in evolution, take on new functions that then open up a whole new avenue for selection and evolution of new capacities of the organism (see also the concepts of "exaptation" by Gould & Vrba, 1982, and of "adaptive specialization" by Rozin, 1976).

However, such side effects of evolutionary selection can also be nonadaptive. In the context of laying out his theory of coevolution of genes and culture, Durham (1991) reports a case in point regarding the differential prevalence of sickle-cell anemia in different but neighboring West African populations. As it turns out, a gene that is adaptive in conferring resistance to malaria (in the heterozygote state) is nonadaptive, even lethal, when it causes sickle-cell anemia (in the homozygote state). In consequence, populations inhabiting areas with a high risk for malaria infection (due to forest clearing and seasonal accumulation of open ponds that allow for mosquito breeding) also develop a higher prevalence of sickle-cell anemia.[1]

Negative side effects of selective adaptations are especially relevant for the biology of aging (see overviews in Baltes, Lindenberger, & Staudinger, 1998; Crews 1993; Finch 1990). Given that selective adaptations are focused on the life span before and around reproduction, late onset malfunctions and disease will not be eliminated from the genetic pool. In fact, late onset nonadaptive characteristics might well accumulate in a species with costly and extended prereproductive phases and high mortality rates in young adults (Charlesworth 1990; Finch 1990; Rose 1991; Williams 1957), as was the case for early hominids. Thus, evolutionary selection in humans most likely has favored various nonadaptive late-life onset by-products of early-onset adaptive characteristics. Such old-age genetic calamities can be brought about by a variety of mechanisms. One of these is captured by the concept of "antagonistic pleiotropy" (Williams 1957) or the "counterpart theory of aging" (P. Baltes & Graf 1996; Birren 1988, 1995; Yates & Benton 1995), which suggests that the long-term effects of developmental growth in early life are detrimental in old age. A case in point is the gene selected for the physiological process of bone growth in childhood, which produces atherosclerosis in old age (hypothetical example by Williams 1957). Another particularly destructive mechanism disfavoring old age may be the coupling of late-onset disease with adaptive characteristics in early life. Thus, in a similar way as sickle-cell anemia is genetically coded along with resistance to malaria, some important resilience factor relevant to early life (e.g., resilience against life-threatening infectious diseases) may, for instance, have the side effect of rendering the individual vulnerable to Alzheimer's disease in old age. Such a systematic mechanism could be expected to produce high prevalence rates of Alzheimer's disease, as has actually been found in very old populations (about 50 percent of adults over ninety years of age; Helmchen et al. 1996).

Life-span trajectories of age-related decreases in evolutionary selection pressure have also been discussed for the realm of psychological functioning (P. Baltes & Graf 1996; P. Baltes, Lindenberger, & Stau-

---

[1] The punch line of this example in the context of Durham's theory of gene-culture coevolution is that the agricultural custom of clearing the forest – thus creating opportunities for open water puddles and thereby mosquito breeding grounds – is the ultimate reason for generating a selective advantage of the sickle-cell-anemia-prone but malaria-resistant gene cluster. In this way, a cultural meme (agriculturally motivated clearings in the forest) directly influenced the gene pool of local populations.

dinger, 1998). Thus, biological aging brings about major restrictions in capacities, decline in physiological and psychological functioning, and vulnerability to disease. All these present a major challenge for the regulation of human behavior and development by the cultural system, societal institutions, and the individual. The sociocultural construction of old age by the society and the individual is, therefore, presented with increasing requirements at higher age levels in adulthood so as to bridge the widening gap between the biological resources and sociocultural expectations associated with old age (see P. Baltes, Lindenberger, & Staudinger, 1998: "age-related increase in need for culture").

In the remainder of this section, a few prototypical biological trajectories and constraints in life-span maturation and aging are considered. A most general biological determinant of development is the length of the life span itself, which provides both opportunities and constraints. Because humans live longer than most other species, the human life span provides substantially amplified opportunities for ontogenetic growth. However, the human life span has an upper limit of about 115 years (Danner & Schröder 1992; Dinkel 1992; Fries 1980).

As noted, in general, the biological resources for physical and mental capacities follow an inverted U-shape trajectory across the life span. During childhood and adolescence the individual's motor and mental capacities develop and mature from a state of complete helplessness and dependence on adult caregivers to complete functioning in a rich assortment of domains. Sometime during adulthood, functioning in each of these domains peaks, levels out, and thereafter declines (Lehman 1953; Simonton 1995). A case in point is neuronal functioning in terms of receptivity to neurotransmitters, which starts to show significant decreases by midlife and progressive losses up to 40 percent by the ninth decade of life (see review in Finch 1986, 1990). Another prototypical case is fertility in women, and to a lesser degree in men, which shows a biologically determined age trajectory from maximum functioning in young adulthood to minimal functioning in midlife. Age-related trajectories of maturation and aging in vital biological systems, such as the immune response (Miller 1990) and cardiovascular and pulmonary functioning (Lakatta 1990), lead to increasing risks for functional decline and disease at higher ages in adulthood and particularly in old age. Other salient trajectories of increase, peak, and decline can be identified in those domains of functioning which the individual has selected as top priority because they are most sensitive to reductions of reserve capacity, which is known to decrease from midlife to old age (Schaie & Hertzog 1983). This is shown in activity-specific age trajectories of peak performance, for instance, in superathletes (Ericsson 1990; Schulz & Curnow 1988), expert mnemonics (Kliegl & P. Baltes 1987), and with regard to late-life dementia being predicted by performance speed in highly trained intelligence tasks (M. Baltes, Kühl, & Sowarka 1992).

Health as the basic biological resource of the individual starts to become more vulnerable during late midlife. In advanced age, individuals become increasingly susceptible to various diseases, chronic conditions, disabilities, and life-threatening illnesses (Brock, Guralnick, & Brody 1990). Eventually, at the upper limits of the life span, the majority of individuals will develop frailty and multiple chronic illnesses, eventually leading to death (Schneider & Rowe 1990).

Given the inverted U-shape trajectory of biological resources, the individual has first increasing and then decreasing physical capacities to attain important goals in life. This implies that during childhood and adolescence certain goals that were hard or impossible to reach earlier (e.g., climbing stairs, learning to write) become accessible and even prescribed as developmental tasks (Havighurst 1973). And, conversely, during midlife and increasingly in old age, certain goals become increasingly hard to obtain (e.g, running at competitive speeds with younger adults), and thus have to be either given up or pursued with increased effort so as to compensate for the physical constraints.

Sociostructural Constraints

The second source of influences pertains to society and its institutions. These *sociostructural constraints* can be identified in terms of the three types of constraints: lifetime-related, chronological age-based, and age-sequential. First, *restricted lifetime* constrains the time extension for future developmental goals and life planning. The fact that there is a limit to the biological life span means that there is a final deadline for everything the individual sets out to achieve in life. This is reflected in sociostructural as well as psychological phenomena. In the realm of social relations, for instance, Carstensen, in her "socioemotional selectivity theory," has proposed and reports compelling evidence that individuals who are close to death or perceive other final endings selectively focus on fewer close emotional relationships (review in Carstensen 1993; see also Lang & Carstensen 1994; Lang, Staudinger, & Carstensen 1995). When considering different domains of life, such as work or social relations, the concept of a final deadline can also be extended to include final deadlines not necessarily associated with the end of life. Career goals in most professions, for instance, have to be achieved before certain defined deadlines (see also Chapter 8) based on age or interpromotion intervals. The latter life-span constraints are based less on biological aging and death than on the social structure of the life course and age-normative conceptions. They can also be conceived of as special or extreme cases of the second type of life-course constraints. Fairly strict and narrow age prescriptions for the exit from certain roles and activities can be found as objectified social institutions in many Western industrial societies. Examples can be found in education (e.g., prescribed age for school entry), career tracks (e.g., military, education, music), and particularly in retirement laws. The fact that in some countries such age-based prescriptions and proscriptions are banned by special anti-age-discrimination laws only illustrates their substantial role in the social system.

The second type of life-course constraint is based on *chronological age.* In most human societies, the life course is composed of an age-graded structure, which stratifies the society into age strata (Riley 1986) and also involves age norms for important life events and role transitions (Hagestad & Neugarten 1985; Kohli & Meyer 1986). In addition to the biological clock of maturation and aging, there are powerful social clocks. Typically, two media of social influence generate, maintain, and transform such socially based age structures. On the one hand, there are objectified social institutions such as laws for child and adolescent welfare ("Jugendschutz"), retirement laws, or prescribed entry and exit ages for the educational system. On the other hand, normative conceptions about age timing are internalized and shared by the members of a given community, and thereby contribute to the notion of good and bad timing of life events and transitions (Hagestad & Neugarten 1985). These two media of social influence naturally influence one another, so that their interface transfers and constitutes social change (Riley 1985, 1986).

Age-chronological constraints are promoted by entry and transition times institutionalized in legislation and state and private companies' promotion rules (e.g., Mayer 1986; Mayer & Müller 1986). Such social institutional constraints provide time-ordered opportunity structures for certain life-course events and thus form part of the "sociostructural scaffolding" of life-course development. Specifically, this implies that, for a given life event, optimal conditions are provided to those the "right" age, while those "off-time" have to swim upstream. Consider, for instance, the availability of student grants for individuals at different ages or life-course periods. In most European countries it is much easier to obtain a study grant at the age of twenty, before one has started an occupational career, than at age forty-five, after having worked in a different occupation for twenty-five years. The same holds for the availability of summer jobs, cheap accommodations, and so forth. Society provides twenty-year-olds with an opportunity structure to study, but not the forty-five-or sixty-year-olds. This means that the "off-time" student has to invest many more personal resources so as to compensate for the lack of sociostructural support.

The third type of life-course constraint pertains to *age-sequential structures* of life-course events and developmental change, which limit the range of potential sequences. This type of constraint is probably most powerful in providing predictability to human life courses. Consider an unstructured scenario in which every event could follow every other event. There would be no way for the individual as well as for society to predict the future from the past. Instead, life courses are typically channeled into sequential patterns or, in other words, biographical tracks (e.g., Geulen 1981). In his/her striving to obtain desirable life-course outcomes the individual is channeled through sequentially organized patterns of opportunities and constraints (Sørensen 1986). So, for example, after completing occupational training one can obtain an entry-level job, followed by the first promotion, and so on. Similar to the chronological constraints, these sequential constraints are generated by multiple sources, such as the state and its laws (on equality in job opportunities based on qualification only). Hence, apart from life-course trajectories in biological resources, there are segregated life-course paths demarcated by social structure and commonly shared notions of normal or desirable biographies.

These age-graded and age-sequential sociostructural constraints narrow down options along given life-course tracks and thereby provide selectivity to individuals' life courses (J. Heckhausen & Schulz 1993a). From a critical perspective, these constraints are viewed as differential and socially unjust allocations of resources to individuals of different social classes (Mayer & Carroll 1987), gender (Mayer, Allmendinger, & Huinink 1991), and race or ethnicity (Jencks 1992), which result in unequal opportunities for social mobility (Dannefer 1987). However, the perspective taken here is nonevaluative and focuses on identifying the function of the societal/individual system, which helps regulate individual life courses. This system is calibrated so that the individual members of society can psychologically manage their life courses (avoidance of volition or planning overload), while the life-course patterns remain reasonably predictable on the societal level so as to safeguard social stability.

Age-sequential constraints are provided by social structure via segregated biographical paths (Blossfeld & Mayer 1988; Featherman & Lerner 1985; Geulen 1981; Kohli & Meyer 1986; Mayer 1986) and prescriptions for sequencing and spacing of life events and transitions (Hogan 1981; Marini 1984; Mayer & Huinink 1990). These age-sequential constraints foster selectivity and can thus be conceived of as a "canalization" of life courses. As discussed in Chapter 1, life-course canalization involves two aspects: choice and focus (see also J. Heckhausen & Schulz 1993a). The first pertains to a restricted and nonrandom set of predetermined developmental pathways (Geulen 1981) and will be referred to as the "mechanism of constraint choice" (see "optimization," as discussed in Chapter 4). This societally provided selectivity mechanism greatly reduces the complexity of individual choices at any given biographical juncture.

The second aspect of sociostructural canalization facilitates the individual's ability to stay on track, or to focus on a given life-course path, by maximizing gains along the track and discouraging shifts to other life-course tracks. The further along the individual has followed a given track, the greater the payoff in terms of acquired functioning (e.g., occupational competence) and access to resources. At the same time, the costs of leaving the track for another life-course path, for which the individual would then be "off-time," increase and discourage the individual to shift tracks. This aspect of canalization might be referred to as the "accumulated effect" mechanism and will become highly relevant for the study of developmental regulation around societal transformation (as in the former GDR, see Studies 5 and 6 in Chapter 6). In sociology this phenomenon has been studied as the sequentially enhanced effect of differential allocations of social resources over the life course (Dannefer 1988; Merton 1968). Merton (1968, 1973), for instance, identified lifetime-sequential cumulations of advantages and disadvantages in scientists' career patterns. To characterize this phenomenon, he adopted the term "Matthew effect" from the gospel of Matthew: "To he who hath, shall more be given, and to he who hath not, shall be taken away, even that which he hath" (cited in Dannefer & Sell 1988, p. 4).

Dannefer has proposed to apply the notion of the Matthew effect to a wider range of life-course phenomena reflecting "aged heterogeneity" (Dannefer 1987; Dannefer & Sell 1988). Used in this more general way, the Matthew effect denotes the spreading out of life-course careers across the life span. Recent research on such accumulated effects has provided empirical support for the idea that interindividual divergence increases across the life span (e.g., Henretta & Campbell 1976; Maddox & Douglas 1974; Rosenbaum 1984; Schaie 1989; Walberg & Tsai 1983).

Constraints Based on Age-Normative Conceptions

The third source of life-course constraints pertains to norms about age timing, life-event sequencing, and the nature of development across the life course (J. Heckhausen 1990a). Age-normative conceptions and their influence on developmental regulation are a major focus of this research and are therefore discussed in more detail. It should be noted that the term "normative conceptions" is used here for conceptions about *typical* or *normal* development.

The Functional Significance of Age-Normative Conceptions

Before considering the empirical findings on normative conceptions about the life course, the role of age-normative conceptions in influencing behavior involved in developmental regulation across the life course is discussed conceptually. In the context of social and developmental psychology, and particularly from a phenomenological perspective, conceptions about age-related change and age stereotypes have been studied as major factors in the perception of self and others (e.g., Fallo-Mitchell & Ryff 1982; Nardi 1973; Ryff & Heincke 1983). However, in this research a different approach to the role of age-normative conceptions is presented. Age-normative conceptions are at the core of the interface between the individual's developmental regulation – that is, the microlevel or psychological approach – and the society's system of age stratification (Riley 1985; Riley Johnson, & Foner 1972) – that is, the macrolevel or sociological approach (Sørensen, Weinert, & Sherrod 1986). Therefore, this section focuses largely on the conceptual interface of life-course sociology and life-span developmental psychology (J. Heckhausen 1990a).

Recently, in the field of life-course sociology, a debate has evolved about the question of to what extent age-normative life courses are actually determined by external societal institutions (e.g., Dannefer 1989; Dowd 1987; Held 1986). What is it that controls individuals' actions directed at shaping their life courses? How do biographies evolve? Kohli (1981) has emphasized these questions as key issues in the interdisciplinary interface of action theory and sociology. He states that the phenomenon of biography marks the intersection of action theory and structure theory, micro- and macrosociology, and highlights the relation between the individual and society.

A set of findings indicating a rather loose connection between external institutional forces and realized life-course patterns in a given population had cast some doubt on the notion that life courses are controlled by societal institutions. For instance, it was shown that even when social institutions were dissolved or eradicated, as in the course of World War II or the Great Depression, the age timing of life transitions (e.g., graduation from school, marriage) did not change (Blossfeld 1987, 1988), and neither did the age-normative conceptions about the age timing of these life events (Modell 1980). Blossfeld (1987, 1988) investigated the age timing of transitions in education during the post–World War II period in Germany and found stable life-event timing even during a period when the societal system had collapsed completely. Similarly, Modell studied the age timing of marriage in the U.S.A. during the 1930s and 1940s, and showed that normative conceptions about the ideal age for getting married remained constant even when people were forced to marry later because of the Great Depression or earlier because of World War II.

Moreover, some life-course sociologists have begun to question the notion of the institutionalized life course (e.g., Dannefer 1989) and even to propose that in modern industrial societies life courses are deinstitutionalized (e.g., Held 1986; Neugarten 1979). Such doubt is based on recent developments toward more flexibility of state-regulated age norms, for instance in legislation about retirement and employment. Moreover, there are also empirical findings that suggest an increased variability in the age timing and age sequencing of life transitions (e.g., Rindfuss, Swicegood, & Rosenfeld 1987). Given that institutional constraints have become more lenient over the past decades (see also Neugarten 1979), how is it that normative patterns of life-event timing still prevail in empirical research about the life course (Hogan 1981; Marini 1984; Modell, Furstenberg, & Hershberg 1976; Modell, Furstenberg, & Strong 1978; Uhlenberg 1974)?

Some fifty years ago, an analogous question troubled sociologists, cultural anthropologists, and historians. Their question was: Why do people regulate their behavior according to certain rules of social conduct, present in each society, without being subjected to external enforcement? Norbert Elias (1969) has raised this question with his great socio- and psychogenetic inquiry into the process of civilization in Western societies. How, he asked, have those regulations of human behavior and affect evolved that are associated with the common-sense concept "civilization"? And how do these processes of civilization relate to long-term historical transformations of society?

Elias answers the questions by showing that external enforcement via societal power has gradually, over centuries, been transformed into internalized rules and norms of conduct and behavior. This process of internalization renders the need for external societal enforcement obsolete. At the same time, the regulations of behavior and affect appear natural and inevitable to the individual member of society (see also Parsons, 1951). More specifically, modern anthropologists argue that social conventions become transformed into institutionalized ways of thinking (Douglas, 1986). Institutional ways of thinking hold advantages over social conventions because conventions as pragmatic rules for social interactions are too transparent and therefore not stable, whereas institutionalized ways of thinking survive and thrive because they appear to be grounded in nature itself. For the individual, they "turn individual thought over to an automatic pilot," and for society "there is a saving of energy from institutional coding and inertia" (Douglas 1986, p. 63). Similarly, Berger and Luckmann (1966), in their sociology of knowledge, argue that reality is socially construed. Social constructions of reality provide societal stability and predictability as well as subjective certainty about a mutually habitualized, and thereby institutionalized, foundation of individual action.

Hence, the puzzling contradiction between a simultaneous deinstitutionalization (in terms of societal regulation) and institutionalization (in terms of observed life-course patterns) of the life course may be solved by assuming an analogous process. Thus, life-course patterns would be expected to have become increasingly regulated by internalized norms about age-appropriate behavior, age-graded events and transitions, and age-sequential rules (e.g., you must finish school first before you can have a family) as societal regulation became more lenient. Thus, age-normative conceptions about the life course internalized by individuals may gradually have replaced external regulations based on objectified societal institutions. Hence, the dynamic between institutionalization and deinstitutionalization of the life course would be just another version of one phenomenon, the internalization of societal norms coupled with a synchronous loss of function on the part of external institutions.

In debates between life-course sociologists and life-span developmental psychologists, some sociologists argue that peoples' age-normative conceptions about the life course are merely epiphenomenal to sociostructural systems of age grading and are not constitutive for homogeneity and variability in populations' life-course patterns (e.g., Marini 1984; Mayer 1987). But maybe the *key* to the problem of conjoint deinstitutionalization and the continued binding force of age-normative regulations lies in just these age-normative conceptions internalized by individuals. Age-normative conceptions may have committing power as internalized, naturalized, and thus unquestionable ways of thinking about human life.

Neugarten and others have studied age-normative conceptions of individuals as social norms (Hagestad & Neugarten 1985; Neugarten, Moore, & Lowe 1965; Neugarten & Peterson 1957). Other life-course sociologists have argued against conceptualizing age-normative beliefs of individuals as social norms; they question whether age-normative conceptions merely represent reflections of statistically dominant behavioral patterns that may have been socialized and modeled to the individual (Marini 1984; Riley 1986). Such passive reflections, according to these researchers, cannot be classified as social norms, because they lack two fundamental characteristics of social norms: (1) they are not behavioral prescriptions in the sense of *ought rules* and (2) they do not elicit social sanctions in the case of transgressions.

However, from the point of view of psychology and the sociology of knowledge, age-normative conceptions about development and the life course may serve as guiding images that regulate behavior. Their binding force may result precisely from the fact that they are *not* enforced by external institutional control but are internalized as frames of reference (see also Parsons's distinction between social control and socialization; Parsons 1951). From attributional psychology, we know that conceptions about what is true for most other people constitute social frames of reference (Festinger 1954) in terms of Kelley's dimension of consensus (Kelley 1967). Such social reference frames function as guidelines for personal aspirations: What most other people can do, I can do too. This also implies, of course, that failing to achieve the level dictated by the social frame of reference entails negative conclusions about the self. If I cannot do what most other people can do, I must be very incompetent. This example relates to the typical case of norm-congruent behavior being perceived of as positive, whereas norm-discrepant behavior is seen as negative. This is not always the case. In some specific cases deviation from the norm may even be highly valued, for instance, if someone attains a desirable status earlier than is prescribed by the norm, or if deviance from the norm constitutes identity (e.g., upward mobility of a late starter).

In general, a need for explanation arises once an individual departs from what is perceived as the norm. Typically, the reasons for norm discrepancies are attributed to the individual's dispositions (see also report, later in this chapter, on study by Krueger, Heckhausen, & Hundertmark 1995). Given that norm deviance is usually evaluated negatively, the target person is then associated with negative dispositions.

Thus, the internalizing of age norms has much more far-reaching implications than merely being a reflection of statistical age norms. Age-normative conceptions are social frames of reference and as such give rise to age-graded levels of goals for individual agents. Failing to attain these aspirations and goals has negative consequences for self-evaluation. In this way, age-normative conceptions, psychologically, are what they have been denied to be in the realm of social institutions: They do have the status of *ought rules*, and failing to abide by them results in *sanctions*.

Hence, age-normative conceptions are both internalized and widely shared among members of a given society. They reflect and at the same time constitute social institutions and can therefore be conceived of as "social constructions of reality" (Berger and Luckmann 1966). As will become apparent in the following review, empirical research in sociology, psychology, and gerontology has mostly focused on normative conceptions based on chronological age. Normative conceptions about age-sequential constraints have not so far been investigated (see prospects for future research, in Chapter 8).

In psychology, the phenomenon of age-normative conceptions has entered empirical research via diverse research traditions. These include research about age stereotypes, age estimates, age-differential attributions of behavior, age-based segmentation of the life course, age-related knowledge systems, and subjective age identification. Age-normative conceptions can provide a social frame of reference for evaluating other people or be used as a normative reference for evaluating one's own life-course status. In the following section, studies focusing on age-graded perceptions of other people are considered, while research investigating the interface of self-related and normative conceptions is considered in the context of social comparisons (see Chapter 7). The following section, which reviews the large amount of literature on age-related normative conceptions, will first consider the phenomenon of age segmentation of the life span, followed by a review of empirical studies on age estimates, age categories, evaluations of age segments, and age norms for behavior and the timing of life events. In this context, some intriguing inconsistencies in research about age stereotypes are discussed and linked to phenomena of self–other contrast (further discussed in Chapter 7). The chapter concludes with a discussion of our own research on normative conceptions about *psychological development* throughout adulthood.

Normative Conceptions about Life-Course Stages:
Age-Timing, Evaluation, and Behavior

Previous research about age-normative conceptions has focused on life-course stages and age categories. This research has provided a rich body of findings regarding laypersons' conceptions about different age groups, the desirability of belonging to either age group, and the expected behavior of different age groups. This body of research lays the foundation for the study of age-normative conceptions about developmental change addressed in the next section. Particularly relevant are the studies on age-normative behavior and life events and the research that uncovers contrasting views about specific old people (including the self) and old people in general. The latter issue will become central when discussing strategies of developmental regulation, in which the self is juxtaposed to the generalized other, in Chapter 7.

Segmentation of the Life Course and Age Categories. The most straightforward question regarding normative conceptions about the life course regards the way in which the life course is segmented into age periods. Shanan and Kedar (1979–80) asked their sixteen- to seventy-eight-year-old subjects to divide the life span into as many segments as they wished. Most of their subjects designated six segments with the following age boundaries: adolescence eleven to twenty years; early adulthood, twenty to thirty years; adulthood, thirty to fifty years; middle adulthood, fifty to sixty years; advanced adulthood, sixty to about seventy years; and late sixties and above. Women of all age groups exhibited a more differentiated view (i.e., identified more age categories) of age segmentation of the life course than men. Middle-aged and old respondents divided the life course into fewer segments than adolescents and young adults.

Fry (1976, 1980) had a representative sample of adult women and men sort cards with person descriptions containing information about gender, family status, children, educational attainment, occupational position, and residence situation. Subjects could use any number of piles to sort the cards. The resulting age segmentation of the life course was highly consensual and reflected a set of combinations of the three dimensions "responsibility-engagement," "reproductive cycle," and "encumberment": Those in their early twenties have fewer social responsibilities, no children, and fewer multiple burdens (establishing a career, finding a partner, etc.); people in their late twenties and mid-thirties have more social responsibilities, are still childless, and are emotionally more stable; thirty-five- to fifty-year-olds have even more social responsibilities, children, and more burdens; and finally fifty- to seventy-year-olds have fewer social responsibilities, no dependent children, and therefore do not feel burdened.

Another set of studies investigated which specific age periods are associated with the age categories "young adult," "middle-aged adult," and "old adult." In an exemplary study by Cameron (1969) young, middle-aged, and old adults provided age boundaries for the categories "young," "middle-aged," "old," and "very old." The resulting age boundaries for the four life-course age segments were as follows: young adults, eighteen to twenty-five years; middle-aged adults, forty to fifty to fifty-five years; old adults, sixty-five to eighty years; and very old adults, over eighty years. Interestingly, a small but significant distortion in these mostly consensual age boundaries was identified for the middle-aged respondents. These subjects advanced the end of midlife from fifty years, considered the end of midlife by young and old respondents, to fifty-five years. At the same time, the middle-aged respondents advanced the onset of old age from sixty to sixty-five years. By both extending midlife and delaying old age, these middle-aged respondents seem to have awarded themselves a reprieve ("Gnadenfrist") before entering the next and less valued age segment.

Drevenstedt (1976) reports similar findings for estimates provided by young and old adults of the onset of young adulthood, midlife, and old age. The resulting age boundaries were congruent with those found by Cameron. However, the old respondents' age estimates were distorted in a way analogous to those provided by the middle-aged respondents in the Cameron's study. Drevenstedt's old subjects delayed the entry age of midlife to forty-two years and, moreover, advanced the onset of old age to seventy years. This way, these older respondents, 50 percent of whom were younger than seventy, could consider themselves neither middle-aged nor old.

The set of studies reported above provided rich evidence for distortions in age segmentations of the life course based on respondents' personal age. Such distortions indicate that age-normative conceptions are far from "cold cognition," but charged with self-involvement (J. Heckhausen & Krueger 1993). As social constructions of reality they are not arbitrary but constrained in their variability vis-à-vis reality. However, age-normative conceptions are highly relevant for the individual personally, because even if the respective age period is not currently her own, it will have been or will become the present self. Behavioral expressions of a dynamic interface between the personal age and age-normative conceptions are closely related to phenomena of strategic social comparison and social downgrading that will be discussed and empirically investigated in Chapter 7.

Evaluation of Age Groups. Another implication of the distortions found is that the different segments of the life course are not valued equally. Direct evidence for this conclusion is found in research about the evaluation of different ages. Tuckman and Lorge (1952) asked young adults and elderly residents in old people's homes (Tuckman & Lorge 1954) to indicate in which of eight decades of life (0–12, 13–19, 20–29, 30–39, 40–49, 50–59, 60–69, 70 years and above) people are most and least happy, free, financially independent, find meaning in life, are needed by others, are respected, and so on. There was consensus between young and old respondents that people are happiest in childhood (0 to 12 years) and young adulthood (20 to 29 years) and most unhappy in advanced old age (more than 70 years). Moreover, young and old subjects agreed that people in their thirties are most fulfilled and in their seventies least fulfilled; that most money is earned in midlife (40 to 49 years) and the least in adolescence (13 to 19 years; childhood was excluded from this question); that most authority and prestige is enjoyed in the fifties and the least in childhood; that most hobbies are pursued in early old age (60 to 69 years) and the least in young adulthood (20 to 29 years); and finally, that religion is of most interest in advanced old age (over 70 years) and least interesting to people in their twenties.

Chiriboga (1978) asked sixteen- to sixty-seven-year-olds which period of life is the best ("absolute top") and which the worst ("rock bottom") both for most other people and with regard to their own past, present, and future lives. There was high consensus in considering the twenties as the happiest and the seventies and eighties the most unhappy time of life, both for one's own personal life and for the life of most other people. Interestingly, adolescence was regarded as a very happy time for most other people but as the most unhappy time in one's own life. Older respondents evaluated their own and higher ages less negatively than young and middle-aged subjects. Women believed that the worst time of their lives had already passed, whereas men deemed the worst was yet to come.

A whole array of studies was dedicated to attitudes and stereotypic conceptions about old age and elderly people (see Green 1981; Harris & Associates 1975, 1981; Lutsky 1980; McTavish 1971). Overall the evidence indicates a negative view of aging and old people in those studies which target aging and old people *in general* (e.g., Golde & Kogan 1959; Harris & Associates 1975, 1981; Kogan 1961; Kogan & Shelton 1962; Palmore 1977; and a critical review in Schonfield 1982). Not all facets of stereotypical images of aging are negative. Some positive aging stereotypes were also identified (Braithwaite 1986; Brubaker & Powers 1976; Hummert 1990, 1993; Thomas & Yamamoto 1975; Thorson, Whatley, & Hancock 1974) and reflected, for instance, in characteristics like wisdom, dignity, patience, calmness, friendliness, and nurturance

(Ahammer & P. Baltes 1972; J. Heckhausen, Dixon, & Baltes 1989; Rothbaum 1983). In a recent study by Hummert and colleagues (Hummert et al. 1994), older respondents generated more complex representations of positive and negative aging stereotypes than middle-aged adults, with young adults giving the least elaborated system of multiple aging stereotypes. Overall, the evidence suggests that older adults and people with higher education and social status (Aisenberg 1964; Bell & Stanfield 1973; Kogan 1961) hold a more positive view of aging.

A discussion of research on aging stereotypes is incomplete without considering the interface between the stereotype and the individual, and its possible adaptive implications. Research contrasting stereotypical images and the evaluation of individuals has revealed great differences between the typical old person and a *specific* old person (Braithwaite 1986; Braithwaite, Gibson, & Holman 1985–86; Crockett, Press, & Osterkamp 1979; Green 1981; Lutsky 1980; Weinberger & Millham 1975) and between the typical old person and perceptions about one's *own* aging (Ahammer & Baltes 1972; Borges & Dutton, 1976; Brubaker & Powers 1976; Harris & Associates 1975, 1981; Milligan et al. 1985; Mueller, Wonderlich, & Dugan 1986; O'Gorman 1980; Schulz & Fritz 1988; Thomas 1981). Numerous studies indicate that specific old people are viewed much more favorably than old people in general or "the typical old person" (Bell & Stanfield 1973; Braithwaite 1986; Connor & Walsh, 1980; Connor et al. 1978). Under certain conditions older persons are regarded even more highly than young persons (Crockett, Press, & Osterkamp 1979; Sherman, Gold, & Sherman 1978; Weinberger & Millham 1975; see reviews in Green 1981; Lutsky 1980; McTavish 1971). These seemingly paradoxical findings can best be explained in terms of psychological attribution theory (Banziger & Drevenstedt 1982; Blank 1987; Green 1984; Reno 1979). When conceptualized in the framework of Weiner's attribution theory (H. Heckhausen 1989; Weiner 1972; Weiner et al. 1971; Weiner et al. 1972; Weiner & Kukla 1970), chronological age as a causal factor for explaining success and failure can assume an ambivalent role. With regard to old people, age can be used to explain failure and thereby excuse the behavior being judged. In contrast, when considering young people, age is considered an advantage, and thus a facilitating factor for success.

A number of studies have systematically contrasted perceptions of typical old and young adults with perceptions of specific old and young adults (Banziger & Drevenstedt 1982; Crockett, Press, & Osterkamp 1979; Reno 1979; Sherman, Gold, & Sherman 1978; Weinberger & Millham 1975) and found stereotypical negative views of the typical old person coupled with selectively favorable views of specific old people described in desirable ways. In the study by Crockett and colleagues (1979), for instance, subjects read the text of a supposed interview with a thirty-six-year-old or seventy-six-year-old widow. In the text the widow describes herself as active and content with her life and reports either socially desirable or undesirable behaviors and either typical or nontypical behavior. The subjects were asked to take notes about the evaluation of the "widow" and finally rate her on a number of scales. The findings indicate that the older target person was invariably evaluated more positively than the younger target person, irrespective of desirable or undesirable target behaviors. The older target appeared more likeable, had fewer typical aging worries (e.g., health, death, loneliness), fewer typical negative (e.g., dependent, nagging) and more positive (e.g., wise, experienced) attributes of aging than the young target.

Green (1981) integrated conceptual and empirical work in this field in proposing that age should be conceptualized as a causal factor that facilitates behavior according to a negative aging stereotype and inhibits behaviors that contradict the aging stereotype. The actual behavior of a person is then evaluated vis-à-vis these age-related expectations. An attributional need only arises when expectations are violated, as in the case of the failing young or the successful old adult. In these norm-discrepant cases a particularly strong disposition for the respective outcome is presumed (Frieze 1984; Green 1979). The failing young adult thus appears as utterly incompetent and the successful old person as extraordinarily able.

In summary, old age carries the explanatory burden for undesirable aspects and at the same time provides the old target with surplus credit for desirable deviations from the aging stereotype. In the context of reporting our own research on self-related and age-normative conceptions about development in Chapter 7, I will return to similar phenomena associated with the contrast between specific cases and age-based stereotypes.

Normative Conceptions about Development in Adulthood

The following section starts with a brief report on early research of age norms. The major part of this section is devoted to more recent research that extends the empirical study of age-normative conceptions to the domain of psychological functioning and its developmental change across adulthood. This work has been conducted in the context of a research project on age-normative conceptions of young, middle-aged, and old adults about development in adulthood at the Max Planck Institute for Human Development in Berlin (J. Heckhausen

1989, 1990b; J. Heckhausen & P. Baltes 1991; J. Heckhausen, Dixon, & Baltes 1989; J. Heckhausen & Hosenfeld 1988; Hosenfeld 1988) and addressed the question whether and which age-normative conceptions exist about developmental change in psychological characteristics.

Early Research on Age Norms.   In the 1960s, theoretical and empirical research on age norms was initiated by sociologists in the United States. Mathilda Riley applied the distinction of three types of age norms proposed by Roth (1963) to the effect of age criteria on the selection of social roles (Riley, Johnson, & Foner 1972). These three types pertained to the three *P*'s: permission, proscription, and prescription. Numerous empirical studies supported the notion that normative conceptions about appropriate age timing of various role transitions in early, middle, and late adulthood are highly consensual, in spite of some interindividual variations related to age and social class (Neugarten, Moore, & Lowe 1965; Neugarten & Peterson 1957; Pincus, Wood, & Kondrat 1974; V. Wood 1973). Most significantly, the respondents not only agreed about the age norms, but also used them as frames of reference for assessing and evaluating their own life-course status. The interviewed adults were able to localize their own biographical position in the social reference frame of age norms and thus identified their own life-course status in various life domains, such as education, work, and family, as "on-time" or "off-time" (Neugarten, Moore, & Lowe 1965; Sofer 1970).

In addition to age norms about life events, Neugarten and colleagues (1965) investigated age-normative conceptions about age-appropriate behavior (e.g., wearing a bikini, doing the twist, living in one's parents' house). Neugarten's study from the 1960s was replicated in the 1970s and 1980s in the United States (Fallo-Mitchell & Ryff 1982; Passuth & Maines 1981; Zepelin, Sills, & Heath, 1986–7) and in Japan (Plath & Ikeda 1975). These more recent replication studies also show a high consensus in age norms about behavioral constraints, although the samples were selected to represent a wide range of ages, social classes, and both genders. Interestingly, consensus and restrictiveness of these age norms were more pronounced with regard to judgments about what "most other people" regard as age normative, as compared to ratings about "your own opinion." This self/other discrepancy in age-normative conceptions, although present, was much less salient in the Japanese sample as compared to the U.S. samples. Moreover, there was a convergence of age-normative conceptions reported for the self and ascribed to most other people across age of respondents. In the Japanese as well as the U.S. samples, older participants viewed their own conceptions about constraints in age-appropriate behavior as similar to most other people's conceptions, whereas younger respondents perceived their own age norms to be more lenient than those of other people. The convergence of perceptions of developmental constraints ascribed to self and others across subjects' age may reflect a cohort effect, in that age norms are perceived to have slackened over the lifetime of the older respondents.

Adults' Conceptions about Developmental Gains and Losses in Adulthood (Study 1).[2] J. Heckhausen, Dixon, and Baltes (1989) conducted a study of adults' normative conceptions about adult life-span change and desirability of psychological attributes. Their work was guided by three basic hypotheses: (1) Age-normative conceptions about psychological development should be shared common knowledge in a given society. People of all adult ages should hold similar conceptions about the age-related change of psychological characteristics in much the same way as previous research has shown overall consensus about age segmentation of the life span and normative timing of important life-course transitions. (2) There should be a systematic shift from expected positive change (gains) to expected negative change (losses) at increasing target ages. The higher the target age, the fewer gains and the more losses should be attributed to it. This prediction concurs with prevailing findings on negative stereotypes of aging. However, in keeping with life-span models of development (e.g., P. Baltes, 1987), which assert potential gains (and losses) at all ages, it was expected that some select growth potential would be expected for all ages, including advanced old age. (3) Based on their accumulated personal experience and exposure to peers' developmental change, older adults should express more elaborate conceptions about development.

Young (20–36 years), middle-aged (40–55 years), and old (60–85 years) women and men responded to a large list of attributes describing personality (e.g., skeptical), social (e.g., friendly), and intellectual (e.g., intelligent) characteristics. Subjects were instructed to consider people in general, not just themselves, and were requested to rate each attribute with regard to the extent it is perceived to increase at any period during adulthood (20–90 years). Attributes identified as change-sensitive were also rated with regard to desirability, expected age at onset (i.e., the age at which increase starts), and the expected closing age (i.e., age at which increase ends) for each attribute on an

[2] The numbering of studies in this monograph does not always follow the chronological sequencing but rather reflects a grouping by topics.

Table 2.1. *Study 1: Eigenvalues of principal components, variance explained by rotated factors, and factor intercorrelations*

			Intercorrelation		
Variable/factor	Eigenvalue	Variance explained	A	B	C
Developmental increase					
A	25.80	13.40	1.00		
B	10.40	7.81	.36	1.00	
C	4.47	7.50	.12	.39	1.00
Desirability					
A	78.21	9.10	1.00		
B	2.99	6.76	.71	1.00	
C	2.15	4.41	.71	.69	1.00
Onset age					
A	39.81	20.81	1.00		
B	4.79	5.48	.58	1.00	
Closing age					
A	28.46	18.97	1.00		
B	5.73	6.54	.41	1.00	

Source: From J. Heckhausen, R. A. Dixon, & P. B. Baltes (1989). Gains and losses in development throughout adulthood as perceived by different adult age groups. *Developmental Psychology, 25,* 109–121. Copyright © 1989 by the American Psychological Association. Adapted with permission.

eight-step scale, representing ages from the twenties through the nineties.

The findings indicated substantial interindividual consensus for expected developmental increase, desirability, and expected onset and closing age. The correlations of item means between and within age groups were substantial (all above .58) and mostly high (above .80). Moreover, Q-technique factor analysis, which intercorrelates individuals across variables – that is, attributes in this case – revealed factor structures with few factors involving rather strong first components (three factors for expected increase and desirability and two factors for expected onset and expected closing age). Table 2.1 shows Eigenvalues, variance explained, and factor intercorrelations. The comparatively large Eigenvalues and amounts of variance explained by the first factors for expected developmental increase, desirability, and expected onset and closing age indicate that there was much agreement about age-normative conceptions. The Q-technique factor analysis, therefore, supports the conclusion that interindividual consensus about expected developmental change in adulthood was high.

In order to investigate the target age-related pattern of desirability of

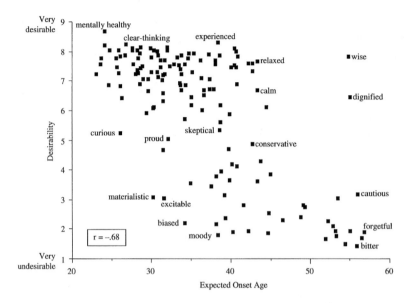

Figure 2.1. Study 1: Mean ratings of desirability and expected onset for 148 change-sensitive attributes. (From J. Heckhausen, R. A. Dixon, & P. B. Baltes [1989]. Gains and losses in development throughout adulthood as perceived by different adult age groups. *Developmental Psychology*, 25, 109–121. Copyright © 1989 by the American Psychological Association. Adapted with permission.)

expected changes, the correlations between expected onset age and desirability and expected closing age and desirability were examined. Figures 2.1 and 2.2 illustrate the target age-related pattern of desirability specifically with regard to expected onset (Figure 2.1) and expected closing age (Figure 2.2).

As can be seen in Figure 2.1, expected onset age and desirability of attributes were highly negatively correlated. Attributes expected to increase early in adulthood were mostly desirable, whereas those expected to increase in later adulthood were predominantly undesirable. Notable exceptions are the attributes "wise" and "dignified," which are highly desirable but also are thought to increase later in life. With regard to expected closing ages (see Figure 2.2), the correlation was also negative, but much less pronounced. Although in general the adults indicated that desirable attributes were somewhat less likely to continue increasing into later adulthood, a substantial number of attributes were in fact expected to exhibit sustained growth. This feature of the target age by desirability pattern supports the expectation that laypersons' conceptions about development might reflect the life-span scientific notion of select but continued growth potential in advanced

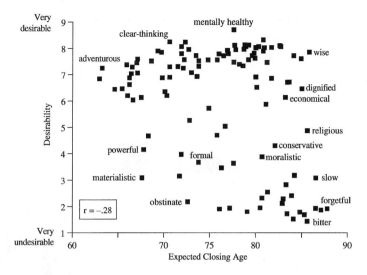

Figure 2.2. Study 1: Mean ratings of desirability and expected closing age for 148 change-sensitive attributes. (From J. Heckhausen, R. A. Dixon, & P. B. Baltes [1989]. Gains and losses in development throughout adulthood as perceived by different adult age groups. *Developmental Psychology*, *25*, 109–121. Copyright © 1989 by the American Psychological Association. Adapted with permission.)

old age. To put the two aspects of age-related timing (onset age and closing age) together and provide an integrated picture of the relative amount of gains and losses across the adult life span, Figure 2.3 displays the percentage and absolute number (see figure insert) of ongoing gains and losses across the seven decades of adult life covered in this study.

As expected, the relative amount of perceived losses gradually increased across the adult life span, with an acceleration of decline occurring around seventy years of (target) age, while perceived gains gradually lost ground in a complementary fashion. The insert to Figure 2.3 gives the absolute numbers and illustrates that at all ages except the last decade (eighty to ninety years) expected gains outnumbered expected losses. At this point it is important to keep in mind that the pool of adjectives did not include all possible changes occurring at higher ages but focused on psychological attributes. A much different picture would most likely emerge, for instance, for a pool of adjectives focusing on health-related aspects of development.

The third aim of the J. Heckhausen and colleagues (1989) study was to identify age differences in the elaboration of age-normative conceptions about adult development. Two aspects of elaboration were investigated: dimensional richness and temporal differentiation. For each age group the number of attributes was identified, which had been

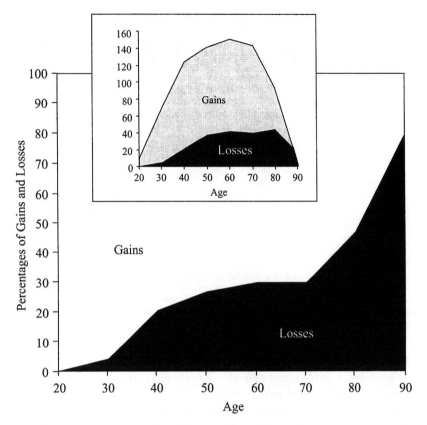

Figure 2.3. Study 1: Quantitative relation of gains and losses across the adult life span. Insert: percentages and absolute numbers. (From J. Heckhausen, R. A. Dixon, & P. B. Baltes [1989]. Gains and losses in development throughout adulthood as perceived by different adult age groups. *Developmental Psychology*, 25, 109–121. Copyright © 1989 by the American Psychological Association. Adapted with permission.)

rated as substantially increasing (rating greater than 5) by at least 50 percent of the age group. Figure 2.4 displays the proportions of attributes endorsed by each age group and by various combinations of age groups conjointly.

Given the high consensus in the sample as a whole, it is not surprising that the largest share of attributes identified by this procedure was common to all three age groups (29%). However, the attributes characterized as change-sensitive only by the old adult group were almost as numerous (26%). Middle-aged and old adults yielded a similar share (26%), while other contributions were much smaller (only young: 3%; only middle-aged: 9%; young and middle-aged: 4%; young and old:

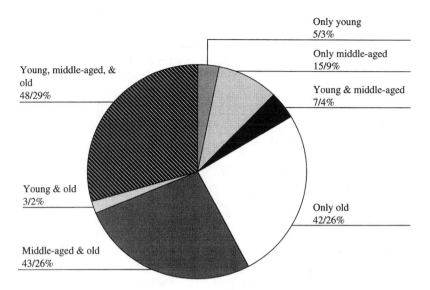

Figure 2.4. Study 1: Attributes perceived as undergoing strong developmental increases by young, middle-aged, and old adults. (From J. Heckhausen, R. A. Dixon, & P. B. Baltes [1989]. Gains and losses in development throughout adulthood as perceived by different adult age groups. *Developmental Psychology, 25,* 109–121. Copyright © 1989 by the American Psychological Association. Adapted with permission.)

2%). Statistical analysis revealed that the young adults endorsed significantly fewer attributes as change-sensitive (63 attributes) than the middle-aged (113 attributes) and the old adults (136 attributes). The middle-aged and old adults did not differ significantly in this respect.

Similar findings were obtained with regard to the temporal differentiation of development-related conceptions. The young adults used the extreme age groups, twenty and ninety years, more frequently than the middle-aged and old adults. Thus, the young adults displayed more of a pattern of expectations about developmental timing reflecting age stereotypes than the middle-aged and old adults. Along with the old adults, middle-aged adults expected the forties and the seventies more frequently to be onset ages. Finally, with regard to age eighty, the middle-aged subjects expressed richer expectations than the young adults, and the old adults more frequently exhibited an even more differentiated image of advanced old age than the young and middle-aged adults, by not only expecting age ninety but also the eighties to be ending markers of developmental increase.

In sum, J. Heckhausen and colleagues (1989) demonstrated substantial consensus about the nature and timing of developmental change in psychological attributes across the adult life span. The overall pattern of expectations involves gradually decreasing gains and increasing losses with later age timing in the adult life span. However, some potential for continued growth is envisaged even for advanced old age. On the basis of consensual normative conceptions about developmental change already present in young adulthood, accumulated personal experience throughout adulthood apparently promotes the elaboration of these normative conceptions, in terms both of dimensional richness and temporal differentiation.

Adolescent Precursors of Age-Normative Conceptions in Adulthood (Study 2). In order to trace back developmental precursors of age-normative conceptions about development, a further study was conducted using the same instructional paradigm as J. Heckhausen and colleagues (1989) but involving adolescents (J. Heckhausen 1989; J. Heckhausen & Hosenfeld 1988; Hosenfeld 1988). Adolescents ranging from eleven to seventeen years of age were requested to rate a large pool of adjectives (see description of J. Heckhausen et al., 1989) with regard to the expected developmental increase during adulthood, desirability, and the expected ages of onset and closure.

In general, the adolescents' conceptions about development in adulthood resembled those found for adults. Desirable changes were expected to predominate in early adulthood, while undesirable changes were ascribed to older ages. The correlation between expected onset and closing ages and desirability were negative (desirability onset age: $r = -.74$; desirability closing age: $r = -.49$). There were also age-related differences with respect to the age timing of developmental stagnation, defined as the point at which expected closings of developmental processes outnumber expected onsets. As shown in Figure 2.5, the expected age of developmental stagnation is represented at the point at which the curves for expected onset and closing cross. As may be expected, the expected age of stagnation is earlier for the adolescents (45.8 years) than for the young adults (54.7 years), and earlier for the middle-aged (53.9 years) compared to the old adults (58.0 years). Developmental differences among the adolescents themselves were also identified. These pertained to two key variables of development, chronological age and the frequency of contact with older people (see Figure 2.6).

Older adolescents endorsed more attributes as subject to developmental change during adulthood than did younger adolescents. This age difference mirrors the age differences found in the study of adults' age-normative conceptions (J. Heckhausen et al. 1989). With increasing age, development-related conceptions about adulthood become richer.

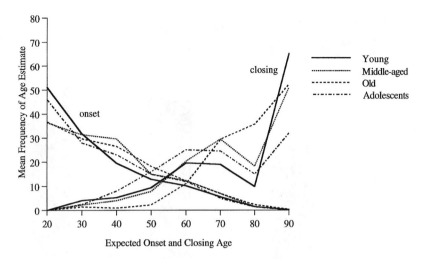

Figure 2.5. Study 2: Mean frequency of decade endorsement for expected onset and closing age; separate for adolescent, young, middle-aged, and old adults. (Adapted from Hosenfeld 1988.)

In addition, frequency of contact with elderly people also increased the richness of development-related conceptions. Adolescents with frequent contacts (at least weekly) to people over sixty-five years of age expected more psychological attributes to increase during adulthood than those who met elderly people only monthly or less.

Conceptions about Controllability of Developmental Change in Adulthood (Study 3). The research on normative conceptions about development was further expanded by an investigation of perceived controllability of expected psychological change (J. Heckhausen & P. Baltes 1991). Perceived controllability is a crucial aspect of laypersons' conceptions about development, because it provides a link between belief systems, values, and goals, on the one hand, and behavior, on the other (for a detailed discussion, see Chapter 7). Depending on whether certain outcomes are perceived as controllable or uncontrollable, individuals decide on the feasibility of action. In the context of age-graded changes, this implies, for instance, that undesirable developmental changes perceived as uncontrollable will not provoke attempts to hinder such decline, whereas negative changes perceived as controllable will elicit active attempts to counteract the loss. J. Heckhausen and P. Baltes (1991) addressed three issues in their study of perceived controllability of expected psychological change across adulthood and old age: (1) We

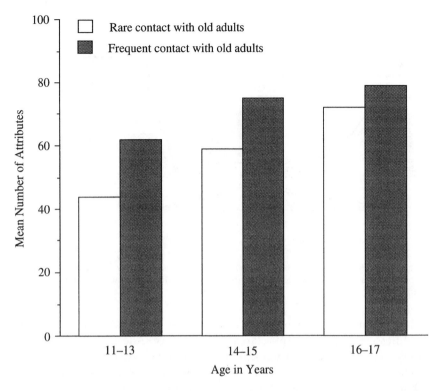

Figure 2.6. Study 2: Mean number of attributes perceived as change-sensitive; separate for different adolescent age groups and groups with frequent or rare contacts with old adults. (Adapted from Hosenfeld 1988.)

predicted that psychological changes expected later in adulthood would be perceived as less controllable than changes expected in earlier adulthood; (2) it was expected that desirable changes would be perceived as more controllable than undesirable changes; (3) we explored potential differences in perceptions of controllability of developmental change between adult age groups in mean level and dimensional structure (across attributes).

A subsample of the young, middle-aged, and old adult subjects involved in the study by J. Heckhausen and colleagues (1989) took part in the study on perceived controllability of change. The questionnaire contained a large number of adjectives describing psychological attributes and selected them so as to include only attributes that were previously rated as change-sensitive in adulthood. Subjects were asked to rate each attribute as to whether they thought its increase could be influenced (facilitated or hindered).

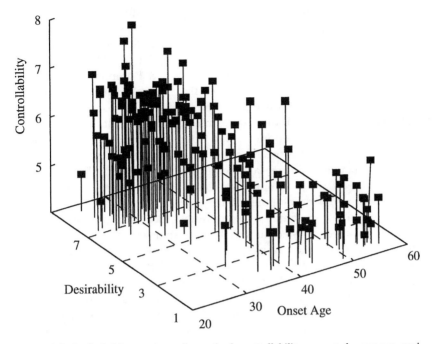

Figure 2.7. Study 3: Mean ratings of perceived controllability, expected onset age, and desirability for 163 change-sensitive attributes. (From J. Heckhausen & P. B. Baltes [1991]. Perceived controllability of expected psychological change across adulthood and old age. *Journal of Gerontology: Psychological Sciences, 46,* 165–173. Copyright © The Gerontological Society of America.)

The findings indicate that perceptions about controllability were consensual. The three Q-technique factors extracted comprised 17, 6, and 5 percent of the variance. Thus, the first factor being substantially larger than the other two indicated a consensus about perceived controllability of developmental change. Moreover, the overall perceptions of controllability of change were optimistic. Most changes were rated as controllable, with the lowest mean controllability rating for the attribute "confused" at 3.8.

The expected age-related decrease in perceived controllability of developmental change across adulthood was confirmed. The correlation between perceived controllability and expected onset age was substantial and negative ($r = -.48$). Figure 2.7 provides a three-dimensional display of perceived controllability, desirability, and expected onset age for each attribute and shows that perceived controllability decreased with increasing ages of expected onset of change. Moreover, desirability and perceived controllability were strongly positively related ($r = .64$).

Desirable changes are perceived as more controllable than undesirable changes. This supports our expectation and suggests that there may be a motivated bias in perceptions of controllability akin to the well-documented "positive attributional pattern" (H. Heckhausen 1987a) or "attributional egotism" (Snyder, Stephan, & Rosenfield 1978). The positive attributional pattern implies that successes are attributed to factors internal to the individual, whereas failures are ascribed to external factors, which the individual cannot control. Similarly, in the context of normative conceptions about development adults may be motivated to perceive positive changes (successes) as controllable and negative changes (failures) as uncontrollable. This way, the individual can take credit for developmental gains while rejecting responsibility and self-blame for developmental losses.

With regard to potential age differences, no mean differences were found. However, Q-technique factor analyses revealed an age-differential distribution of subjects across factors (see detailed description of analysis and results in J. Heckhausen & P. Baltes 1991). The first factor was substantially larger than the other two. Moreover, the first factor was shared among the young and middle-aged adults and included only one old person. This factor involved particularly low controllability ratings for late-onset psychological decline (e.g., for the adjectives sad, nagging, forgetful, confused, weak). Thus, older subjects differed from young and middle-aged adults in viewing developmental decline in old age as more controllable. Moreover, the relationship between desirability and perceived controllability of psychological change varied in strength across age groups. Older ($r = .78$) and middle-aged ($r = .69$) adults expressed a closer relationship between desirability and perceived controllability than young adults ($r = .35$). Thus, the older adults were more likely than the young adults to perceive gains as controllable and losses as uncontrollable. This finding can be interpreted in the context of motivated biases. Beliefs about controllability that are consistent with the positive attributional pattern are effective as motivated biases only for the attribution of outcomes which have already occurred, but not prospectively. For instance, when a loss has already occurred it is helpful to reject personal responsibility for it, but when a future loss is feared, it is not adaptive to expect no personal control. Thus, older adults who take a retrospective view of large segments of the adult life span are more motivated to use attributional biases than young adults. Young adults have a prospective viewpoint on the life course. Motivated biases that discourage active attempts to counteract negative developmental change would in fact be maladaptive for them.

In sum, J. Heckhausen and P. Baltes (1991) showed that perceptions about controllability are part of normative conceptions about life-span development. Perceptions of controllability are optimistic and systematically vary with expected age timing and desirability of change. Age-related differences, in general, are small. However, older adults perceive developmental losses in old age as more controllable than do young and middle-aged adults. Moreover, older and middle-aged adults exhibit a greater tendency toward a positive attributional pattern than young adults. This may be due to the different temporal vantage points from which the age groups view the life span as either in the past or the future.

Age-Normative Conceptions and Social Perception (Study 4). A further aspect of the research program on age-normative conceptions about development in adulthood concerned the role played by normative conceptions in the social perception of stereotype-congruent and -incongruent persons. Age-related conceptions about development and respective age stereotypic categories might serve as organizers of social perception. Similar to other dimensions of social classification (e.g., gender, social class), age information might carry assumptions about various human characteristics that are typically associated with certain age levels. Thus, people might expect a forty-year-old, for instance, to be married, have children, and be settled in his or her occupation. These age stereotypes are used to make social judgments more efficient. However, what happens if a given individual departs from such stereotypes? The "attribution of contrast" model (J. Heckhausen 1990a; Krueger, Heckhausen, & Hundertmark 1995) assumes that persons who deviate from the age stereotype of their age group are perceived as atypical and surprising. Moreover, the "attribution of contrast" model also proposes that stereotype-incongruent persons will elicit a search for causal attribution, which will usually result in the ascription of more extreme personality dispositions than in the case of stereotype-congruent persons.

Krueger and colleagues (1995) conducted a study to test the "attribution of contrast" model. Young, middle-aged, and old women and men were presented with vignettes describing a target person's age, occupation, and family status. In the experimental group the age of the target person was given as forty-five years, while in the control group no age information was given. The target characters varied systematically by age status for the work and the family domain. The age status in the family or the work domain was either on time (i.e., resembling the age stereotype for forty-five years), delayed (i.e., resembling the age stereotype for thirty years), or advanced (i.e., resembling the age stereotype for sixty years). All possible combinations of on-time, advanced, and delayed family and work status generated nine vignettes, which were presented to all subjects in the experimental group.

Subjects were asked to rate the target person on a number of variables: typicality for middle-aged adults, apparent age, how surprising the work and family status was, likability, respect, ascribed satisfaction with family and work situation. Moreover, participants were requested to provide ratings of causal attribution for the respective life situation in terms of the target's own personal control, personality, the influence of powerful others, and general life-span circumstances. In addition, open-ended responses were collected with regard to the first impression of the target person and the causal explanation for the target's current life situation.

The findings indicate a successful test of the "attribution of contrast" model for social perception of stereotype-congruent and -incongruent persons. As expected, target persons in the experimental condition (age of forty-five years given), who were developmentally delayed or advanced were perceived as less typical than persons who appeared to be developmentally on time. Thus, the experimental variation of information contained in the vignettes did succeed in generating perceptions of the target person being "on" or "off" in terms of age-related timing of family and work status.

The predicted interaction of experimental versus control condition and developmental age (advanced, on-time, delayed) was significant. This interaction implies that apparent developmental age only affected the judgment (e.g., of surprise) when the chronological age of forty-five years was given (i.e., experimental condition). Figure 2.8 displays mean ratings of surprise in the experimental and the control condition for three privotal vignettes: family and work status on time (i.e., typical for a forty-five-year-old), family and work status advanced, family and work status delayed. Surprise ratings are displayed separately for the family and the work status, because they were assessed specifically for the two domains. The top panel shows subjects' mean ratings of surprise over the family domain, while the bottom panel shows mean ratings of surprise over the work domain.

Surprise ratings were higher in the experimental conditions of advanced or delayed timing compared to on-time targets. No such difference was found in the control condition, where no information about the target person's chronological age (i.e., forty-five years) was given. Thus, enhanced surprise was due to the contrast between a chronological age of forty-five years and advanced or delayed timing of family and

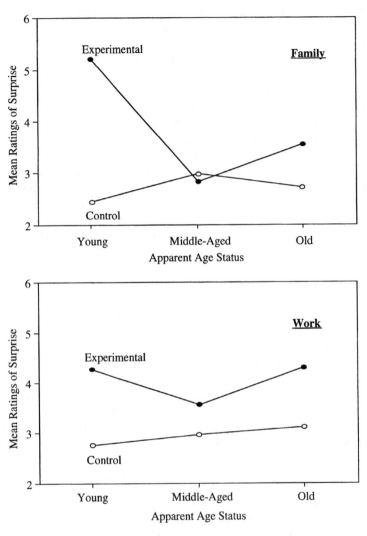

Figure 2.8. Study 4: Mean ratings of surprise with regard to the family and work status of target persons in social perception. (From J. Krueger, J. Heckhausen, & J. Hundertmark [1995]. Perceiving middle-aged adults: Effects of stereotype-congruent and incongruent information. *Journal of Gerontology: Psychological Sciences, 46,* 165–173. Copyright © The Gerontological Society of America.)

work status. A similar pattern of results was found for the number of words written in the open-ended responses about causal explanations for the target's life situation. Again, the interaction between experimental versus control condition and developmental age was significant. Delayed and advanced targets in the experimental but not the control condition elicited longer statements about causal explanations. These findings support the "attribution of contrast" model.

With regard to the evaluation of the target person, findings partially conformed to the prediction based on the "attribution of contrast" model that off-time targets in the experimental condition should be rated more extremely. The predicted pattern of findings was obtained only for women and female targets. Given that gender of subject and target were matched (due to restricted resources a completely crossed design was not realized), it is unclear whether the predicted pattern was produced by women exclusively or was elicited by female targets exclusively. For females, developmental delay was more negatively evaluated than being on time, and developmental advancement was evaluated more positively than being on time.

Further support for more extreme evaluations of off-time targets in the experimental condition came from the open-ended responses to the question about the first impression and about causal explanations, which were coded on a desirable–undesirable scale. For both women and men, developmentally older (i.e., advanced) and on-time target persons received more favorable evaluative statements than developmentally younger (i.e., delayed) target persons. In accordance with predictions based on the "attribution of contrast" model, this pattern pertained only to the experimental condition, when the target persons were identified as being forty-five years old.

Thus, convergent evidence in support of the "attribution of contrast" model was found for reactive (item rating) and operant (open-response) measures of target evaluation. It should be added that the evaluative preference for developmental advancement found in this study may be due to the life domains sampled and should therefore not be generalized. It is quite conceivable that other vignettes or more extreme timing (e.g., teenage pregnancy) could elicit negative evaluations of developmental advancement.

Further analyses investigated the relative impact on family status and work status of typicality ratings, surprise, evaluation, life satisfaction, and causal attribution. This was possible because developmental status (on-time, delayed, or off-time relative to chronological age) in the work and the family domain were varied independently in the vignettes, thus yielding incongruent targets (e.g., family advanced, work delayed). The

Table 2.2. *Study 4: Means and significant ANOVA results for ratings of on-time and off-time target persons in the two domains*

Variable (Source of Variance)	Delayed	On-Time	Advanced	F	p	η^2
Typicality						
(FamAge)	4.17	5.76	5.03	33.5	.001	.28
Liking						
(FamAge)	5.81	5.67	5.66	5.6	.004	.06
(WorkAge)	5.20	5.58	5.81	10.9	.001	.11
Respect						
(FamAge)	5.23	5.73	5.67	7.8	.004	.08
(WorkAge)	5.28	5.47	5.86	6.9	.001	.07
Surprise about family life						
(FamAge)	4.43	2.79	3.61	42.2	.001	.31
Satisfaction with family domain						
(WorkAge)	6.02	6.15	6.47	5.1	.007	.06
Satisfaction with work domain						
(WorkAge)	5.44	6.33	6.75	31.2	.001	.26
Personal control in family domain						
(FamAge)	6.25	6.13	5.76	11.8	.001	.18
Personal control in work domain						
(WorkAge)	6.27	6.64	6.99	9.8	.001	.04
Personality in family domain						
(FamAge)	6.20	6.23	5.97	7.8	.001	.08
Personality in work domain						
(WorkAge)	6.44	6.40	6.87	6.4	.002	.07
Powerful others in work domain						
(WorkAge)	5.26	5.75	5.99	10.0	.001	.10
Circumstances in family domain						
(FamAge)	5.46	5.15	5.55	3.8	.025	.04

Note: FamAge = apparent age status in the family domain; WorkAge = developmental age in the work domain.
Source: From J. Krueger, J. Heckhausen, & J. Hundertmark (1995). Perceiving middle-aged adults: Effects of stereotype-congruent and incongruent information. *Journal of Gerontology: Psychological Sciences, 46*, 165–173. Copyright © The Gerontological Society of America.

question was whether the developmental status in the two life domains would exert independent, partial, or interactive effects on how the target person was perceived. Independent effects imply that the developmental status of each domain specifically impacts on ratings regarding the respective domain. In the case of partial effects, domain-specific impacts are present only for one, but not the other. Interactive effects imply that the effect of the developmental status in one domain is moderated by the developmental status in the other. This is the case, for instance, when a developmental delay in the work domain is viewed less negatively because the target person has to deal with a family life that is developmentally advanced (i.e., involves more children). Table 2.2 shows the three means (for the delayed, the on-time, and the advanced target person), the respective F-statistic, level of significance, and effect size. The rows give the information for each variable (e.g., typicality, liking) with respect to the predictor or source of variance, family age (FamAge), or work age (WorkAge).

As can be seen in Table 2.2, the findings overall indicate that the developmental status in the family and the work domain exerted independent effects on the way the target person was perceived in the respective domain. Interactive effects were not found, while partial effects were present in some cases. Family status affected the subjects' ratings of typicality and surprise, whereas work status predicted satisfaction ratings in both domains.

In sum, Krueger, Heckhausen, and Hundertmark (1995) demonstrated that conceptions about age-appropriate family and work status provide a normative framework for social perception. Developmentally off-time persons are perceived as atypical and surprising, and they elicit a search for causal attributions because they contrast with the commonly accepted stereotype about the age group.

Summary

In this chapter, the basic propositions of life-span developmental psychology are first discussed as a broad conceptual framework. According to this perspective, development is a process of continuous gain and loss in various dimensions of functioning throughout life, which is subject to intra- and interindividual variation depending on age-normative, nonnormative, and historical influences and contexts. Developmental regulation is scaffolded by constraints based on the biology of human development and aging, the social structure and sociocultural context, and age-normative conceptions shared by individuals in a given society. In general, such constraints can be classified as lifetime-related, chronologically age-related, and age-sequential. Fundamental examples of biology-based and sociostructural constraints are briefly sketched, while research in age-normative conceptions is reviewed in more detail.

Research on age-based segmentation of the life span, age estimates, and age categories has indicated that chronological age provides structure and meaning to the human life span and gives rise to stereotypical conceptions about age groups that are widely shared in a given society.

However, some specific interindividual differences can also be found and may reflect the personal position of the respondent on the life-span age axis. Similar evidence is found in the area of research about the evaluation of age groups and aging stereotypes. Although normative conceptions about old age present a negative image of aging, specific old people are in contrast to this negative view. Such a specific–general contrast often results in more positive evaluations and favorable causal attributions for specific older target persons, who are viewed as favorable exceptions to the general negative stereotype associated with their age group. In addition, early investigations of age norms initiated by sociologists were reported that indicate the pervasiveness and prescriptive power of age-normative conceptions about the timing of life events and transitions and about age-appropriate behavior.

Our own research extended the study of age-normative conceptions to the realm of psychological change. Age-normative conceptions about developmental change in psychological attributes were found to be highly consensual both within and across adult and even adolescent age groups. They conformed to a negative view of aging, but also involved expected growth even in advanced age. Age differences were small, but where present they reflected more elaborate conceptions of older compared with younger adults. Moreover, evidence for motivated biases with regard to controllability conceptions about change was found. While adults of all ages perceived desirable change to be more controllable than undesirable change, this tendency was particularly pronounced in older adults. It may be that this is a way to avoid self-blame for past undesirable events while facilitating ascription of desirable changes to oneself. Finally, age-normative conceptions also play a crucial role in the perception of others. Attaining an age-congruent developmental status versus being advanced or delayed influences how target persons are perceived and evaluated. Incongruencies of the target person's developmental status with age-normative conceptions violated subjects' expectations and elicited surprise, a search for causes ("attribution of contrast" model), and extreme evaluations.

The conceptual and empirical work reviewed in this chapter shows that the life course provides a context for individual action that is highly structured in terms of age-gradedness and sequential organization. Biological, sociostructural, and age-normative opportunities and constraints thus furnish a framework for the individual's efforts to regulate her own development.

3   Primary and Secondary Control across the Life Span

Now that the fundamental requirements for developmental regulation and the biological sociostructural and age-normative constraints have been outlined in the previous chapter, this chapter will address the means of control available to the individual to meet the demands of developmental regulation. The basic functional characteristics of control-related behavior and its change across the human life span are conceptualized in the life-span theory of control (J. Heckhausen & Schulz 1995). First, conceptually important dimensions for distinguishing various kinds of control-related behavior are discussed. Subsequently, relevant findings from diverse areas of research pertaining to all age groups from infancy to old age are considered and integrated into the new theoretical framework.

Humans strive to produce behavior-event contingencies and thereby to exert control over the environment. This fundamental motivator of behavior is shared with many other species, at least with all mammals. Numerous studies on both humans and nonhuman mammals have shown that behavior-event contingencies bear reinforcing potential in their own right, irrespective of consummatory behavior (White 1959). Thus, for instance, children as well as rats prefer rewards that are contingent on their own behavior over rewards that are noncontingent on their own behavior (Singh 1970).

A deeply rooted desire for behavior-event contingencies is adaptive, because it provides a generalized motivator for adaptive action that reaches in scope far beyond a restricted set of drive-related goals. The fundamental striving for mastery lends reinforcing potential to an unlimited universe of new goals. This way, the organism becomes motivated to develop various new behavior patterns and goal-directed strategies, thus overcoming the previous restriction to tightly bound stimulus-response associations in drive-related behavior. A more differentiated and rich repertoire of behavior enables the individual to control the environment, not only with respect to immediate needs, but

62

also with respect to the more long-term ecological conditions for its own future development, an ability nonexistent in lower species. Humans thereby become the producers of their own development (Lerner & Busch-Rossnagel 1981).

Earlier theories of control have acknowledged the fundamental human striving for behavior-event contingencies (e.g., Bandura 1982b; Rodin 1986; Skinner 1985; White 1959). Complementary research on noncontingent behavior-event relations indicated their devastating effects on behavioral regulation (Abramson, Seligman, & Teasdale 1978; Seligman 1975).

Recent innovations in this field of research have emphasized the assumption of a basic striving for control (Rothbaum, Weisz, & Snyder 1982) and put forward the notion that control striving extends to behaviors directed at "fitting in with the world and 'flowing with the current'" (ibid., 1982, p. 8). Starting from the argument that most apparently passive and introverted reactions to loss of control are in fact attempts to maintain perceived control, namely by adapting the self to the environment, Rothbaum and colleagues (1982) proposed a two-process construct of control, comprised of primary and secondary control. *Primary control* refers to individuals' attempts to "gain control by bringing the environment into line with their wishes." In contrast, *secondary control* captures individuals' attempts to gain control by "bringing themselves into line with environmental forces" (ibid., p. 5). Specifically, the authors propose that secondary control is achieved with regard to expectations ("predictive control"), causal explanations ("interpretive control"), by alliance with a powerful other ("vicarious control"), or with luck ("illusory control"). Related, although distinct, concepts (see also review in Flammer 1990) include problem versus emotion-focused coping (Folkman et al., 1986), active versus avoidance coping (Holahan & Moos 1987), and assimilation versus accommodation (Brandtstädter & Renner 1990).

In their life-span theory of control, Heckhausen and Schulz (1995) have defined primary and secondary control as follows: "Primary control refers to behaviors directed at the external environment and involves attempts to change the world to fit the needs and desires of the individual. Secondary control is targeted at internal processes and serves to minimize losses in, maintain, and expand existing levels of primary control" (J. Heckhausen & Schulz 1995, p. 284). From using these definitions for empirical research and discussing them with other researchers in the field, it became clear that in order to prevent a confusion of terminology it is useful to differentiate between primary (and secondary) control, primary (and secondary) control striving, primary (and secondary) control strategies, primary control potential, and perceived control.

Primary control refers to behavior-event contingencies achieved by an individual. *Primary control striving* refers to an individual's motivation to produce behavior-event contingencies. *Primary control strategies* address the behavioral and cognitive means by which an individual attempts to produce behavior-event contingencies. Long-term *primary control potential* means an individual's capacity to produce behavior-event contingencies on a long-term, typically life-span encompassing basis. This capacity comprises behavioral (e.g., abilities, skills) and motivational resources (e.g., self-esteem, perceived personal control, beliefs about controllability). *Perceived control* refers to the individual's beliefs or conceptions about his/her own capacity to produce behavior-event contingencies.

Secondary control refers to an individual's effective influence over his/her own emotions, motivational states, and mental representations in general. *Secondary control striving* means an individual's motivation to influence his/her own emotion, motivation, and mental representations. Finally, *secondary control strategies* refer to the cognitive and behavioral means employed to influence internal processes.

In the course of the argument to be presented in the following sections, it will become clear that these distinctions are essential, although they may seem minor at this point. Primary control itself, for instance, is conceptualized to follow a very different, that is inverted, U-shape trajectory over the human life span, as compared to the trajectory of primary control striving, which is expected to be fairly stable throughout life. Moreover, the concepts given above involve different degrees of relevance to a psychological perspective on developmental regulation as well as different degrees of empirical accessibility. Whereas primary control itself, and particularly the long-term potential for primary control, extends in conceptual and empirical scope far beyond psychology – involving, for instance, biological characteristics and social resources – the concept of primary control striving is more intrinsically psychological and more accessible to empirical measurement. The empirical studies to be discussed in later chapters focus on investigating primary and secondary control striving rather than on determining realized primary control itself, or even estimating long-term potential for primary control.

The Primacy of Primary Control

Rothbaum and colleagues included self-to-environment adjustments as acts of control with an intent to strengthen the claim that human behavior is dominated by striving for control. However, their two-process model of control also bears the potential of weakening this claim. Building on their distinction between primary and secondary control, some researchers have recently proposed that the two types of control are equivalent in their functional value (Azuma 1984; M. Baltes 1995; Trommsdorff, Essau, & Seginer 1994; Weisz, Rothbaum, & Blackburn 1984). Whether an individual turns to primary or secondary control, in their view, depends on the availability of primary control, the value system of the relevant society, or even the subjective preference of the individual. This position may be characterized as "relativistic." According to this relativistic conception, individuals might forsake primary control in order to serve secondary control needs. Thus, secondary control can hold primacy over primary control under certain conditions – for instance, in collectively oriented cultures (Azuma 1984; Essau 1992; Essau & Trommsdorff 1993; Seginer, Trommsdorff, & Essau 1993; Weisz, Rothbaum, & Blackburn 1984) or in old age (M. Baltes 1995, 1996; Lang et al. 1994).

The fundamental assumption of such relativistic conceptions is that the ultimate goal of human behavior is to maximize subjective well-being. Such reasoning seems plausible at first glance; what else could human behavior be aimed at if not well-being? However, various common patterns of behavior conflict with it. Two prototypical phenomena that contradict the primacy of the well-being assumption will be discussed here: upward adjustments of aspiration levels and habituation to positive affect.

First, when individuals attain certain levels of performance, they usually adjust their levels of aspiration upward (H. Heckhausen 1965; Lewin et al. 1944). To maximize well-being, individuals would have to stick to attained levels of performance. Elevation of aspiration levels is incompatible with the assumption of well-being as the ultimate criterion of functioning. Rather, individuals strive to extend their mastery to previously not managed activities, and thereby to increase their long-term potential for primary control. It is important to note that such promotion of long-term control potential may be bought at the expense of short-term difficulties in primary control; barely manageable tasks have a relatively high failure rate. We shall return to conflicts between short-term and long-term primary control below.

Another case in point is habituation to positive affect (Brim 1992). Even after extremely positive events, individuals usually only briefly experience strong positive affect, which quickly dissipates and gives way to a more neutral emotional state. If the psychic system were focused on optimizing subjective well-being, positive affect would be maintained at least until a negative event overrode it. Frijda (1988) has captured this phenomenon in the "law of hedonic asymmetry" (Schulz & J. Heckhausen, 1997). Adaptation to positive affect is swift because positive affect is contingent upon change. Conversely, negative affect persists under continuously adverse conditions. Thus it seems that the human mind has evolved to optimize effective interactions with the environment rather than to maximize subjective well-being, or, in Frijda's provocative words, "the human mind (is not) made for happiness but instantiating the blind biological laws of survival" (Frijda 1988, p. 354).

In contrast to the relativistic stance, the universalist position asserts that the ultimate goal of human behavior is to maximize primary control across the life span, irrespective of culture, age, or other contextual factors (J. Heckhausen & Schulz 1993a, 1995; Schulz, Heckhausen, & Locher 1991). The universalist position emphasizes the primacy of primary control. Individuals operate to increase, maintain, or defend against losses to their potential to exert control over the environment. Due to selectivity and failure proneness, the two fundamental characteristics of human behavior discussed in Chapter 1, maximizing primary control across the life span does not always mean exerting primary control whenever it is possible. The individual has to select specific goals and refrain from pursuing other options of control. Moreover, the individual has to protect herself against the negative effects of failure on motivation for future attempts at primary control. Both these functions, selectivity and failure buffering, require the usage of secondary control strategies. A more detailed model of how selectivity and failure buffering are achieved by primary and secondary control strategies is discussed in Chapter 4. In sum, the underlying agenda of human behavior, especially with regard to developmental regulation, is to develop and cherish the long-term resources for primary control in terms of time, energy, cognitive and motor skills, and most importantly motivation. This purpose of behavior requires both primary and secondary control strategies.

Although secondary control is necessary to cope with selectivity and failure, it should not become a goal in itself. Instead, secondary control serves long-term primary control. Once secondary control becomes self-serving, the individual will fall prey to pathological delusions. If subjective well-being and optimism as such were the criteria of adaptive control behavior, excessive self-aggrandizement and illusory hopefulness would be the result.

The two phenomena discussed above (upward adjustment of aspirations, habituation to positive affect) speak to the universalist position as much as they conflict with a relativist position, which would propose functional primacy for well-being. All three behavior patterns work toward optimizing long-term primary control. First, upward adjustments of aspiration levels promote the acquisition of new skills, since learning is optimized at medium levels of difficulty (H. Heckhausen 1991). Upward adjustments of aspirations are especially important under the conditions of substantial ontogenetic plasticity, as is the case in human life-span development. Second, habituation of positive affect helps the organism to keep up motivation for attaining goals and thereby to improve its emotional state (Schulz & J. Heckhausen, in press). A sedentary bliss would discourage attempts to change the environment. Emotions may serve as mediating mechanisms to regulate human behavior, such as to promote long-term primary control, but, according to a universalist control perspective, they are only a regulatory mechanism and not the purpose itself (J. Heckhausen & Schulz 1994).

However, the examples considered also raise the issue of conflict between long-term and short-term primary control. What is adaptive for long-term primary control in terms of challenging goals, for instance, might raise problems for maintaining short-term primary control; difficult tasks are easy to fail at. Thus, upward adjustments of aspirations might benefit the individual for long-term future competence but expose him/her to experiences of failure in the immediate future. Hence, the crucial question is: How does someone "know" what adaptive challenges to primary control[1] are and where to find them?

Moreover, one of the most difficult tasks in coping with a loss of short-term primary control is to know when to keep trying and when to give up. How does the individual know which adaptive, manageable challenges are worthy of persistent effort and which maladaptive, excessive demands are to be avoided and defended against?

It might be that, for the most part, we do not have to search for mysterious foresightedness in people's judgments about adaptive and maladaptive challenges, "worthwhile" and "troublesome" goals, and life tracks. Instead, there might be more basic mechanisms on the individual and societal level which safeguard that people's life-course investments follow a latent, nonexplicit "wisdom." One could even assume that, in the normal case, there is no need to assume that individuals are even aware of protecting their long-term primary control. Instead, for the most part developmental regulation is covered by biologically determined behavioral dispositions and sociostructural constraints, so that the individual only needs to take over regulatory tasks at certain conjunctures or under unusual nonnormative conditions.

---

[1] In another context I have referred to such adaptive challenges as "good" stress (J. Heckhausen & Schulz 1993b).

Secondary Control Facilitates Primary Control

Secondary control strategies help the individual to manage the two basic challenges of any human behavior: selectivity and compensation for failure. Most control and coping research has focused on the former aspect, the buffering of failure or losses by cognitively based intrapsychic processes. Indeed, the compensatory need after failure is manifold. Failure experiences result in feelings of frustration and thus involve an inefficient drain of energy. Moreover and more importantly, failure experiences present a threat to self-esteem, mastery (Harter 1974), and perceived self-efficacy (Bandura 1982a). And finally, severe loss may lead to lowered general expectations about the controllability of events, and eventually may result in helplessness (Abramson, Seligman, & Teasdale 1978; Seligman 1975). These negative effects of failure or loss on the potential for primary control can be compensated for by secondary control strategies. The means involved in compensatory secondary control are discussed in more detail in Chapter 4.

The other major function of secondary control has previously not been ascribed to secondary control. However, J. Heckhausen and Schulz (1995) propose selectivity as one of the two major functions of secondary control. Because of the great repertoire of human behavior, resources such as attention need to be focused in order to produce desirable action outcomes. Selective secondary control (see more detailed discussion in Chapter 4) typically means, not only that the commitment to a chosen action alternative is strengthened, but also that alternative goals which might compete for action resources are actively ignored.

A Taxonomy of Control Strategies

J. Heckhausen and Schulz (1995) propose a taxonomy for classifying control strategies that involves a set of conceptually orthogonal dimensions. In addition to the fundamental distinction between primary and secondary control itself, the dimensions veridicality, functionality, and aspect of action identify control-related behavior in a three-dimensional space. Table 3.1 juxtaposes the three conceptually orthogonal dimensions and shows prototypical strategies in each category of secondary control.

In the following section the three dimensions will first be considered. Thereafter, the prototypical strategies in each of the twelve categories will be discussed. First, the dimension of *veridicality* characterizes control strategies with regard to the degree to which they reflect valid

Table 3.1. *Three-dimensional model of secondary control: Functionality and veridicality in different action phases*

		Functional	Dysfunctional
Veridical	*Expectancy*	Social comparison with age peers	Self-handicapping
	Value	Give up on unattainable goals	Dwell on unattainable goals
	Attribution	Make accurate attributions	Make pessimistic attributions
Illusory	*Expectancy*	Positively biased behavior–outcome appraisals; "I could if I wanted to"	Extremely exaggerated behavior outcome appraisals; "I can attain anything I want"
	Value	Devalue unattainable goals; sour grapes	Increase value of unattainable goals
	Attribution	Egotistic attributional bias	Self-blame for uncontrollable events

Source: From R. Schulz & J. Heckhausen (1996). A life-span model of successful aging. *American Psychologist, 51,* 702–714. Copyright © 1996 by the American Psychological Association. Adapted with permission.

accounts of reality. Veridicality of primary control is more easily determined because it can be objectively assessed in terms of known cause–effect relations in the physical world. In the case of secondary control, veridicality is less clearly discernible; but in some cases, such as in the self-perception of competence at a given task, veridical and illusory cognitions can be identified.

The second dimension regards the *functionality* of a control strategy and reflects the degree to which a strategy is adaptive in promoting long-term primary control (see also criteria for optimization, Chapter 4). It may seem surprising that the functionality dimension is conceptualized as orthogonal to the veridicality dimension, because in many instances primary control is best promoted by veridical assessments of reality. However, there are also important exceptions. Veridical representations of reality may become dysfunctional when primary control potential in a given domain is extremely limited and the acknowledgment of this loss of control creates despair and thus severely impairs the motivational and emotional resources of the individual for future primary control in other domains. This may be the case, for instance, with severe disabilities and illnesses. However, illusory control may be very dysfunctional if it misleads and thus compromises primary control.

The third classifying dimension regards the aspect of action addressed by control strategies: *expectancy* of goal attainment, *value* of goal attainment, and *causal attribution* of action outcome. This classifying dimension applies only to secondary control strategies, since primary control refers to the action itself. Secondary control of outcome expectancy includes such phenomena as optimism (Scheier & Carver 1992; Scheier, Weintraub, & Carver 1986; Schwarzer 1994), defensive pessimism (Norem & Cantor 1986a, 1986b), adjustment of aspiration level, and strategic selection of social reference group. Goal values may become subject to secondary control by phenomena such as the "sour grape" effect (Elster 1983), goal substitution, and other changes in the goal hierarchy. Finally, secondary control of attributions might bear out egotistic attributional patterns and related phenomena commonly referred to as "life lies."

After considering the three dimensions, the prototypical strategies in each cell of Table 3.1 will be discussed. The first class of strategies involves those dealing with the expectancy of goal attainment. A veridical and functional way to generate outcome expectancies is the *social comparison with age peers*, because this lays the basis for realistic and age-appropriate standards. In contrast, *self-handicapping*, such as avoiding effort in order to protect oneself against disappointment and self-blame, is dysfunctional. Self-handicapping may ameliorate the negative impact of failure, but at the same time it minimizes the chances for success. On the illusory side (lower section of Table 3.1), *positively biased behavior-outcome appraisals* can at the same time be illusory and functional. For instance, in acquisitional processes, positively biased estimates of one's competence may be adaptive, because they motivate the investment of effort and in the end achieve higher competence, thus overcoming the individual's own illusion. In contrast, *extremely exaggerated behavior-outcome appraisals* are dysfunctional, because they result in unrealistic aspirations and inappropriate action means. Such an overambitious individual is set up for recurrent failure.

The second class of strategies is directed at the value of action outcomes. *Giving up on an unattainable goal* represents a veridical and functional way to cope with failure, because inefficient investments of resources are avoided and the individual is free to commit herself to new or substitute goals. In contrast, persistent *rumination about unattainable goals* drains the individual's resources and threatens self-esteem without achieving anything. On the illusory side (lower section of Table 3.1), *devaluing unattainable goals* ("sour grapes") may represent a distortion of reality in the sense that a previously valued goal is now demoted. However, such a bias is functional because it helps the individual to disengage from the unattainable goal and reinvest resources in more realistic goals. The dysfunctional version of this strategy is *increasing the value of unattainable goals*. This phenomenon is probably rare, although it is commonly known in certain contexts (e.g., unrequited love).

Finally, the third class of strategies addresses causal attributions of action outcomes. In *accurate attributions* functionality and veridicality converge. Attributions that reflect valid cause–outcome relations allow an optimal use of feedback information contained in the outcome and therefore foster future adjustments of action means. On occasion, *pessimistic attributions* may be veridical, but they also have high costs. The individual may be exposed to feelings of helplessness and depression. In favorable contrast, the *egotistic attributional bias* allows the individual to take credit for success while blaming failure on external causes. This attributional pattern is very common (Snyder, Stephan, & Rosenfield 1978) and even distinguishes mentally healthy from depressed individuals (Alloy & Abramson 1979; Lewinsohn et al. 1980). Finally, *self-blame for uncontrollable events* is nonveridical and dysfunctional. It does not reflect reality and also threatens self-esteem, thereby undermining future action potential.

Life-Span Developmental Changes in Primary and Secondary Control

In an earlier article, Schulz (1986) proposed applying the distinction between primary and secondary control to maturation and aging-related change across the life span. According to this approach, control strategies shift in accordance with the developmental change in primary control potential and the developmental availability of secondary control strategies. Figure 3.1 shows hypothetical developmental trajectories for primary control capacity and secondary use of control across the life span (Schulz & J. Heckhausen, 1996) and for primary control striving.

The life-span theory of control asserts that primary control holds functional primacy in the system of control. Therefore, primary control striving is expected to remain high and stable throughout the life span. It is the capacity for primary control that undergoes substantial age-related change. Thus, primary control is postulated to increase very rapidly in infancy and early childhood. During later childhood and adolescence, primary control most likely still increases, but not as rapidly as in early childhood. More moderate still will be the growth of

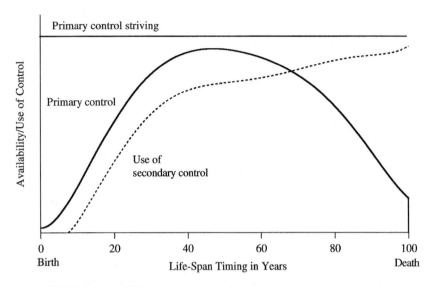

Figure 3.1. Hypothetical life-span trajectories of primary control striving, primary control capacity, and use of secondary control process. (From R. Schulz & J. Heckhausen [1996]. A life-span model of successful aging. *American Psychologist, 51,* 702–714. Copyright © 1996 by the American Psychological Association. Adapted with permission.)

primary control during early adulthood. Sometime in midlife, overall primary control probably begins to stagnate – that is, processes of growth and decline are balanced. In advanced adulthood and old age, primary control can be expected to decline, moderately at first and more radically toward the end of life. In spite of the decreasing capacity for primary control in advanced age, the life-span theory of control would predict that the *striving* for primary control should be stable across adulthood, because primary control still holds *primacy* over secondary control.

The trajectory representing the use of secondary control process in Figure 3.1 reflects two developmental constraints. First, the use of secondary control is determined by the requirements of primary control at any given developmental stage. And second, the use of secondary control is constrained by its own developmental course. Secondary control strategies have to be generated or acquired before they can be put to use for the purposes of action selectivity and failure compensation. Their development requires a somewhat advanced cognitive system; therefore, secondary control is not used in the very first years of life.

In early adulthood a substantial repertoire of secondary control strategies becomes available, although in middle and later adulthood a further elaboration and differentiation of secondary control strategies probably takes place (Hundertmark 1995). However, from early adulthood onward it is the requirements of primary control in terms of compensating for losses and volitional selectivity that mainly determine the use of secondary control strategies. Consequently, the decline in primary control that comes with aging produces an upsurge of secondary control in old age.

The Development of Control-Related Behavior during Infancy, Childhood, and Adolescence

In the early segment of the life span, before humans reach physical maturity, primary control capacity shows major growth. This growth is accompanied by substantial advances in the development of beliefs about action, control, and competence (see review in Flammer 1990; J. Heckhausen 1993; J. Heckhausen & Schulz 1995). However, the striving for primary control is a built-in motivational system from the first days of human life onward. A fundamental drive to control the environment has been demonstrated for neonates, who detect, learn, and take pleasure in behavior-event contingencies (Janos & Papousek 1977; Papousek 1967). This striving for behavior-event contingencies extends to other mammals (see review in White 1959). Rats, monkeys, and other mammals have been shown to prefer nonconsummatory responses, which involve behavior-event contingencies, to event-event contingencies.

In contrast to what is known about other mammals, humans develop this striving for primary control into a more generalized expectancy of contingent behavior-event relations. This notion has been captured in various concepts, such as mastery motivation (Harter 1974), self-efficacy (Bandura 1982a), "Funktionslust" (K. Bühler 1919), "effectance" motivation (White 1959), and perceived control (Rotter 1966). The developmental precursor to and foundation of these phenomena is captured in Watson's concept of "generalized contingency awareness" (Watson 1966, 1972).

It is important to note that in early childhood these generalized expectancies about one's own effectance typically are gross overestimations of the actual level of personal control (Weisz, 1983). Preschoolers, for instance, are convinced that they can control chance events by their own skill and effort (Weisz 1980, 1981; Weisz et al. 1982). It is not until mid-childhood that children acquire more accurate conceptions about their own control potential. This trajectory is also depicted in Figure 3.1. Far from being merely an example of immaturity, the early overestimations of personal control may well have adaptive value (Bjorklund & Green 1992). Because infants and young children experience rapid developmental progression, a fixed and therefore conservative assessment of their own control potential would be a hindrance rather than an aid to developmental advancement.

Generalized expectations about behavior-event contingencies provide the basis for an even more radical advancement in behavioral regulation that occurs toward the end of the second year. At that age the child becomes able to reflect the outcome of an action back to herself (Geppert & Küster 1983; H. Heckhausen 1980, 1982; J. Heckhausen 1988). Action outcomes become sources of information about the self. Self-reflection also paves the way for anticipated positive self-regard. The child can now imagine in advance that she will feel competent after succeeding at a task. This provides a powerful motivational mechanism for any future goal-related activity, because it allows for persistence in activities that lack immediate rewards (delay of gratification; Mischel, Shoda, & Rodriguez 1989).

But the ability to reflect action outcomes back to the self also involves major risks. Failure experiences become a threat to perceptions about one's own competence and thereby may undermine motivational resources for future primary control. The individual therefore needs secondary control-type strategies to counteract and compensate for these negative effects on self-esteem. One is reminded of Gould's argument about the not-selected-for side effects of evolutionary selection that in the further progress of evolution become major constraints and structural requirements (Gould 1977).

At three or four years of age children begin to react to failure with embarrassment and shame, emotional indicators of negative effects on self-esteem (Geppert & Heckhausen 1990; H. Heckhausen 1980, 1984). Currently there is no systematic empirical research about the emergence of secondary control strategies at this early age. However, there are some episodic accounts of failure reactions in three-and-a-half-year-olds that include denial of failure, excuses, and reinterpretations of the outcome as a success (see H. Heckhausen 1974).

The development of secondary control strategies in childhood and adolescence has only recently received attention in empirical research (Compas 1987; Compas et al. 1991a). Using open-ended reports about real-life stressors (Compas et al. 1991b; Compas & Worsham 1991; Curry & Russ 1985; Wertlieb, Weigel, & Feldstein 1987), chronic medical conditions (Band & Weisz 1990), and hypothetical stress scenarios (Altshuler & Ruble 1989; Band & Weisz 1988; Flammer 1990; Flammer, Züblin, & Grob 1988), these recent studies indicate that secondary control strategies, such as distracting oneself from a stressful stimulus, are increasingly used during middle childhood and early adolescence. The cognitive developmental prerequisites of advanced types of secondary control strategies are particularly elucidated by a study conducted by Band and Weisz (1990). They investigated the use of primary and secondary control strategies in adolescents suffering from juvenile diabetes. In addition to age as a marker of developmental status, Band and Weisz also assessed the cognitive level of the youngsters. Formal operational thinking substantially increased the use of secondary control strategies (e.g., "I tell myself I can still live a full life") compared to primary control (e.g., "taking insulin to control my sugar"). Ironically, use of secondary control strategies in the cognitively more advanced adolescents also decreased the behavioral and medical adjustment to the illness. Secondary control may thus have served as an excuse not to engage in appropriate health-care behavior.

In sum, primary control striving is a powerful motivator from the beginning of life onward. The development of primary control is facilitated by the emerging secondary control capacities in childhood and adolescence, and by the time the individual reaches physical maturity a basic repertoire of secondary control strategies is available.

Control-Related Behavior during Adulthood and Old Age

Given that basic strategies of secondary control are in place by early adulthood and that primary control striving remains the central concern throughout life, one should expect stability in control-related behavior throughout adulthood. However, in advanced age the potential for primary control is increasingly restricted. This should not lead to a decrease in striving for primary control, but in order to be effective primary control should focus on goals that are age-appropriate and therefore controllable. In addition, secondary control becomes more essential for maintaining the potential for primary control at older ages in the life span. Recent empirical research on age-appropriateness of primary control striving is presented in Chapter 7, while research relevant to the latter prediction about age increases in salience of secondary control is reviewed in this chapter.

The Stability of Primary Control Striving across Adulthood. In this section, empirical studies will be discussed which speak to the prediction that primary control striving should remain stable across adulthood. Peng and Lachman (1993; Peng 1993) investigated control-related behavior in eighteen- to sixty-four-year-old U.S. Americans and Chinese living in the United States. In accordance with the stability prediction, Peng and

Lachman did not find age differences with regard to self-reported primary control striving. Secondary control indicators, in contrast, exhibited age-related increases from young adulthood (25 to 39 years) to middle (40 to 59 years) and from middle adulthood to old (over 60 years). This pattern of findings suggests that secondary control strategies were increasingly used at older ages to maintain primary control in spite of aging-related restrictions.

However, findings by Brandtstädter and Renner (1990) are inconsistent with this conclusion. In partial convergence with the concept of primary and secondary control, they propose two coping tendencies: assimilative and accommodative. Their conceptual distinction differs from the theory of primary and secondary control in that Brandtstädter and Renner exclude intentional processes from the accommodation category. Accommodation, in their view, is not intended, but "happens" to the individual ("Widerfahrnischarakter"; see also Brandtstädter & Greve 1992; Brandtstädter & Renner 1992). Two scales measuring dispositional preferences in goal striving were developed to indicate interindividual differences in the preference for assimilation and accommodation. "Tenaciousness of goal pursuit" (item example: "When faced with difficulties I usually double my efforts") characterizes assimilative coping, while "flexibility of goal adjustment" (item example: "I find it easy to see something positive even in a serious mishap") is associated with accommodation (Brandtstädter & Renner 1990; Brandtstädter, Wentura, & Greve 1993). The items of these two scales, however, do not emphasize the intentional versus accidental distinction and therefore can also serve as a measurement device for primary and secondary control (see studies reported in Chapters 7 and 8). In a cross-sectional study of German adults ranging in age from thirty-four to sixty-three years, Brandtstädter and Renner found an age-related decrease in tenacious goal pursuit and an increase in flexible goal adjustment. Thus, the findings on flexibility are consistent with the prediction that secondary control increases with age, while the decline in tenaciousness does not agree with the stability prediction.

Recent data from three cross-sectional studies (J. Heckhausen 1994a, 1997; J. Heckhausen, Diewald, & Huinink 1994a; Hundertmark 1995; J. Heckhausen, Schulz, & Wrosch 1998; see detailed reports in Chapters 7 and 8) of German adults only partially converge with Brandtstädter and Renner's findings on tenaciousness. Using the tenaciousness and flexibility scales with samples of adults ranging in age from twenty to eighty-five years, we consistently found stability of tenacious goal pursuit throughout adulthood. Flexible goal adjustment, in contrast, showed the predicted age-related increase. Factor analyses and structural modeling were used to resolve the apparent inconsistency between our findings and those of Brandtstädter and colleagues (see detailed report in Chapter 7). In our data the tenaciousness scale comprised two subscales: one involving the positively and one the negatively phrased items. Interestingly, these two scales show differential age trends, with the positive items exhibiting age-related increase and the negative items showing decrease.

Less direct but convergent evidence for the stability of primary control striving can be found in the literature on age differences in perceived control. Overall, the findings indicate that generalized and internal control remains stable throughout adulthood and well into old age (Brandtstädter & Rothermund 1994; Brandtstädter, Wentura, & Greve 1993; Grover & Hertzog 1991; Lachman 1986a, 1986b, 1991; Lachman & Leff 1989; Reker, Peacock, & Wong 1987; Smith et al. However, with regard to domains of functioning such as health and intellectual capacities, which are specifically affected by aging-related decline, age-related shifts in perceived control are found in some studies (Beisecker 1988; Brandtstädter, Krampen, & Greve 1987; Brandtstädter & Rothermund 1994; Keller, Leventhal, & Prohaska 1989; Lachman 1986a, 1986b; Lachman & Leff 1989; Reker, Peacock, & Wong 1987). In particular, older adults acknowledge a greater influence of external factors (Brandtstädter & Rothermund 1994; Brandtstädter, Wentura, & Greve 1993; Lachman 1986a, 1986b, 1991).

The Primacy of Primary Control in Adulthood. Stability of primary control striving across adulthood alone does not necessarily imply a preference for primary control. However, other evidence about the striving for primary control and about reactions to loss of control support the notion of the primacy of primary control. A large body of observational, experimental, and survey studies demonstrates that individuals at all adult ages readily use opportunities to directly control outcomes in their lives. Various field experiments show that older people benefit in mental and physical health from control-enhancing interventions in their life ecologies (Langer & Rodin 1976; Reich & Zautra 1989; Rodin & Langer 1978, 1980; Schulz 1976; Schulz & Hanusa 1980). Similarly, observational and experimental studies conducted with disabled elderly people living at home or in long-term-care institutions demonstrate a strong desire for independence and the beneficial effects of environments that provide high levels of primary control (Bowsher & Gerlach 1990; Timko & Moss 1990; Wahl 1991).

Research on the detrimental effects of loss of control provides complementary evidence for the importance of primary control opportunities. Loss of control associated with financial problems, for instance, was shown to lead to increased distress among samples of Americans,

Japanese, and Canadians (Krause & Baker 1992; Krause, Jay, & Liang 1991). Older adults who have control over whether or not they work report higher physical and mental well-being (Herzog, House, & Morgan 1991). Similarly, older individuals who are subject to involuntary retirement tend to have more difficulty adjusting to retirement, more illnesses, impaired physical status, and more depressive symptomatology (Swan, Dame, & Carmelli 1991). Finally, medication-related restrictions in activity were a strong predictor of depression among elderly outpatients suffering from cancer, even if the medication reduced pain (Williamson & Schulz 1992a, 1992b). In sum, these studies show that restrictions in opportunities and potential for primary control are abhorrent and lead to negative mental and physical consequences.

Secondary Control Strategies for Coping with Age-Related Losses. Apart from predicting maintained primary control striving across the life course, the life-span theory of control (J. Heckhausen & Schulz 1995) also predicts that at higher ages primary control striving increasingly relies on support from secondary control strategies. Secondary control should increase in salience in older adulthood, because decline and losses become more frequent and severe, and reserve capacity decreases (on reserve capacity see also P. Baltes 1987; Kliegl & P. Baltes 1987). Such declines are also acknowledged by older adults, as can be seen in research on normative conceptions about aging, reported in detail in Chapter 2 (J. Heckhausen & P. Baltes 1991; J. Heckhausen, Dixon, & Baltes 1989; J. Heckhausen & Krueger 1993).

Evidence for the prediction that secondary control strategies are used increasingly at higher ages in adulthood comes from a variety of research fields. However, direct empirical evidence is still scarce, as few researchers in the field of coping with adverse events in the medical, domestic, and family domains focus on age comparisons. Except for direct age comparisons, which in general support an increased use of secondary control with age, some researchers have investigated responses to controllable and uncontrollable stress. Given that controllability of stressors can be expected to decline in old age, this research supplies relevant evidence for our prediction.

Blanchard-Fields and Irion (1988) investigated young and middle-aged adults' coping strategies in controllable and uncontrollable situations. They distinguished between problem- and emotion-focused coping, a distinction that converges with the distinction between primary and secondary control. Both young and middle-aged adults preferred problem-focused coping in controllable situations while resorting to emotion-focused coping in uncontrollable situations. Folkman, Lazarus, Pimley, and Novacek (1987) found that younger adults identified more problems in the domains of work and finances and used proportionately more active, interpersonal, problem-focused coping, such as confrontation, seeking social support, and planful problem solving. Older persons, in contrast, were more concerned with problems in the domains of environmental and social issues, home maintenance, and health, and accordingly used more passive, intrapersonal, emotion-focused coping, such as distancing, acceptance of responsibility, and positive reappraisal. In their research on coping with severe disability, Schulz and Decker (1985) demonstrated the impressive capacities of elderly persons with spinal-cord injuries to adapt emotionally to their impaired condition. One of the ways these people came to terms with their disability was to emphasize the importance of "brain" over "brawn" in defining the quality of their lives. Moreover, using religion as a coping strategy was identified by Koenig, George, and Siegler (1988) as an effective means for dealing with aging-related challenges.

Another class of relevant phenomena in this regard is associated with self-protective or enhancing reference frames. Research on readjustments of reference frameworks indicates that strategic selection of criterial (ideal self), temporal (past, future self), and social comparison standards is used by older adults to maintain well-being in spite of aging-related losses. Ryff (1991), for instance, found that older adults downwardly adjust their ideal self so as to reduce the discrepancy with the actually attained status. Similarly, Lang, Görlitz, and Seiwert (1992) found that in older more than in younger adults developmental trajectories perceived to be ideal converged with those perceived to be realistic. In addition, elderly adults viewed their past more positively than younger adults, and thereby possibly compensated for less promising future developmental prospects. In convergence with these findings, Brandtstädter and colleagues (1993) report that older adults view their past selves more positively than their present selves and expect a decline in the future. Moreover, their data show that conceptions about desired self follow life-span trajectories that mirror perceptions about the actual self, and thus provide a compensatory standard of reference. Not surprisingly, perceived self-deficits remain stable across age in the adults studied by Brandtstädter and colleagues (1993). Further empirical support for the adjustment of reference frames comes from research on strategic social comparisons, discussed in detail in Chapter 8.

One way to control the impact of aging-related threats to the self is to invalidate the information contained in the loss or to redefine the self-relevant domain so as to render the information irrelevant. Greve (1990; Brandtstädter & Greve, 1994) has found evidence that elderly people who experience losses in certain domains of functioning (e.g., remembering a shopping list) show such *immunization mechanisms* to protect the self in that they downgrade the diagnostic relevance of lost skills for more general domains of functioning (e.g., intellectual competence).

The adaptive nature of flexible goal adjustments in old age is supported by research conducted by Brandtstädter and colleagues (Brandtstädter, Wentura, & Greve 1993; Brandtstädter & Greve 1992, 1994; Brandtstädter & Rothermund 1994). First, as reported above, Brandtstädter and Renner (1990) found age-related increases in the tendency to adjust goals flexibly across middle adulthood. An additional sample of younger and older adults covered an age range from eighteen to eighty-nine years. This larger data set also revealed a continuous increase in flexible goal adjustment across adulthood (Brandtstädter, Wentura, & Greve 1993).

Direct evidence for the protective effects of flexible goal adjustment comes from studies that investigate its role as a moderator variable for the effects of stress on mental adjustment (Brandtstädter, Wentura, & Greve 1993; Brandtstädter & Renner 1990). Brandtstädter and Renner (1990) investigated the moderator effect of flexible goal adjustment on the relation between perceived distance from goal attainment and satisfaction with goal attainment. For seven goal domains (social recognition, occupational efficiency, harmonious partnership, empathy, family security, prosperity, and self-esteem), flexible goal adjustment had a compensatory effect in terms of protecting well-being against perceived distance from desired goal states. Converging evidence is also reported by Brandtstädter and Rothermund (1994) for perceived importance of goal, a proxy variable to readiness to give up a certain goal. The subjective importance of a given goal moderates the effect of goal-specific control perceptions on general conceptions about personal control. Moreover, in a study on coping with aging-related health problems, flexible goal adjustment was found to moderate the effect of perceived health problems on depressive symptomatology (Brandtstädter, Wentura & Greve 1993). Interestingly, tenaciousness of goal pursuit exhibited a similar moderator effect, thus suggesting that primary control striving may also serve as a protector against health-related threats to mental adjustment. The authors interpret the latter effect as indicative of adaptive coping with challenges that call for both tenacious and flexible coping. A different pattern of moderator effects emerges when perceived situational constraints are the predictor variable. Again, flexibility of goal adjustment compensated for negative effects of adverse conditions on well-being. However, tenaciousness of goal pursuit amplified the negative impact of perceived situational constraints on well-being. Finally, the valence of future developmental prospects was protected from the negative impact of age restrictions when subjects had a higher tendency to adjust their goals flexibly. In sum, these studies demonstrate that secondary control type strategies can protect the individual's motivational and emotional resources for primary control.

Secondary Control by Strategic Social Comparison.   Social comparisons are a particularly flexible means of reframing reality without compromising the validity of self-related perceptions. One's own behavior can be made to look relatively superior when it is compared downward with that of inferior others (in terms of behavior or capacity) and relatively inferior when compared upward with that of superior others. It is the social frame of reference which produces these differences in relative evaluation. The perception of one's own behavior and the processing of feedback for future improvement of one's own behavior is unaffected by this strategy of secondary control. This has great advantages in terms of avoiding the potential negative effects of positive illusions, which could give rise to unrealistic and therefore futile goals for primary control that would ultimately lead to a depletion of motivational resources.

Upward social comparisons are conducive to motivating and modeling growth in primary control. In this way, comparisons with superior others serve as a secondary-control means to selectively focus motivation on a chosen goal. Thus, for example, a youngster might orient himself toward and compare himself with a successful baseball player and in this way be motivated to invest as much effort and time as his hero invested when he was a youngster his own age. Conversely, downward social comparisons assure the individual that he is doing better than some other people. In this way, negative effects of losses and failure on emotional and motivational resources can be prevented and, thus, secondary control achieved. Such secondary control via downward social comparison is probably most necessary after experiences of losing or decline in control. An older adult suffering from mild arthritis, for example, might compare herself to an elderly neighbor who is bedridden and constantly in pain. In Chapter 7, specific hypotheses about the function and age-gradedness of upward, downward, and lateral comparisons will be developed and relevant empirical research (Studies 7, 8, and 9) will be discussed.

The Functional Limits of the Control System.   To conclude this chapter, scenarios that overtax the individual's control potential are briefly considered. Although, as shown in the previous review of control-related behavior, the capacity of the human mind to protect and maintain the potential for primary control is substantial, there are limits to this capacity. Helplessness as a response to extreme experiences of noncontingency between behavior and outcomes is a long-standing topic of research (Abramson, Seligman, & Teasdale 1978; Alloy & Abramson 1979; Seligman 1975). Most prominently in this area, the learned helplessness model provides a control-based explanation for the occurrence and maintenance of depressive disorders. Although J. Heckhausen and Schulz's life-span model of primary and secondary control was not originally designed to account for pathological processes, but to emphasize the adaptive nature of the control system, it does allow for predictions about boundary conditions for its functioning. Schulz, J. Heckhausen, and O'Brien (1994) have proposed a model of control in the disabling process that ultimately results in depression. Under conditions of increased life expectancy in the general population, the process of physical disability can be conceived of as a normative life event. However, its relentlessly progressive and uncontrollable destruction of primary control ultimately demoralizes the individual to the point of depression. During initial stages, the individual will successfully adapt to his/her continually worsening condition by adapting his/her behavior and resorting to compensatory means (Verbrugge & Jette, 1994). Moreover, secondary control strategies such as downward comparisons with more severely affected persons may help the individual to maintain well-being, perceptions of personal control, and hopefulness. However, when independent functioning is no longer possible in the long run, secondary control strategies will also appear futile for refurbishing long-term primary control. At this point, the individual is no longer able to protect him- or herself from negative affect, and even clinical depression (Kennedy, Kelman, & Thomas 1990; Williamson & Schulz 1992a, 1992b).

A particularly devastating effect on the control system can be expected when substantial losses in primary control occur suddenly and unexpectedly. In such a situation the individual has no time to adapt and anticipatorily compensate through secondary control processes. After experiencing a stroke, for instance, the individual's motivational and emotional resources may be inadequate to buffer the immediate threats to primary control. Thus, when such losses of primary control occur suddenly, and substantially disrupt the individual's experience of primary control, depressive symptomatology and long-term negative effects are frequently the outcome (Schulz, Tompkins, & Rau 1988; Tompkins, Schulz, & Rau 1988). However, even under such unfortunate circumstances, people may eventually overcome the collapse of the control system and reestablish an elaborate control within the constraints set by the disability. A particularly interesting case is the loss of primary control due to unexpected and radical changes in a social or economic system that deprive individuals of economic and occupational opportunities. The socioeconomic transformation of East Germany after reunification is a case in point, and offers a unique opportunity to study the effects of a loss in constraints provided by a social structure and its regulation of life-course patterns. In Chapter 6, this East German case of radical sociohistorical transformation is discussed as a testing ground for the limits of developmental regulation. Age cohort differences in developmental ecologies are discussed and findings (Study 6) presented about the conditions that bring about a collapse of the control system.

Summary

J. Heckhausen and Schulz's (1995) life-span theory of control distinguishes two fundamental types of control-related behavior: primary and secondary. Primary control is directed at affecting changes in the external world, while secondary control addresses the internal world of the individual. Primary control holds functional primacy over secondary control. Secondary control serves primary control by promoting volitional commitment to selected action goals and by compensating for the negative effects of control loss on the motivational resources of the individual. Either type of control can be veridical or illusory and functional or dysfunctional. Moreover, control behavior can occur in different phases of action and address either of three aspects: expectancy of goal attainment, value of goal attainment, or causal attribution of action outcome. Within each of these subcategories, a rich set of phenomena is discussed in the context of the life-span theory of control. Moreover, a review of control-related behavior is given, covering the entire life span from infancy through adulthood to old age. Primary control striving is present from the first days of life and prevails until the end. The potential for primary control, however, shows an inverted U-shape with a radical increase in childhood and declining pattern in old age. Accordingly, the individual needs to employ secondary control to make amends for the age-related decline in primary control potential. Secondary control strategies are developed in middle childhood and adolescence, so that by early adulthood a basic repertoire of strategies is available. Secondary control is used increasingly in middle adulthood and old age. Flexible goal adjustment, one prototypic instantiation of secondary control, has been shown to buffer effectively the negative effects of aging-related losses on well-being. Although the adaptive potential of the human control system is substantial, there are also limits to its effectiveness. Particularly under conditions of severe, sudden, and unexpected loss in primary control, the control system of primary and secondary control may collapse.

4   A Model of Developmental Regulation across the Life Span

In Chapter 2 the biological, sociostructural, and age-normative constraints to the individual's developmental regulation were discussed. This chapter focuses on the role played by the individual in regulating life-span development in the context of these constraints and presents a theoretical model. As argued in Chapter 2, constraints to developmental options are not merely restrictions, but serve as a scaffold to keep the developmental options manageable and help the individual to focus on crucial developmental challenges at any given point in the life course.

Selection, Compensation, and Optimization

As we have seen, the fundamental requirements of developmental regulation across the life span are the management of selectivity and the compensation of failure (Chapter 1). P. Baltes and M. Baltes (M. Baltes 1987; P. Baltes 1987, 1991, 1993; P. Baltes & M. Baltes 1990; P. Baltes, Dittmann-Kohli, & Dixon 1984; Marsiske, Lang, P. Baltes, & M. Baltes 1995) have proposed a metamodel of "selective optimization with compensation" (SOC), which is most relevant here because it involves the aspects of selection and compensation. In the P. Baltes and M. Baltes model, life-span development is conceptualized as a process of continuous selection in the investment of motivational and cognitive resources. This selection process helps the individual to deal with aging-related decline in the ratio between developmental gains and losses and decreasing reserve capacity. Adaptive capacity serves as the criterion for successful development and is optimized when individuals (1) selectively maximize their performance in specific domains of functioning and (2) compensate for aging-related losses and restricted reserve capacity so that essential levels of functioning are maintained. In a recent article (Marsiske, Lang, P. Baltes, & M. Baltes 1995) the definitions of the three components – selection, compensation, and optimization – were restated as follows: "The component of *selection* (my emphasis) refers to the (conscious or unconscious) choice of particular behavioral domains or goals for continued development (growth or maintenance)" (p. 45).

> In the most fundamental sense, *optimization* reflects the view that development is the internally and externally regulated search for higher-level, efficacious, and desirable levels of functioning . . . optimization reflects the notion that – for the targeted domain(s) of functioning – the outcome is expected to be an increase in adaptive fitness (p. 47). . . . Of the three components in the selective optimization with compensation model, optimization . . . is the only component with an *a priori* valence and direction: It always serves the purpose of enhancing or maintaining desired end levels of functioning. (p. 48; my emphasis)
>
> The final component of the model, *compensation,* results particularly from internal and external limits and losses in the range of plasticity, reserve capacity, and contextual opportunities. In other words, limits and losses which concern both the person and the context may be sources for compensation. . . . compensation summarizes strategies of adjustment, such that the functional impact of losses and limits on resources are minimized by relying upon other internal or external resources that are not part of a previously effective behavior system. (Marsiske et al. 1995, p. 49; my emphasis)

The selective optimization with compensation model seems particularly well suited to account for the life-span dynamic of gains and losses in terms of the management of selectivity and failure. P. Baltes and M. Baltes indicate that their selective optimization with compensation model is a general theoretical orientation which needs specific explications and/or modification when applied to a concrete developmental event or outcome. One way to consider the present work is to view it as being stimulated by the selective optimization with compensation model but as proposing an independent theory. The particular topic addressed in this theory is primary and secondary control and their interactive dynamics across the life span (J. Heckhausen & Schulz 1995; J. Heckhausen & Schulz 1998; Schulz, Heckhausen, & Locher 1991; Schulz & J. Heckhausen 1996). This theory and its elaboration with regard to a set of strategies involved in developmental regulation (J. Heckhausen & Schulz 1993a) will be presented in the following sections.

The Model of Optimization in Primary and Secondary Control (OPS Model)

Based on their life-span theory of control, J. Heckhausen and Schulz (1993a, 1995, 1998; Schulz & J. Heckhausen 1996) have proposed a life-span model of developmental regulation that involves both selectivity and failure compensation as basic requirements of human behavior

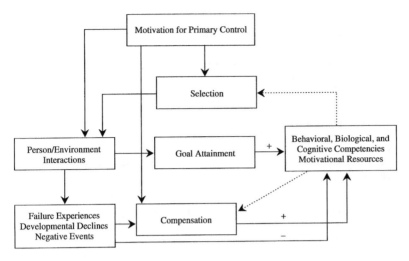

Figure 4.1. A life-span model of successful development. (From R. Schulz & J. Heckhausen [1996]. A life-span model of successful aging. *American Psychologist, 51,* 702–714. Copyright © 1996 by the American Psychological Association. Adapted with permission.)

and primary and secondary control as the two fundamental types of control-related behavior.

In a model of successful development, Schulz and J. Heckhausen (1996) specify the sequential demands and adaptive outcomes of primary and secondary control as they result from the requirements for selectivity and compensation in a given developmental challenge. This model is shown in Figure 4.1.

As can be seen in Figure 4.1, the motivation for primary control is the central driving force of human behavior: Motivation for primary control provides the impetus and regulation of the individual's interactions with the environment; motivation for primary control motivates person–environment interactions. The impact of primary control striving is mediated by a selection process that determines particular action goals to be pursued (in the context of the OPS model, it is optimization). As we shall see later (OPS model, see below), person–environment interactions also involve secondary control processes to focus motivational resources on a chosen action goal.

Any person–environment interaction will result in a positive (success) or negative (failure) outcome. Goal attainment will stabilize or enhance future action resources both in terms of competencies and with regard to motivational resources, such as perceived efficacy and self-esteem. Three types of failure or loss experiences can be identified. First, failure

Table 4.1. *OPS-Model: Optimization in primary and secondary control*

Optimization
—adaptive goal selection: long term and age-appropriate goals
—management of positive and negative trade-offs for other life domains
   and future life course
—maintain diversity, avoid dead ends

Selective Primary Control	*Selective Secondary Control*
—invest effort, abilities	—enhance goal value
—invest time	—devalue competing goals
—learn new skills	—enhance perception of control
—fight difficulties	—anticipate positive consequences of goal attainment

Compensatory Primary Control	*Compensatory Secondary Control*
—recruit others' help	—goal disengagement (sour grapes)
—get others' advice	—self-protective attributions
—use of technical aids	—self-protective social comparisons
—employ unusual means	—self-protective intra-individual comparisons

---

Source: Adapted from J. Heckhausen & Schulz 1995.

experiences are inevitable at any age in the context of acquisitional processes, which typically are most efficient at moderate levels of difficulty. Second, failure or loss experiences may be associated with aging-related decline (e.g., losing the ability to walk to the store). And finally, nonnormative events in the lives of individuals (e.g., disability due to an accident) provide a third source of failure or loss. These failure experiences may undermine action competencies and motivational resources, and therefore need to be compensated for to protect the individual from long-term restrictions on primary control potential. Compensatory processes serve to maintain, enhance, and restore action competencies and motivational resources. When discussing the model of optimization in primary and secondary control (OPS; J. Heckhausen & Schulz 1993a) in greater detail below, it will become clear that specific primary and secondary control processes compensate for deficiencies in behavioral or action competencies and motivational resources, respectively.

The model of optimization in primary and secondary control (see Table 4.1) conceptualizes optimization as a higher-order process, which regulates the use of four types of control strategies, which in turn address the basic requirements of selectivity and compensation.[1] Optimi-

---

[1] The OPS model (J. Heckhausen & Schulz 1993a) is related to P. Baltes and M. Baltes's SOC model but differs from it in three major ways:

zation determines the choice of a goal to pursue and thus directs the employment of the four control strategies. For instance, a person might decide to focus on pursuing her career for the next few years rather than on building a family. In order to put this decision into practice, various behavioral and motivational processes have to be orchestrated; in other words, the use of control strategies has to be optimized. Thus, the person will make sure that as much time and effort as possible is spent in career-related activities, that she is absolutely convinced of doing the right thing, and that she is not being distracted or even suffers regret (e.g., for not having a family), and so forth. The three aspects of optimization (adaptive goal selection, management of trade-off, and maintenance of diversity) will be explicated in greater detail in the next section, where criteria of adaptiveness are discussed. At this

(1) The OPS model is hierarchical. Optimization is conceptualized as a higher-order process, which regulates the operation of four types of strategies. The main process involved in optimization is making decisions about which domain or goal to invest in, so that the long-term, that is, life-span encompassing potential for primary control, is optimized. These decisions are based on age-normative conceptions, perceived challenges, personal preferences, and long-term developmental planning. Optimization represents the choice aspect of selectivity, while the focus aspect of selectivity (see distinction between choice and focus aspects of selectivity as discussed in Chapter 1) is covered by selective primary and selective secondary control. (Note that the SOC model proposes a different grouping of selection processes: Choice is subsumed under selection, while focused resource investment comprises selective optimization.) Based on a particular choice, optimization processes activate either of the four processes or combinations thereof, so as to attain the chosen goal while maximizing the long-term potential for primary control. Thus, for instance, when someone has decided to try very hard to get promoted, the person will not only activate selective primary control but also make sure that he is not distracted by other goals (selective secondary control), and even recruit other people's help and advice (compensatory primary control). In this process of selective investment in primary control, the individual should also consider the possible negative long-term consequences, for instance, in terms of draining resources or missing opportunities in other domains. The guiding principles and fundamental success criteria for optimization are further elaborated later in this chapter.

(2) The dimension of selection refers to the focus and not the choice aspect of selectivity (see Chapter 1). While goal choice is a matter of the higher-order optimization process, primary and secondary selection serve to focus the individual's resources on a chosen goal. This involves both investment of resources for a chosen goal and a motivational disengagement from nonchosen goals. In the theoretical framework of the SOC model, select and focused investment of resources (e.g., practice) has previously been identified with the optimization component (P. Baltes & M. Baltes 1990; Marsiske, Lang, P. Baltes, & M. Baltes 1995).

(3) Finally, the OPS model integrates the life-span theory of primary and secondary control with a model of selectivity and compensation. This means that the OPS model can address phenomena of primary control as well as secondary control. This makes it possible to identify behavior directed at the external world as distinct from that directed at the inner world of the individual. While primary and secondary control work hand in hand, it is important to have conceptual distinctiveness, since it provides the potential for theoretical conceptualization and empirical investigation of sequentially organized processes in developmental regulation.

point, the four types of control strategies regulated by optimization will be considered more closely.

The four strategies are characterized in terms of the two dimensions selectivity and compensation and of primary and secondary control (see Table 4.1). The model assumes that the two requirements of developmental regulation, selectivity and failure compensation, can be mastered by the two modes of control: primary and secondary. The model thus comprises four prototypical strategies: primary selection, secondary selection, primary compensation, and secondary compensation (see more detailed discussion of these strategies below).[2]

In the following section each of the four strategies will be considered in more detail. Selectivity involves both primary and secondary control. The individual needs to selectively invest resources in a chosen goal and also achieve and maintain a motivational commitment to that goal. *Selective primary control* refers to the focused investment of internal resources, such as effort, time, abilities, and skills required for the chosen goal. Developing relevant skills and abilities by processes of acquisition and practice are also included, as well as persistence when fighting difficulties. All these resources can be directly controlled by the individual. An example would be the academic who has decided to write a particular article. She will try to do her best, dedicate the most productive time of the day to the task, and search out the relevant information.

Selective secondary control targets internal representations that are motivationally relevant for goal pursuit. Relevant representations include the value ascribed to the chosen goal, the values associated with alternative goals, the perceived personal control of goal attainment, and the perceived personal control of nonchosen alternative goals. Thus, to be effective, selective secondary control should enhance the value of the chosen goal and its consequences while devaluing nonchosen alternatives. Moreover, the individual might boost the perceived personal control of goal attainment so as to add a posteriori support to the decision. In terms of the example about writing an article, the academic might imagine her feeling of accomplishment when the article finally appears in print, remind herself that alternative activities (committee work) do

---

[2] Flammer's four-stage model of control strategies partially converges with the OPS model with regard to "direct control" (a summary concept of primary control), "reactance, ex aequo: indirect control" (similar to compensatory primary control), and "secondary control" (a summary concept of secondary control) and also includes "loss of control/ relinquished control" (Flammer 1990). Flammer postulates a universal ontologic-domain-specific sequence among these four control strategies, so that direct control precedes reactance, reactance precedes secondary control, and secondary control precedes loss of control.

not yield such an enjoyable outcome, and tell herself that she has the relevant skills and competencies to complete a good article.

Compensation for failure or losses also works through both primary and secondary control means. *Compensatory primary control* is required whenever the physical or mental (reserve) capacities of the individual are insufficient to attain a chosen goal. This may happen in older adults due to aging-related decline, but also in infants, children, or inexperienced individuals in general due to immaturity or insufficient skill. Compensatory primary control refers to the use of external resources, either in terms of external assistance or in terms of action means that are not typically involved in the respective activity. External assistance could be given by other people (help, advice) or by technical aids (wheelchair, hearing aid). Employment of unusual means comes into play when certain activity-inherent skills are incapacitated or otherwise unavailable. An example is lipreading, which may be used by people with hearing loss to compensate for the lack of acoustic cues in speech perception (Bäckman & Dixon, 1992; Tesch-Römer, 1993). An extensive review of compensatory phenomena in human functioning is provided by Bäckman and Dixon (1992; see also Seifert, 1969), who mainly focus on primary control–type functioning.

Compensatory secondary control serves to buffer the negative effects of failure or losses on the individuals' motivational and emotional resources for primary control (e.g., generalized success expectancies, optimism, self-efficacy beliefs, self-esteem). Baltes and colleagues have referred to similar phenomena as "resilience of the self" (P. Baltes & M. Baltes 1990; Staudinger, Marsiske, & Baltes 1993). Compensatory secondary control strategies include disengagement from prior goals (the "sour grapes" phenomenon; Elster, 1983), self-protective patterns of causal attribution, strategic social comparison with inferior others (i.e., downward comparison, see Chapter 7), and strategic intraindividual comparisons involving self-serving temporal or interdomain comparisons. Returning to the article-writing example, we might imagine that the academic finds it impossible to complete the text. She then might tell herself that this article was really not a good idea to begin with, would lead her too far astray from her real interests, that other activities such as writing up a new and interesting set of data would be much more rewarding, that the failure to complete the article was not really her fault, and that other academics her age have fewer publications than she does anyway.

The four types of control strategies are not in themselves functional but might well have dysfunctional consequences if used in a nonoptimized way. For example, the two strategies related to selectivity, selective primary and selective secondary control, can be maladaptive in two ways. They may be dedicated to the *wrong choice* or they may represent a *too narrow focus*. A wrong choice may lead to a developmentally dead end. In this case, resources are invested inefficiently and the individual unnecessarily deprives herself of time, energy, and opportunity for pursuing alternative life-course options. A too narrow focus of investment makes the individual vulnerable, because losses in the selected area of functioning cannot be compensated for in other domains, which have been neglected. Both, dysfunctional choice and dysfunctional focus, can be exemplified by a youngster who wants to be a superathlete but really lacks superior talent. This person will invest a great deal of time and effort in athletic practice, neglecting other domains, such as education, of behavioral and motivational resources. The investment will be futile in the chosen domain of functioning and also have long-term detrimental consequences for other domains, which have been ignored.

The two compensatory strategies, compensatory primary and compensatory secondary control, also have dysfunctional potential. Compensation may be *premature* or turn out to be too *short-lived*. Premature compensation may cause a person to give up developing internal resources for primary control or even give up primary control altogether before its potential is fully exploited. One example of this is nursing-home residents who seek excessive help, which results in dependency and helplessness in the long term, although it may serve short-term affiliation needs because the dependency-seeking residents receive more social attention from the staff (M. Baltes 1996; M. Baltes & Silverberg 1994; M. Baltes & Reisenzein 1986). Some argue that for elderly nursing-home residents, affiliation goals are more important (Carstensen 1993) than autonomous self-care (M. Baltes 1995, 1996). However, with regard to self-care, this type of compensation is dysfunctional because it prevents the individual from selectively investing effort to increase, or at least maintain, primary control of self-care activities. The life-span theory of control, with its emphasis on primary control (J. Heckhausen & Schulz 1995; Schulz & J. Heckhausen 1996), would give priority to maintaining basic aspects of functioning (like autonomous self-care) and thus judge such premature dependency-seeking behavior as dysfunctional.

Hence, it becomes clear that the four types of control strategies need to be regulated by a higher-order process that activates and deactivates them in view of long-term criteria of adaptiveness. These criteria of adaptiveness will now be discussed.

Criteria of Adaptiveness

In gerontological research on successful aging there is a long-standing debate on the criteria of adaptiveness (see reviews in M. Baltes & Carstensen 1996; P. Baltes & M. Baltes 1990; Schulz & J. Heckhausen 1996). The different approaches fall into three broadly defined classes: those using absolute standards, those proposing relative standards, and those advocating subjective standards. Some researchers have also proposed combining these three types of criteria (M. Baltes & Carstensen 1996; P. Baltes & M. Baltes 1990).

In the typical case, *absolute standards* are derived from optimal or at least normal levels of functioning in a given domain. In this vein, researchers focus on peak performances in athletics (Ericsson 1990; Schulz & Curnow 1988; Schulz, Musa, Staszewski, & Siegler, in press), artistic domains (Ericsson, Krampe, & Tesch-Römer 1993; Simonton, 1994), or the sciences (Simonton 1984, 1988). Others have used normal or nonpathological biomedical functioning as indicators of successful aging (e.g., Rowe & Kahn 1987). These absolute standards are applied universally to all individuals irrespective of their position in the life course, genetic makeup, physical state, or social status-based opportunities. Another characteristic of this approach, and also of the relative standard, is that there is general consensus in a given society about identifying and valuing higher as compared to lower performance.

The approach using *relative standards* is also based on consensual dimensions of functioning. However, in contrast to absolute standards, relative standards take into account the performance conditions for a given individual. Thus, the same performance is valued more highly if attained by an individual who has to function under less favorable conditions, such as older age, a disability, or a deprived social background. The criteria of successful performance are thus adjusted to a frame of reference that may be defined by interindividual or intraindividual comparison (temporal comparison of an individual's performances).

Finally, some researchers propose to use *subjective standards* of performance, which are entirely idiosyncratic to the individual. The criterion of success is not based on objectively assessable performances but on the individual's subjective psychological experience. According to the subjective approach, it is the individual's feelings of accomplishment, self-worth, and fulfillment that make up successful aging. Thus, individuals may have downwardly adjusted their aspirations excessively and still be regarded as successful by subjective standards, because they feel satisfied with their functioning. Some research on accommodative coping comes close to this position, because the accommodation of goals is valued as adaptive irrespective of its costs for short-and long-term primary control (e.g., Brandtstädter & Rothermund 1994; Ryff 1984, 1985). Another case in point is the view that dependent behavior in old age is adaptive even when not warranted by actual disability (M. Baltes 1995, 1996). In our view (Schulz & J. Heckhausen 1996), subjective criteria of successful aging are problematic, because they prevent and exclude any consensus-based assessment of successful functioning, permit every phenomenon to be interpreted a posteriori as successful (see also P. Baltes & M. Baltes 1990), and therefore potentially hinder scientific progress in the field of successful aging.

The criterion adopted by Schulz and J. Heckhausen (1996) for their recent model of successful development through the life span builds on our life-span theory of control (J. Heckhausen & Schulz 1995). The fundamental criterion for human functioning can be defined in terms of the primacy of primary control. As discussed in Chapter 3, human functioning is adaptive if and insofar as it promotes and maintains the potential for primary control across the life span. This criterion implies that at any point in the life span the individual strives for primary control, using the opportunities and taking into account the constraints at the particular time in her life. It is important to stress the life-span encompassing nature of this criterion, because, as will be shown, short- and long-term primary control may be incompatible in certain cases. Schulz and Heckhausen thus take a relativist stance with regard to the life-span timing of particular control strivings. What is functional control striving at a certain point in the life span may be dysfunctional at another. Thus, for example, it makes sense to want to raise a child in early adulthood, but it is much less feasible at age fifteen or at age fifty. However, whatever the opportunities and constraints are at any given age, it is adaptive for the individual to strive for primary control for those goals that are attainable. It is the totality of realized primary control across domains of functioning and across the life span that makes up a successful life.

How does the individual regulate the goal selection for control striving across the life span so as to satisfy this general and ambitious criterion? Schulz and J. Heckhausen (1996) propose three general principles of optimization in developmental regulation: selection of age-appropriate developmental goals, maintenance of diversity of functioning, selectivity of resources, and management of trade-offs between domains and life-span phases (see top of Table 4.1). Each of these three principles will now be discussed.

First, the individual should exhibit *age-appropriate goal selection*. This implies that age-graded opportunities for goal attainment are made use of and constraints are observed. Developmental regulation is most effective if the individual takes advantage of conducive societal and biological age contexts in the life course. Deviating from normative age structures is possible but costly. Individuals who go against the age-graded opportunity structure in their selections of developmental goals need to support this deviance by extra investments of resources to make up for lacking societal (or biological) support. In addition, long-term rather than short-term goals help to adaptively organize developmental regulation over longer lifetime segments.

Second, it is essential that the individual maintain *diversity* (variability) in functioning. Maintaining diversity helps to avoid the vulnerability that comes with too narrow specialization. Moreover, and most importantly, diversity provides the "raw material" for new developmental advancements in the life-span future that are unprecedented by prior developmental attainments. In this way, diversity in human development is analogous to the role of variability in evolutionary change. Variability provides the material upon which selection, the basic evolutionary process, can work. The principle of diversity has important implications: for instance, for socialization agents who bring up or educate children. Early in their development children should be exposed to a variety of domains of functioning so that they are challenged, develop diverse skills, and, most importantly, have the opportunity to develop their genetic potential in select domains of functioning.

Third, developmental regulation across the life span involves the *management of positive and negative trade-offs* between domains and life-span phases. Selective investment in a given domain at a certain point in the life course often has important implications for other, alternative domains competing for resource investment and for other phases of the life span. These implications may be positive or negative. In general, broad skills and abilities (e.g., general education, health) involve positive trade-offs to other domains and other life-span phases, whereas narrow and intensive investment patterns (e.g., practicing to become a world-class athlete) involve higher risks for negative trade-offs to other domains and later phases of the life span. This chapter will conclude with a discussion of positive and negative short- and long-term trade-offs and the ways in which an individual may optimize primary control potential across the life span when confronted with such trade-offs (see also J. Heckhausen & Schulz, 1993b).

Positive and Negative Trade-Offs

To open this section, we need to consider the distinction between "proximal causes" and "distal causes," two concepts that figure prominently, for instance, in sociobiological theories about "inclusive fitness" (Wilson 1980). Proximal causes are mechanisms that directly and concurrently cause a given behavior. Distal causes, in contrast, refer to the ultimate implications of a given behavior for inclusive fitness (i.e., reproductive success) of the respective gene. Those behaviors and their proximal causes that optimize the distal cause of inclusive fitness are favored. In this way the distal causes become the ultimate sources of the proximate causes. However, what actually generates the behavior in a specific individual at a given point in time are genetically predesigned behavioral programs or dispositions that produce reactions to certain environmental conditions in certain ways – the proximal causes.

From an anthropological point of view (e.g., Douglas 1986), it can even be argued that not only individuals but also societies usually attain adaptive functioning not by consciously aiming at distal causes. Instead, basic mechanisms function as proximal causes for regulating individuals and social institutions. Across phylogenetic and historical change, specific sets of such proximal causes evolve to generate social systems and suitable societal members who are capable of adaptive functioning directed at distal causes such as cultural productivity.

Although the conflict between long-and short-term primary control presents, of course, the more challenging regulatory task, it is important to consider the nature of positive trade-offs. These cases, where short- and long-term primary control work in tandem, are frequent, present opportunities for important developmental advances, and do not pose a particular challenge to the individuals' developmental regulation. However, they help to highlight the issues involved in optimizing life-span development when confronted with short-term/long-term and interdomain conflicts. Congruence of short- and long-term primary control can also be characterized as an adaptive challenge. A typical and noncomplicated case of adaptive challenge is one in which aspirations are gradually adapted upwardly. It is not sufficient to stick with already achieved primary control, because this would not allow for developmental progress. In short-term/long-term tandem scenarios, the long-term primary control potential of the individual is realized in small steps, in which short-term primary control is elevated in incremental amounts. These situations typically are of the universal development type. Primary control potential is gradually increased within a given domain. What, then, could be, the proximal cause that helps the individual to find adaptive challenges in this type of situation?

The most plausible candidate is the general preference for moderate discrepancy or intermediate difficulty. Indeed, optimal arousal at moderate discrepancy is a basic mechanism of behavioral and even sensory regulation. Wilhelm Wundt (1874) was probably the first to describe the curve of arousal with intermediate levels producing the most positive affective reactions. Thereafter, the idea of moderate discrepancy was incorporated in Helson's adaptation level theory on sensory habituation (Helson 1948), Hebb's activation theory (Hebb 1955), and Berlyne's general theory of curiosity, exploration, and aesthetical preference (Berlyne 1960, 1971). The idea of moderate discrepancy or intermediate difficulty became the cornerstone of theories of motivation, such as in McClelland's general theory of motives (McClelland et al. 1953), Atkinson's risk-taking model (Atkinson 1957), and Csikszentmihalyi's research on intrinsic motivation and flow, "beyond boredom and anxiety" (Csikszentmihalyi 1975). It is at medium levels of difficulty that processes of acquisition are optimized. In the field of development, Brim (1992) discusses a set of common, yet stunningly adaptive strategies involved in keeping up ambition across radical changes in developmental ecologies throughout the life span. In a nutshell, these varied, extensive, and long-lasting research traditions reveal that the human mind is not made to rest on its laurels, but is designed to seek out adaptive challenges to develop its capacity to control the environment.

After considering the frequent cases where short- and long-term primary control work in tandem, potential conflicts between these controls will be discussed. Such conflicts are the testing ground for adaptive regulation of primary control. These conflicts are situations in which short-term primary control jeopardizes long-term primary control and thus has to be given up. Such short-term/long-term conflicts are characteristic of the human life course. Behavioral demands are not uniform across the life span. Instead, the human life course has an age-sequential structure of opportunities and constraints related to biological change and socially institutionalized life transitions. Thus, in order to increase, maintain, and regain primary control across the life span the individual constantly needs to adapt her goals to new chances for growth and new risks for decline. This sometimes involves disengaging from old goals and engaging in new. However, giving up old goals should not be done too easily, for accumulated investments would then be given up prematurely.

There are three types of short-term/long-term conflict situations: first, the case of too costly success in a short-term goal; second, the case of highly probable failure in a short-term goal; and third, the case of too costly failure in a short-term goal.

Let us consider the situation of "too costly success" first. Given that resources are limited and have to be invested selectively, new goals can often only be pursued at the expense of old goals. Even sure tracks to mastery in a given domain can become a problem when they compete for resources with upcoming age-normative developmental tasks. The athletic career can again serve as a case in point. Extensive athletic training may present no particular problem in mid-childhood, but it can seriously jeopardize educational attainment and thereby long-term career prospects once the demands in college become more challenging and a competition for time investment arises.

Moreover, a given goal may become increasingly difficult to pursue, so that it absorbs excessive resources and its performance-capacity ratio (Brim 1992) becomes dysfunctional. Consider, for instance, an expected and overdue job promotion that becomes increasingly difficult to achieve with increasing age. Pursuing this goal will become very costly in terms of time and effort and will thus drain resources from other goals (e.g., maintaining a lively social network) and future activities (e.g., developing a hobby). In this case, the individual probably needs to disengage from the goal, thus using a secondary control strategy to compensate for the feelings of loss. Disengaging from the old goal does not, however, necessarily require an awareness that future resources will be drained if it is further pursued. Instead, more trivial proximal causes regulate the individual's behavior. In the case of a long-standing success track at work, for instance, the individual might become bored with her old goals and search for novelty and change. Thus, boredom is an adaptive mechanism that can motivate exploration and risk taking in the pursuits of new goals.

Second, there is the case of high-probability failure. In general, highly failure-prone strivings would be avoided to start with because medium-level difficulty would be preferred. However, in life management the likelihood of success and failure is often not easily assessed beforehand. An individual whose goal is to become a well-known artist might simply underestimate the obstacles involved. Another scenario of unexpected difficulty is that one has missed the ideal timing. Many common goals in life involve age-normative timing, which comes with promotive opportunity structures (e.g., Hagestad 1990; Havighurst, 1952; Neugarten 1979; see also discussion in Chapters 2 and 5 on normative and nonnormative age timing and developmental tasks). Thus, missing that timing makes the goal (e.g., bearing a child, achieving an academic degree) much more difficult to achieve, because it has to be attained in spite of a lack of biological feasibility (e.g., fertility) or institutional support (e.g., availability of stipends). In such scenarios, the individual needs to avoid inefficient use of resources for uncertain outcomes. Again, however, this optimization principle does not need to be consciously represented because proximal mechanisms help the individual to do the right thing. For one thing, the preference for moderate difficulty, as discussed above, will help to avoid such situations to start with. However, once encountered, unexpected obstacles and failure will lead to anger and frustration, so that the goal domain becomes a less preferred or even aversive field of action. Moreover, the anticipated blow to self-esteem in case of failure after all this effort might also motivate a disengagement.

Finally, there are short-term/long-term conflicts based on the fact that failure in a short-term task would be too costly in the long run, and thus further pursuing the short-term goal becomes too risky an enterprise. The excessive costs of failure might involve external or internal consequences. An example of high external costs would be the case of pursuing a career in athletics, which might prevent investment in education and thus result in an occupational and financial crisis in case of failure. High internal costs of failure typically accompany intensive personal commitment; the higher the commitment, the greater the negative effect of failure on the individual's life planning and self-esteem. For example, women who want to have children are typically highly committed to this goal. However, when they encounter difficulties, the internal costs of engaging in extensive fertility programs are great. The greater the internal investment in pursuing the wish to have children, the more devastating the emotional consequences of an ultimate failure. With sufficiently high costs of failure, the need to protect long-term motivational and emotional resources might become more important for long-term primary control than the potential gain in case of success. In this case of too costly failure, disengagement from the short-term goal is adaptive. Again, the individual does not need to be aware of this optimization principle in order to protect long-term resources. Instead, proximal causes related to the short-term goal itself will often be sufficient to motivate disengagement. The individual might fear the imminent internal and external consequences of failure even if they have not been frequently experienced in the past.

Prototypical examples of short-term/long-term conflicts are goal engagements and disengagements around developmental deadlines (e.g., the "biological clock" for childbearing, see more detailed discussion in

Chapter 5). Developmental deadlines are adaptive challenges because they provide a time structure for the individual's life planning. In sociobiological terminology, one could say that age deadlines are proximal causes for goal disengagement-engagement cycles. Age deadlines help to ensure that long-standing goals are not continuously postponed but finally pursued with enhanced tenaciousness. And when the deadline has passed, they provide an opportunity finally to disengage from an old goal and thus set free resources to pursue new and more timely ones.

Summary

A model of developmental regulation is presented that involves the basic requirements of life-span development, selectivity, and failure compensation. Heckhausen and Schulz's OPS model is discussed in regard to its relations to and differences from the SOC model proposed by P. Baltes and M. Baltes. The OPS model involves two conceptually orthogonal dimensions: selectivity and failure compensation, on the one hand, and primary and secondary control, on the other. Four prototypical strategies are defined by this conceptual scheme: selective primary, compensatory primary, selective secondary, and compensatory secondary control. These four strategies are in and of themselves neither functional nor dysfunctional. In order to be functionally adapted to the promotion of long-term primary control across the life span, they need to be regulated by a higher-order process, referred to as optimization. Criteria for the adaptiveness of optimization in developmental regulation are discussed in detail. A subjective approach to defining criteria of adaptiveness is rejected. Preference is given to an approach that emphasizes the primacy of primary control in a life-span encompassing perspective. Thus, relative standards are used in order to accommodate the life-span changes in potential for primary control and the trade-offs involved. When taking the universalist stance on the primacy of primary control, the question arises of how the individual regulates the use of primary and secondary strategies to promote long-term primary control. This involves not only congruence, but also conflicts between short- and long-term primary control. It is proposed that such long-term/short-term trade-offs do not usually require wisdom-type problem-solving abilities, but are typically regulated by comparatively simple proximal mechanisms in the individuals' behavioral makeup or in social institutions. Proximal mechanisms, such as preferences for moderate incongruence or difficulty, usually are sufficient to steer the individual through the perils of short-term/long-term management, so that the distal cause of optimizing primary control across the life span is attained. Prototypical examples of adaptive developmental challenges are age-normative deadlines for developmental tasks, which are discussed in the next chapter. They provide the proximal causes of engaging in urgent developmental tasks and disengaging from obsolete goals, so that overall primary control is optimized across the life span. Hence, such proximal mechanisms represent adaptive constraints that facilitate and scaffold developmental regulation on the part of the individual.

5 Developmental Goals as Organizers of Developmental Regulation

This chapter introduces the concept of developmental goals. Developmental goals are conceptualized as organizers of developmental regulation. An action-theoretical framework based on recent innovations in motivational action theory (H. Heckhausen 1987a, 1987b, 1987c, 1989; H. Heckhausen & Kuhl 1985) is utilized. Although motivational action theory provides the general theoretical framework for our research, action directed at development constitutes a particular case. Development-related action is embedded in and shaped by its action field, the human life course, which entails particular types of constraints. These biological, sociostructural, and age-normative constraints to life-span development were discussed in Chapter 2. This chapter examines a specific type of age-graded constraint: age-normative deadlines for the attainment of developmental goals.

I shall start with a comparison between the concept of "developmental goals" and other related concepts and, subsequently, introduce an action-phase model developed for general motivated behavior. This model will then be extended to include the concept of action deadlines and be applied to behavior directed at developmental goals.

Developmental Goals and Related Concepts

Although the early phase of revival of the life-span approach was in general characterized by a greater emphasis on explanatory or boundary factors for individual development, there were also early pioneers of the study of life-span changes in individuals' motivation and attempts to take an active part in their developmental course. The latter emphasis has become particularly influential in a more recent upsurge of interest in this topic (see also review in Brandtstädter 1990). In his stage theory of psychosocial development, Erikson proposed a fixed sequence of age-normative challenges that give rise to developmental crisis, which need to be successfully resolved in order to allow further psychosocial growth (Erikson 1959, 1963). With regard to adulthood, Erikson conceptualized three stages of crisis during which the individual has to manage the conflict between two opposing poles: intimacy versus isolation in young adulthood, generativity versus stagnation in midlife, and ego integrity versus despair in old age. During each stage of development the respective conflict is expected to dominate the individual's strivings and concerns.

C. Bühler (1933, 1953, 1962) was a pioneer in the study of biographies. She and her students identified two types of life events, biological and biographical, which bring about life curves following an inverted U-shape, with the biological trajectory showing an earlier decline than the biographical. Later Bühler developed the conception that the individual's behavior is motivated by a set of five basic life tendencies or "life themes": satisfaction of needs, adaptive self-limitation (adjustment), creative expansion, establishment of inner order, and self-fulfillment (C. Bühler 1962). These five basic life tendencies become salient during different phases of the life span, which Bühler divided into ten subsegments, five of which cover adulthood. The work of Thomae and his colleagues in the Bonn Longitudinal Study of Aging (see reviews in Lehr & Thomae 1987) to investigate the role individuals play in constructing their biographies (see also Fisseni 1985; Kruse & Lehr 1989; Lehr 1982; Olbrich 1985; Olbrich & Thomae 1978; Rudinger & Thomae 1990; Schmitz-Scherzer & Thomae 1983) can be viewed as a continuation of this research tradition. Thomae and colleagues identified "Daseinsthematiken" (life themes) and their changing realization across the adult life span in the Bonn Longitudinal Study of Aging (Thomae 1976).

Finally, Havighurst developed the concept of developmental tasks to capture the interface of "drive toward growth of the individual with the demands, constraints, and opportunities provided by the social environment" (Havighurst 1973, pp. 9f.). Developmental tasks are age-normative challenges to individual development (e.g., finding an occupation in late adolescence or early adulthood) that are jointly produced by the processes of biological maturation, the cultural pressures of society, and the desires, aspirations, and values that characterize the individual's personality (Havighurst 1953). Successful mastery of developmental tasks leads to satisfaction and happiness and enables and promotes further psychological growth, whereas failure endangers further progress and the mastery of developmental tasks in later phases of the life span. While some of the specific developmental tasks described by Havighurst (1952, 1953) appear outdated from today's perspective, the general approach has become widely accepted in developmental psychology (e.g., Lehr 1984; Oerter 1978, 1986; Thomae 1975).

A motivational or "organismic" (Hultsch & Plemons 1979) approach to life-span development has recently acquired a new flourish. Lerner and Busch-Rossnagel (1981) took the lead with their book on "individuals as producers of their own development." Although most of the contributions to this book focus on the responsiveness of the environment to stable features of the individual (e.g., attractiveness, gender, temperament), it has promoted an upsurge of interest in the role of the individual as an active agent in his/her own development, who attempts to influence it in accordance with personal values, preferences, motives, and goals (Brandtstädter 1984, 1986; Dannefer 1989; Filipp 1987; Flammer 1988; Silbereisen, Eyferth, & Rudinger 1986).

The concept of developmental goals adopted in this research can be distinguished from other related concepts in three ways. First, developmental goals typically have developmental processes as their target of action (e.g., become independent from my parents, prevent aging-related memory loss). Thus, the unique action field for developmental goals is the life course. This specific action field entails a certain structure based on age-related and sequential constraints in life-span development. In this regard, the concept of developmental goals shares features with the concept of personal life tasks (Cantor & Kihlstrom 1987), which is also associated with age-graded, specific sociocultural settings.

Second, the concept of developmental goals relates to, but is distinct from, recent propositions about the impact of individuals on their life courses. Brandtstädter's notion of action directed at regulating development (Brandtstädter 1984, 1989) is probably closest to the present approach. However, within Brandtstädter's model of development-related action the goal states are broad values similar to motives (e.g., self-esteem, social recognition, satisfying friendships). Moreover, development-related action is conceptualized as one kind of action among others, without taking into account the specific structural constraints of the life course as action contexts.

And third, developmental goals are conceptualized in the theoretical framework of a recent innovation in motivational action theory, namely the "Rubicon model of action phases." The Rubicon model accounts for systematic differences in the actor's motivational approach to his/her own action projects in the different sequential phases of action regulation. The Rubicon action phase model is extended to include developmental deadlines as age-normative markers of goal disengagement.

Developmental goals can be represented at various goal levels, and accordingly they encompass a range of temporal extensions (e.g., future time perspectives). The most general level is addressed in the concept of "motive" (McClelland 1985; McClelland et al. 1953), "unity theme" (Murray 1938), or "life theme" (C. Bühler 1933; Csikszentmihalyi 1985). Motives or life themes are general motivational orientations conceptualized as traits of an individual involving long-term and/or ever recurrent goals (e.g., striving for academic achievement). Somewhat more specific to the individual, and not necessarily encompassing the life course (disengagement is possible), are "current concerns" (Klinger 1975, 1977) and "identity goals" (Gollwitzer 1987). "Personal projects" (B. Little 1983), "personal strivings" (Emmons 1986), "personal goals" (Brunstein 1993; Wadsworth & Ford 1983), "life goals" (Nurmi 1991, 1992), "personal life tasks" (Cantor & Fleeson 1991; Cantor et al. 1987), and "intentional changes" (Tough 1982) are goal representations on an even lower level in terms of specificity and time perspective.

Numerous empirical studies have revealed that goals embracing a medium range of future time extension are common and important features of adult-motivated behavior. Moreover, such goals have important influence on subjective well-being (Brandtstädter 1989; Brandtstädter, Krampen, & Greve 1987; Brunstein 1993, 1995; Emmons 1986; Palys & Little 1983) and determine what people think and do in their everyday activities (Cantor & Fleeson 1994; Emmons & Diener 1986; Klinger, Barta, & Maxeiner 1980). An important precursor of the recent revival of goal-related concepts in motivational psychology is the concept of "current concerns" introduced by Klinger (1977; Klinger, Barta, & Maxeiner 1980). Current concerns refer to the process of motivational goal commitment, which extends from the onset of engagement to eventual disengagement and has a major influence on attentional processes, thought content, and frequency (Klinger, Barta, & Maxeiner 1980). Once a person is committed to a given goal, this engagement cannot easily be deactivated. It takes major reasons (e.g., irreversible obstruction) and effort to overcome the commitment and disengage from the goal, and this often involves negative affect.

More recently, Little introduced the concept of "personal project" as a set of interrelated acts extending over time, that are intended to maintain or attain a state of affairs foreseen by the individual (B. Little 1983, p. 276). Little developed the hypothetical construct of personal projects as a new unit of analysis in personality psychology based on a long-forgotten proposal by Murray (1938, 1951) to study serials in human behavior. "Serials" refer to enterprises that are organized sequentially over extended time. Little emphasizes the temporal characteristics of "personal projects" in terms of "psychological specialization – selective channeling of orientation and abilities in the course of an individual's progressive adaptations to the environment" (B. Little 1983, p. 275). Personal projects go through four stages in their "life course": inception, planning, action, and termination. B. R. Little (1983) was the first to develop a methodology for assessing projects or goals that combines open-ended idiosyncratic information with standardized and quantifiable ratings. Subjects first write down a list of personal projects and then rate each of them on various rating scales. This methodology has since been used by numerous researchers in this field. In a first study using the combined open-ended and rating-scale methodology to assess personal projects, Palys and B. R. Little (1983) investigated the impact of personal projects on life satisfaction. Engaging in subjectively important, enjoyable, and challenging projects promoted higher ratings of life satisfaction. Moreover, life satisfaction was promoted when a social network also shared project involvements. Similarly, Ruehlman and Wolchik (1988) found that the amount of social support in goal-related activities predicted interindividual differences in subjective well-being and, when lacking, predicted psychological distress.

Emmons (1986, 1989) adopted the goal-assessment approach combining open-ended and quantitative methods to study personal strivings. He asked his subjects to nominate what he calls "personal strivings" and then collected ratings of each of these goals for a number of marker variables such as importance, perceived past attainment, effort investment, between-striving interdependence or conflict, specificity, social support, and expected success. In a series of studies (Emmons 1986, 1989, 1991, 1992a, 1992b; Emmons & King 1988) various characteristics of the strivings had significant impact on subjective well-being. Negative affect, for instance, was related to low-perceived probability of success, conflict among personal strivings, and ambivalent feelings about striving fulfillment. Positive affect, in contrast, was predicted by importance, past fulfillment, and value of personal strivings. Brunstein (1993) longitudinally investigated the relationship between university students' personal goal strivings and subjective well-being over a period of fourteen weeks, thus covering one semester. Changes in goal attainability over the longitudinal span influenced subjective well-being. However, this relation depended on the degree to which subjects were committed to the goals. Low-commitment goals influenced subjective well-being only slightly, even if conditions for goal attainment deteriorated. In contrast, for high-commitment goals favorable changes in goal attainability boosted subjective well-being, while a deterioration of goal attainability dampened it. Converging evidence comes from a study comparing students undergoing psychological counseling to other students (Salmela-Aro 1992). Students in counseling reported more personal projects directed at changing the self and indicated a lower sense of accomplishment in these projects.

In the context of research on personal meaning systems, Dittmann-Kohli (1991, 1995) also investigated young and old adults' conceptions about their personal future. In contrast to other work in this area, Dittmann-Kohli did not use a completely open-ended assessment strategy, but instead employed a sentence-completion paradigm. Subjects completed sentence roots such as "In the coming years. . . ." The findings indicate that future-related personal conceptions reflected normative role changes and developmental tasks of the respective age group. Young adults named more often than older adults education, career, family building, and financial scenarios as domains involving expected future changes. Older adults, in turn, expressed a greater interest in social relationships and leisure-time activities, such as travel. In general, the older adults exhibited far more concern about maintaining achieved states of functioning and satisfaction than the younger adults, who appeared much more hopeful about improvements in various domains of life.

Nurmi (1989a, 1989b) studied hopes and fears in adolescents' future orientation. The assessment of hopes and fears was similar to the methodology used in other research about personal goals (e.g., Emmons 1986; B. Little 1983). Adolescents' goals and interests predominantly reflected the typical developmental tasks of late adolescence and early adulthood (Havighurst, 1952), such as completing education, starting an occupational career, founding a family, and attaining appropriate financial support. In further studies, Nurmi and colleagues extended the research on so-called life goals to adulthood and old age (Nurmi 1992, 1993; Nurmi, Pulliainen, & Salmela-Aro 1992; Salmela-Aro 1992). Adults' life goals reflected the developmental tasks of their respective age groups (Nurmi 1992): Young adults were most interested in goals concerning future education and family; goals named by middle-aged adults were mostly related to their children's welfare and to their property; while old adults were most concerned with health, retirement, leisure activities, and general world issues (e.g., peace, the environment). Nurmi and colleagues (1992) also investigated adults' beliefs about personal control over their life goals. In general, older adults' goals were associated with less personal control. However, the authors propose that this finding is due to increased interest in low-control goals in older adults (e.g., health, peace), rather than to decreased control estimates irrespective of goal domain.

Rapkin and Fischer (1992a, 1992b) also studied personal goals in older adults, investigating the relationship of goal profiles and subjective well-being. They found that goal profiles reflecting disengagement and reduced activity were negatively related to well-being, while goal profiles reflecting an orientation to improvement and activity were associated with better general satisfaction.

Cantor proposes "personal life tasks" as an inherently developmental concept of goal orientation (Cantor & Fleeson 1991, 1994; Cantor et al. 1987; Cantor et al. 1991; Zirkel & Cantor 1990). Life tasks represent "the individual's version of culturally prescribed, age-graded tasks. Life tasks are the tasks that people see themselves as working on and devoting energy to in a particular life period. They take place in a daily life context, sometimes encompass many projects or activities, and typically unfold over substantial periods of time" (Cantor & Fleeson 1991, p. 338).

In a longitudinal study, Cantor and colleagues applied their life-task approach to the transition of young students from home and high school to college life. Subjects were asked to describe their personal tasks and subsequently to match the nominated tasks to age-graded tasks typical for their peer group (e.g., for college students, "doing well academically," "being on my own, away from family"). Cantor and Fleeson (1991) report that during the college years, nominated life tasks decrease in diversity of domains. Whereas first-year students named life tasks relevant to various domains and often phrased them in generic ways (e.g., "Getting to know new people"), senior-year students had narrowed down their interests to fewer domains and specified those in idiosyncratic terms (e.g., "Leading the student group that I am a president of"). Thus, over the course of four years, the students had selectively adopted age-normative tasks and specified them as personal life tasks.

Age-graded shifts in the underlying motives between different age-normative settings were also found (Zirkel 1992; Zirkel & Cantor 1990). For first-year students undergoing the transition to college life, those who were absorbed by the developmental task of becoming independent showed particular emphasis on achievement goals (Zirkel & Cantor 1990). The inverse was true for students in their senior year, who would be graduating. Here, those individuals who were preoccupied with attaining independence shifted their predominant concern from the academic to the social domain (Zirkel 1992).

Moreover, Cantor and colleagues (1987) identified interindividual differences in fundamental strategies of tackling life tasks. The college students' approach to life tasks differed in the optimism/pessimism dimension. One group of students subscribed to a defensive-pessimism strategy of intentional confrontation with failure-related anxieties, which helped them to buffer the detrimental effects of failure by anticipating them. In contrast, another group of students motivated themselves by anticipating success, postponing self-protection concerns until after an unexpected failure.

Finally, research on personal life tasks was integrated with the concept of "possible selves" developed by Markus and colleagues (Markus & Nurius 1986; Cantor et al. 1986). Possible selves characterize dynamic components of the self-concept that relate to hoped for or feared future developments. At variance with other goal-related concepts, possible selves do not imply a commitment to a certain goal; rather they reflect wishes that are not necessarily grounded in reality. Cross and Markus (1991) investigated hoped for and feared selves in subjects varying in age from eighteen to eighty-six years. Young adults focused on occupation and family-related hoped for and feared selves, while older adults were most concerned about physical and health aspects of the self. Moreover, it was shown that the complexity of the self-system in terms of multiple possible selves predicted the degree of affective responses to negative and positive events related to the respective life task (Markus & Wurf 1987). More complex possible selves gave rise to moderate affective reactions, whereas self-systems involving only few dimensions afforded more extreme affective reactions, both for better and for worse. Moreover, these relations only hold within a given time frame. Thus, complexity of present or actual selves only affects affective reactions to present events, while future possible selves have a unique impact on affect resulting from future events.

Action-Phase Model of Developmental Regulation around Developmental Goals

In the next section of this chapter, a sequential action model is discussed as a theoretical framework for the evolution, transformation, and deactivation of developmental goals over the life course. This sequential action model represents an integration of the life-span theory of control with the Rubicon model of action phases. The new model allows specific predictions about the adaptivity of certain control strategies in volitional and motivational action phases (see also Wrosch & Heckhausen, in press).

Before discussing the new model, the Rubicon model of action phases will first be introduced as a theoretical foundation. Subsequently, the extended sequential action model for developmental regulation around developmental goals is developed and some initial empirical examples are reported.

The Rubicon Model of Action Phases

H. Heckhausen (1991) developed the Rubicon[1] model of action phases, which divides the action process into four major sections: predecisional motivation, preactional volition, actional volition, and postactional motivation. During the *predecisional phase*, the individual considers the advantages and disadvantages of diverse action alternatives (e.g., taking a job offer and moving to another city) so as to reach a decision about what to do or, in other words, form a goal intention. Once a goal intention is formed, the individual is pushed across the decisional "Rubicon" and enters the next phase, when weighing pros and cons is no longer appropriate. After crossing the Rubicon the main concern switches from what to do (e.g., whether to move) to how and when to do it (e.g., where to find an apartment in the new city). In the postdecisional (post-Rubicon) *volitional phases* (preactional and actional phases) the individual is committed to a certain action goal and focuses on how to implement it. Accordingly, information processing before and after the decisional Rubicon differs radically in form and function. First, during the *preactional volitional phase* action opportunities are considered and the planning for action is completed. Thereafter, once an appropriate opportunity for action is present, the individual is set up for actually initiating the anticipated activity in the *actional phase*. While planning and performing the action, the attentional and motivational resources have to be focused on the intention rather than be spread among competing action opportunities. Moreover, volitional strength during the two volitional phases should increase reactively when the individual encounters an obstacle or temporary failure in goal pursuit. After completing the action, successfully or not, the individual enters another motivational stage, the *postactional phase*, during which the action outcome is evaluated, causal attributions are considered, and inferences about future action are drawn.

During both motivational phases, predecisional and postactional, the

---

[1] The Rubicon metaphor refers to Roman general Julius Caesar's decision to have his legions cross the Rubicon river in northern Italy, knowing this act would instigate a civil war. The irrevocable nature of the Rubicon crossing is evident in Julius Caesar's exclamation, "alea iacta est!" ("The die is cast!").

individual needs to be veridical and diverse in considering possible factors for decision and inferences (e.g., she must consider the pros and cons of the old and new job and city as objectively as possible). The motivational mind-set is therefore referred to as "deliberative" (Gollwitzer, H. Heckhausen, & Steller 1990b). In the context of the OPS model, the control processes involved in this deliberative mind-set are conceptualized as optimization of goal selection. In contrast to the predecisional phase, the volitional phases require a biased enhancement of goal commitment and a narrow focus on action-relevant factors (e.g., after deciding to move, the individual has a growing preference for the new city and is alert to information about it). The volitional mind-set is thus labeled "implemental" (Gollwitzer, Heckhausen, & Steller 1990). The relevant control processes for the volitional phase are selective primary and selective secondary control.

H. Heckhausen, P. Gollwitzer, and their colleagues have been able to show the multiple effects of the deliberative and implemental mind-sets on cognitive-motivational indicators – such as intentional and incidental memory, response latency, perceptual readiness, and vocal shadowing under dichotic listening conditions – in various experimental and real-life settings (Beckmann & Gollwitzer 1987; Gollwitzer 1990, 1993; Gollwitzer, H. Heckhausen, & Ratajczak, 1990a; Gollwitzer, Heckhausen, & Steller 1990b; Gollwitzer & Kinney 1989; H. Heckhausen & Gollwitzer 1986, 1987).

Gollwitzer has proposed to apply the Rubicon model of action phases to the realm of identity striving (Gollwitzer 1986, 1987; Gollwitzer & Wicklund 1985). Because of the life-span encompassing nature of identity striving, Gollwitzer's concept of "identity goals" is most relevant from a life-span developmental point of view. Identity goals target overarching, long-term commitments to a certain identity status (e.g., becoming a physician). They stretch out over extended periods of time, involve multiple subgoals, and are redefined and continually extended as subgoals are attained. Thus, identity goals can only be approached but never reached. They set the individual up for a continuous search for action opportunities to complete his/her identity. Consequently, striving for identity goals is not easily discouraged. Given that the individual is in a continual volitional phase with regard to his/her identity goal, obstacles and failures should instigate increased persistence rather than a reconsideration of alternatives.

Research on self-completion supports the appropriateness of the Rubicon model for behavior directed at identity goals (Gollwitzer 1986, 1987). Wicklund and Gollwitzer (1981) compared subjects who were firmly committed to their identity goals with subjects who were as yet unsure whether a given identity was appropriate for them. When confronted with an identity-relevant failure experience (e.g., the feedback that their personality was unsuitable for their professional ambitions), only the committed subjects stepped up their efforts toward self-completion whereas noncommitted subjects even reduced their efforts. This pattern of findings converges with the Rubicon model, because committed subjects should be in a volitional state and thus tend to increase goal striving when obstructed. In contrast, noncommitted subjects in the predecisional motivational phase can be expected to treat a failure experience as negative information that decreases their motivation.

Further evidence comes from studies on symbolic self-completion. An early study on college students committed to identity goals associated with certain activities, such as dancing, might serve as an example (Gollwitzer, Stephenson, & Wicklund 1982). Prior to the experiment, the actual degree of training in the respective activity was assessed. In the experiment itself, one group of subjects was made to feel incomplete in their identity by negative feedback about identity-related personality characteristics. In subsequent public self-reports, those subjects who felt incomplete, either in terms of reported previous training or due to experimentally provided negative feedback, reported more positive self-descriptions than those who were not made to feel incomplete in their identity. Thus, the "incomplete" subjects portrayed themselves unrealistically with a distinct bias for self-completion, presumably to compensate for the experienced threat to their identity goal. Similar findings were obtained for students with the identity goal of becoming physicians and private business managers (see review in Gollwitzer 1987).

Extension and Application of the Action-Phase Model to Developmental Regulation

The present approach uses the concept of "developmental goals" to capture the basic action unit in the pursuit of developmental goals. Developmental goals provide an important medium through which developmental regulation – that is, optimizing selection and compensation via primary and secondary control – has its impact on behavior. They target future outcomes of development that the individual tries to attain within a medium time range (i.e., five to ten years) and can either reflect strived-for gains or avoidance of losses. Developmental goals are contingent upon the structure of opportunities and constraints encountered at various stages of the life span.

In analogy to the Rubicon model of action phases, it is proposed that individuals pursue developmental goals in sequentially ordered phases of motivational and volitional processing. On four levels (from top to bottom) Figure 5.1 identifies critical transition points, boundaries of, and characteristic processes and functions of five action phases in the pursuit of developmental goals. First, the two critical Transitions are the "Rubicon," when intentions are formed, and the "Deadline," when the action ecology shifts to more constraints and less opportunities, and thus goal attainment becomes highly unlikely (see also J. Heckhausen 1996; J. Heckhausen & Fleeson 1993; Wrosch & J. Heckhausen, in press). This deadline marks a point in time, after which action opportunities are no longer available or radically reduced.[2]

Second, the extended model of action phases includes a further differentiation of predeadline actional phases into a nonurgent and an urgent phase. This is so because the deadline, with its shift to unfavorable opportunities, sets up a stage of urgency for primary control striving as the individual approaches the deadline (see "urgent" phase in model, Figure 5.1).

Thus, on the level of control processes (see third level from top of Figure 5.1) the predecisional phase is marked by optimization-type control processes, when the individual considers the conditions and consequences of selecting a particular developmental goal. After crossing the Rubicon, selective primary and selective secondary control processes are required. However, in the urgency phase created by the deadline, increased investment in selective primary and selective secondary control as well as in compensatory primary control (e.g., recruitment of external assistance when available resources prove insufficient) is expected. After passing the deadline, goal intentions become futile and need to be deactivated. Thus, in analogy to the Rubicon transition (but in inverse sequence), the deadline transition marks a shift between volition (implemental mind-set) and motivation (deliberative mind-set). Specifically, the pre-/postdeadline transition for those who fail the deadline (see postdeadline "failure" condition in model, Figure 5.1) affords a radical shift from intense primary control striving to compensatory secondary control (e.g., goal disengagement, self-protective attributions). In contrast, those who achieve their developmental goal be-

---

[2] One could also extend the concept of developmental deadlines beyond the time dimension to situational action opportunities in general. Such a general concept might be labeled *transition to a condition of lost opportunities* and would include situations when, in the process of goal striving, the external or internal prerequisites for goal attainment are lost. Examples would be a teacher who in his early career is confronted with radically vanishing job opportunities in the school system, or an athlete who in the process of training for peak performance suffers an incapacitating and irreversible injury.

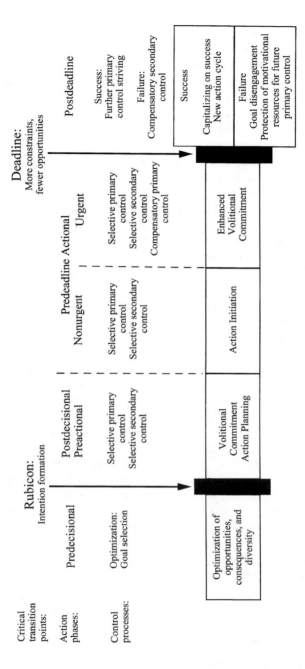

Figure 5.1. Extended model of action phases: Rubicon and Deadline.

fore passing the deadline (see postdeadline "success" condition in model, Figure 5.1) can invest in further primary control striving and capitalize on the action resources strengthened by their success.

Finally, the functions of each phase are characterized as follows (see bottom level of Figure 5.1). During the predecisional phase, the individual tries to arrive at a goal selection that optimizes his/her future diversity, opportunities, and consequences of goal striving. The postdecisional preactional phase is dedicated to volitional commitment to the selected goal and action planning. Typically, sometime during the nonurgent phase, action is initiated. The phase of urgent predeadline functioning will have to be charged with enhanced volitional commitment so as to meet the deadline. After crossing the deadline, the successful individual will try to capitalize on his/her success and enter a new action cycle, either in the same domain and building on its prior achievements or in a different domain that had been neglected during the deadline-ridden phase of life. Those individuals who pass the deadline without achieving their goal will have to disengage from the goal and put effort into protecting their motivational resources for future primary control striving.

Age-Normative Developmental Deadlines. In the context of life-span development, goal deadlines are set according to age norms about the life-span timing of life transitions and events. The individual is viewed as an agent regulating his/her own development and life course by actively pursuing goals (primary control) and by mentally adapting to changes (secondary control). This developmental regulation occurs within specific constraints provided by the structure of the life course, which is based on biological and sociocultural factors as well as constraining conditions inherent to the idiosyncratic biography of the individual. Although at first sight such constraints may appear to impoverish the individual's regulation potential, the present approach views them as adaptive challenges to developmental regulation. They not only relieve the potential burden of an overload of developmental options, but also structure individuals' life courses so as to make optimal use of age-graded opportunity structures, thereby scaffolding their developmental regulation. Socially conveyed age norms for life events and transitions (e.g., getting married, bearing a child, settling into a profession) help the individual to choose the appropriate age timing for investing in primary control to attain a given developmental goal. Social age norms are particularly pronounced in the case of life events and transitions that apply to the majority of members of a given society.

These can be conceived of as *normative developmental goals* and are also known as *developmental tasks* (Havighurst, 1952).

Most developmental tasks of the life course involve normative conceptions about their age-related timing. This is a long-standing topic of life-span developmental and life-course sociological research (see reviews in Hagestad 1990; J. Heckhausen 1990a, 1990b; Settersten 1992). Members of a given society have common conceptions about when one should get married, have one's first child, start an occupation, reach the peak of one's career, retire, and so on. Some of these conceptions will be based on objective conditions, for instance, the timing of childbirth, and others will involve more culture-specific constraints. In any case, age norms for life-course events and transitions give structure to the life course and help both the individual and the society to manage the challenges associated with the variability of life courses.

Age-normative deadlines are a special and extreme case of age norms in that they represent the uppermost limits of normative age ranges. These deadlines mark a final timing constraint for attaining a developmental goal; any further postponement is impossible, or at least extremely costly, because the goal then has to be attained without the appropriate structure of opportunity; missing the deadline will therefore mean that the goal will never be attained in one's lifetime. A prototypical example is the "biological clock" for childbearing, which sets a consensually accepted deadline for fertility in the early forties. Generally, a woman who wants to have a child sometime in her life has to fulfill this goal before age forty or give it up altogether.

Hence, age deadlines can be expected to have a more radical effect on behavior than more malleable age norms. Interestingly, Carstensen's socioemotional selectivity theory involves a similar concept, "endings" (Carstensen 1993). When approaching "endings" such as the end of life (Frederickson & Carstensen 1990), a social ending such as a geographical relocation (Carstensen & Frederickson 1992), or the end of a period of living in a certain city, individuals are expected to shift their selection of social contacts away from informational and self-relevant purposes to focus on socioemotional needs. The common feature of developmental deadlines and "endings" is the notion that personal control for achieving important goals drops radically in association with passing a certain point in time, and that this drop in personal control effects a radical change in the personal priorities and concerns of the individual.

Hypothetical Model of the Life Course of Developmental Goals. Developmental goals evolve as anticipated developmental outcomes typically just before the age-normative change or life-course transition is expected. During life-course periods, which the individual, based on age-normative conceptions, perceives as most conducive for goal attainment, developmental goals are activated (see selectivity aspect of optimization, Chapter 4). The individual will select developmental goals appropriate to a given developmental or life-course challenge (e.g., establish a career in early adulthood). This often implies both disengagement from previous goals that have become less accessible or unattainable and engagement in new goals for which action opportunities are becoming available (e.g., terminating general education plans and pursuing a career). This process of goal engagement and disengagement in accordance with age-graded developmental tasks was empirically investigated in Study 5 and will be further discussed in Chapter 6.

Moreover, the individual may consider the implications of pursuing a particular goal in view of its effect on diversity and positive or negative trade-offs for other goals (see requirements of optimization, Chapter 4). For instance, a young woman may wonder what the career implications would be of having a child now compared to in the future. When considering such trade-offs, precautions may be taken to allow for reevaluations of the feasibility and payoff of goal striving (e.g., what happens if the career slows down as the biological deadline for childbearing approaches). Such opportunties for reevaluation are particularly important with regard to life-span developmental action, as wrong decisions can have very long-term and devastating consequences. Under such conditions it would appear adaptive to use strategies that permit a reassessment of the decision taken. Thus, developmental projects might often involve multiple Rubicons. This means that the choice of a certain track receives a reevaluation after being tried. Such reevaluations might be anticipated even before deciding on a goal, so as to put to rest concerns about long-term costs, or alternatively be designed in the phase of preactional volition by setting up criteria and opportunities for reentry in a motivational state. Interestingly, such "probational periods" are also socially institutionalized in the occupational and family domains (e.g., probation period or premarital engagement).

The chosen developmental goal then becomes elaborated and individualized and gives rise to a structure of subgoals (see also concept of project serials; B. Little 1989) as it is actively pursued. In the preactional phase of volition, the individual will consider the relevant action opportunities and put him/herself into a conducive mind-set for searching out and recognizing relevant opportunities (e.g., looking out for opportunities such as parties in order to meet members of the opposite sex). For age-normative developmental goals, mental models about normative developmental tracks provide an adaptive constraint to developmental regulation in the volitional phases of goal striving (e.g., the transition from college to university and graduate studies). They prevent a reentry into motivational processing (i.e., pondering alternatives) while pursuing the developmental project. This might be so because sequential segments of the track are so closely linked that transitions between them do not appear as points of choice but merely as opportunities to continue with project-relevant action. Thus, at such transitions implemental intents are enacted instead of goal attainment assessed and new intentions formed. This channels the individual along and thus helps to minimize the motivational effort required for "staying on track."

As the individual approaches the expected age deadline for the respective goal (e.g., as she becomes a little too old to start an apprenticeship), goal attainment becomes more urgent, and consequently volitional commitment to the goal should be enhanced. Primary control striving under such urgent conditions should require more investment of resources (selective primary control) and may also involve unusual means or external assistance (compensatory primary control). Moreover, alternative goals that may derail the deadline-relevant goal need to be neutralized (selective secondary control).

The postactional phase is reached when one of two conditions applies: Either the developmental goal is attained or it becomes clear that the goal is unattainable because, for instance, the deadline has passed. In the case of success, the individual should capitalize on this success in terms of promoting long-term primary control. This can be done by setting new aspirations and further subgoals in line with the chosen goal track. For example, a successfully published article on a new theoretical model can be used as the stepping-stone for an ambitious research grant proposal. Alternatively, after attaining success in one domain the individual might decide to switch primary control resources to other domains, especially if the previous goal pursuit has deprived other goal domains of resources and thus endangered an essential level of diversity. Thus, for example, the scientist who has been granted tenure might decide to dedicate more time to her family and social life.

In contrast, in the case of failure, when the developmental deadline for a given developmental goal has irrevocably passed, the respective goal should be deactivated (compensatory secondary control) so as not to hinder the pursuit of other, more timely goals. For example, a manager who is approaching retirement but has not achieved the top position he has been striving for would probably do well to let go of this unrealistic goal.

In this way, age deadlines help to make sure that long-standing goals are not continuously postponed but are finally pursued with enhanced tenaciousness. And when the deadline has passed, they provide an opportunity finally to disengage from an old goal and thus free resources to pursue new and more timely goals.

Challenge to Developmental Regulation Presented by Age-Normative Deadlines. The interesting challenge to developmental regulation provided by age-normative deadlines is the rapid and radical shift from a situation of urgency, when the deadline is approaching, to a situation of final and irrevocable failure, when the deadline has passed (J. Heckhausen & Fleeson 1993). This involves a radical shift from enhanced efforts for primary control to a secondary control-type disengagement from the goal. The mind-set before and after the deadline should be quite different because it is based on different functional requirements. When approaching the deadline, urgent primary control striving requires a mind-set that can be characterized in three ways: content, focus, and form (see a more detailed account in J. Heckhausen & Fleeson 1993). First, the content of thought should reflect enhanced goal commitment and center on the actual performance of the action. Second, the focus of attention should be narrowed to action-relevant aspects such as action opportunities and feedback. And third, the form of processing should be single-minded in terms of excluding all competing tendencies and heightening perceptions of controllability and likelihood of success. In contrast, after the deadline has passed, secondary control requires a mind-set that turns away from the goal, buffering negative consequences (e.g., egotistic attributions, goal devaluation) and opening the search for new goals that might substitute for the original goal.

Moreover, the urgency/disengagement shift described above can be expected to vary with a number of characteristics of the developmental ecology and individual goal commitment. First, the shift should be more radical the more irrevocable the deadline is (e.g., "biological clock"). Second, a less radical primary/secondary control shift would be expected when the goal and its deadline can be substituted (e.g., adopting a child). Third, under conditions of low goal controllability the individual will be more likely to shift away from primary control. Fourth, the more personal significance a goal holds for a given individual, the less likely is disengagement. And fifth, the social sanctioning that follows certain deadline failures will enhance the tenaciousness of primary control striving and hinder disengagement.

It should be noted that the urgency/disengagement shift in developmental regulation around deadline transition represents a prototypical, possibly exaggerated scenario. However, the individual can be expected to be aware of the deadline-related changes in opportunities for goal attainment long before the situation of urgency actually arises. Thus, anticipatory optimization of selection and compensation in primary and secondary control might prompt the individual to not wait until the deadline has passed but to disengage in anticipation so as to avoid major long-term costs in motivational and emotional resources (J. Heckhausen & Schulz 1993b). As discussed in Chapter 4, developmental optimization involves the management of diversity, selectivity (including age-appropriate choices), and intergoal (interdomain) trade-offs. These requirements of developmental optimization were illustrated in different scenarios of long-term/short-term conflicts.

Short-term/long-term conflict scenarios are particularly relevant to developmental regulation around deadlines. One may ask, for instance: What happens if the deadline-relevant goal involves too many resources, thus presenting a case of "too costly success"? What happens if failure at the deadline goal becomes very likely? And what happens if failure at the deadline goal becomes very costly? Under conditions of high-cost and low-success probability, people shift from engagement in primary-goal pursuit to secondary-goal disengagement even *before* the deadline has actually passed. When individuals fear they have little control over the outcome, they will try to lower the long-term costs of failure by avoiding too much investment. Thus, optimized developmental regulation also means anticipation of the long-term costs and disengagement from the risky goal before the deadline has passed.

Summary

Developmental goals are conceptualized as long-term action units in developmental regulation. Related concepts such as developmental tasks, current concerns, personal projects, personal strivings, personal life tasks, and identity goals are reviewed and discussed in terms of their similarities to and differences from the concept of developmental goals. The concept is distinct from other goal-related concepts in three ways: (1) in the focus on developmental regulation across the life span; (2) in conceptualizing the individual as an agent of developmental processes around specific age-graded developmental tasks; and (3) in applying an action-theoretical model encompassing four phases – predecisional motivation leading to the decisional Rubicon, preactional volition after crossing the Rubicon, actional volition, and postactional motivation. In an extension to the action-phase model, the concept of developmental deadlines is introduced as an age-normative marker for disengagement from goals that have become unattainable because the appropriate age timing has been missed. Developmental deadlines are based on biological, sociostructural, and age-normative constraints to the age timing of developmental tasks. Developmental deadlines involve adaptive challenges to developmental regulation because they provide predictability and chronological and sequential structure. Thereby, they help the individual to make use of age-graded opportunity structures and to organize resource investment for important goals within specified windows of age timing. Based on the extended action-phase model and on the OPS model of developmental regulation (see Chapter 4), a hypothetical model of the life course of developmental goals is outlined. This model illustrates how developmental goals might serve as the medium through which developmental optimization is realized in sequential action phases, during which primary and secondary control strategies are employed according to the requirements of the respective action phase. The particular challenge presented by developmental deadlines is that they require a radical shift from urgent primary control as the deadline is approaching to compensatory secondary control as the deadline has passed. The theoretical model of action phases in developmental goal striving, presented in this chapter, furnishes an extensive research program. While most of this research still needs to be done (see prospects for future research, Chapter 8), a first set of relevant studies is reported in the next chapter.

6 Developmental Regulation in Different Life-Course Ecologies

In order to be effective, individuals' attempts at developmental regulation have to be adapted to the particular type of challenge present in the developmental ecology of the individual. According to the life-span theory of control, the key dimension for characterizing challenges is the degree of primary control available in a given developmental ecology. In this chapter, two types of challenges to developmental regulation will be considered: those associated with aging in later adulthood and those resulting from radical sociohistorical change. First, these two challenges are conceptually analyzed in terms of the specific demands they raise for the individual's developmental regulation. Based on this conceptual analysis, operationalizable hypotheses about characteristics of developmental regulation under conditions of aging and sociohistorical transition are derived. Subsequently, findings from two relevant empirical studies are discussed with regard to these predictions. It should be noted that the two studies were not originally planned as empirical investigations of the theory. Instead, the studies were conducted concurrently with the development of the life-span theory of control. However, these studies yield important findings that are consistent with the theoretical propositions of the theory of control.

The first study (Study 5) allows one to directly juxtapose aging-related and sociohistorical challenges to developmental regulation by investigating a sample of adults from East and West Berlin who vary in age between young adulthood and old age. Second, a representative survey of East Germans (Study 6) is reported that addresses the question of whether sociohistorical transitions differentially affect developmental regulation in different age/birth cohorts.

Two Prototypical Challenges to Developmental Regulation

Under normal and stable conditions (i.e., no major developmental or sociohistorical change), developmental regulation requires relatively little effort because the investment of control resources is regulated by the opportunities and constraints encountered in the given developmental ecology. The individual does not need to exert particular energy or intentional and conscious efforts to modify his/her own behavior. However, across the life course the structure of opportunities and constraints changes, and the individual undergoes major transformations with regard to the capacity to exert primary control (see Chapters 2 and 3). Insofar as these changes are age-normative, they provide a predictable challenge to the individual and are shared commonly within a given age cohort. However, there are also changes that are not age-normative but unique to a given historical period, or even to an individual ("nonnormative factors," P. Baltes 1987). In this chapter, I will extend the conception of developmental challenge beyond age-normative requirements and include the demands placed on developmental regulation by a radical transformation of social structure due to an unexpected and sudden sociohistorical event. Moreover, I will discuss hypotheses about how these developmental challenges affect the striving for primary and secondary control, as well as about the specific kinds of control strategies individuals may employ to master these challenges.

Aging-Related Challenges

As discussed in Chapter 2, as age increases the individual is confronted with more and more developmental losses and increasing constraints on developmental growth. This holds in both the realm of social roles and biological functioning. Although there is some scope for interindividual variability (e.g., Nelson & Dannefer 1992) and intraindividual plasticity (e.g., Kliegl, Smith, & Baltes 1990), aging-related losses eventually are inescapable for everyone. Both social and biological constraints reduce the individual's potential for primary control.

In order to maintain present primary control for ongoing goal strivings and to protect the motivational resources needed for primary control in the future, the individual has to employ *specific control strategies*, especially those based on secondary control (see Chapters 3 and 4). More specifically, aging-related decline in primary control potential for given goals requires that primary control resources be invested more selectively. Such striving for *selective primary control* (see OPS model discussed in Chapter 4) in old age involves engagement with age-appropriate goals and also implies disengagement from age-inappropriate goals. The latter can be conceptualized as attempts at *selective secondary control*, which prevent alternative options from distracting resources from the chosen goal. When even focused investment of given primary control resources proves insufficient to maintain functioning in the domain at hand, *compensatory primary control* strategies, such as recruiting help or using technical devices, are called for. Finally, when certain goals become unattainable due to aging-related decline in primary control, the individual has to disengage from such goals by using *compensatory secondary control* strategies. It should be noted that goal disengagement does not only happen due to a lack of primary control. Old age also offers some select opportunities for developmental advancement that may prompt older individuals to shift their interests away from obsolete goals to domains still holding developmental promise. In sum, older individuals can be expected to invest primary control resources selectively in age-appropriate goals while disengaging from age-inappropriate goals that have become unattainable or irrelevant. Secondary control strategies will become more important in old age in various ways: for shielding given goal strivings against distractions, for buffering negative effects of control loss with regard to a given goal, and for facilitating goal changes. These general hypotheses about developmental regulation of aging-related challenges are based on the OPS model and provide the conceptual foundation for deriving specific predictions for Study 5 (see introductory section to Study 5 below).

Challenges Presented by Sociohistorical Change

Sociohistorical change transforms the societally based structure of opportunities and constraints for developmental regulation. As was discussed in Chapter 2, selectivity and failure compensation, the two fundamental requirements of human behavior, are achieved not only by individuals' efforts but to a large extent are also provided by social structure (see also J. Heckhausen & Schulz 1993a). The "windows" for individual decision and regulation are probably quite narrow compared to what is channeled by age-chronological constraints and life-course tracks. Although to some these sociostructural constraints may seem like a disadvantage and unduly restrictive, they help the individual to stay on track, provide a predictable structure of future outcomes for planning, and set her/him free to focus on essential decisions and selected goals.

Under conditions of radical sociohistorical change all these advantages are lost. This is the situation in the former German Democratic Republic (GDR) during reunification with the Federal Republic of Germany (FRG). Within months, after the fall of the Berlin Wall, the former social structure collapsed and gave way to a chaotic aftermath that still has not been entirely replaced by the social structure adopted from the West German state. But it is not only the loss of social structuring for one's own life planning that accompanies radical sociohistorical changes. Individuals also lose their selective investments in life courses embedded in the former social structure, which have now become incompatible with the new social system. Ironically, those who were best adapted to the previous social system may be more disadvantaged in the new social structure than those who were less well fitted to the previous societal niche.

However, radical societal change involves not only losses but also the potential for gains. Given that the social structure exerts fewer and weaker constraints in a situation of social transformation, the individual also has the potential for greater upward mobility. Thus, effective action directed at optimizing one's future life can achieve better life-course outcomes than under normal conditions of a stable society. On the other hand, no or ineffective action can be particularly costly. Thus, a focus on primary control should be particularly adaptive in a situation of radical societal transformation.

It is difficult to think of a historical event that parallels the specific challenges presented to individuals' developmental regulation by the collapse and radical transformation of East Germany in the context of reunification. However, in terms of the general challenges to individual's developmental regulation, other major sociohistorical events do bear similarities. A case in point is the Great Depression in the United States and its effects on individuals' behavior and life courses, as has been studied by Glen Elder and his colleagues (e.g., Elder 1974; Elder & Caspi 1990). Elder and Caspi, for instance, found that young adults affected by the Great Depression did not react with resignation but rather with increased striving for control ("control cycles") during the turmoil of the worldwide economic collapse.

The congruent feature of the Great Depression and the sociostructural transformation in the former GDR is the increased risk of negative life-course outcomes, coupled with the remaining potential for personal control over one's future life course. An individual in this situation can either struggle to master the challenge and, if successful, attain a superior position in society that may not have been attainable under normal societal conditions; or, alternatively, if the individual gives up or is unsuccessful at primary control, he/she loses all previous life-course investments. Thus, there is a polarized winning versus losing alternative, which calls for increased efforts to optimize primary control in order to be among the winners and avoid becoming a loser in this changed sociostructural situation. For adults in the former GDR, one can therefore expect increased striving for primary control, with a likely emphasis on economic survival and prosperity (J. Heckhausen 1994a, 1997). This general hypothesis about developmental regulation when confronted with a radical sociohistorical transition will be translated into specific predictions about differences between East and West Berliners' control-related behavior.

Developmental Regulation in Young, Middle-Aged, and Old East and West Berliners (Study 5)

In a study involving East and West Berliners at various age levels, the two challenges to developmental regulation were investigated with regard to their effects on control striving in the context of pursuing developmental goals (see also J. Heckhausen 1994a, 1997). The two challenges to developmental regulation addressed in this research both represent substantial threats to the individual's striving for developmental goals. They differ, however, with regard to the degree of personal control available. With regard to aging-related changes, the individual has little potential actively to influence the course of development. In contrast, sociostructural transformation in the former GDR renders individuals' control more influential, because greater social mobility is possible.

Based on the hypotheses developed above for the two types of challenges, a specific scheme of predictions about primary and secondary control striving can be derived for aging-related and sociohistorical challenges. For investigating the validity of these hypotheses one would ideally have employed a questionnaire targeted at the strategies of developmental regulation addressed in the model of optimization in primary and secondary control (OPS model; J. Heckhausen & Schulz 1993a). However, given that Study 5 and the life-span theory of control were developed conjointly, such an instrument was not yet available. Therefore, other indicators for the four strategies of developmental regulation proposed by the OPS model were used. This includes an existing two-scale measurement instrument by Brandtstädter and Renner (1990), which measures tenacious goal pursuit and flexible goal adjustment, two concepts that are consistent with the primary versus secondary control distinction for the domain of goal engagement versus goal disengagement.[1]

[1] The Brandtstädter and Renner Scales were used in various studies, and it is only recently that we have developed a new measurement instrument for primary and secondary control strategies in developmental regulation (J. Heckhausen, Schulz, & Wrosch 1998).

Specifically, selective primary control striving was expected to be reflected in age-appropriate goal selection, striving for gains, and high tenaciousness in goal pursuit. Attempts at compensatory primary control should be shown in the selection of goals directed at the avoidance of losses. Selective secondary control striving is expected to involve optimistic expectations about goal attainment, lack of satisfaction with present life, anticipated improvement for future life, and greater urgency. Finally, compensatory secondary control strategies should involve a high flexibility of goal adjustment, satisfaction with current life, and disengagement from obsolete goals. Based on the use of these indicators for various aspects of developmental regulation the following scheme of predictions can be derived.

Developmental regulation confronted with *aging-related challenges* will be associated with three major characteristics. First, older subjects, compared to younger subjects, should express an *awareness of the decreased potential for developmental growth*. Such an awareness is the subjective precondition for adjusting developmental regulation to aging-related challenges. An awareness of decreased potential for growth should be indicated by less optimistic expectations about the likelihood of attaining goals and by lowered perceptions of personal control over goal attainment. Second, *selective primary control* should be reflected in goal strivings that are focused on *age-appropriate developmental goals*. This selection of age-appropriate goals should be complemented by disengagement from previously attainable but now less attainable (or even unattainable) goals. Moreover, age-graded goal selection should also lead to a greater concern with avoiding losses and a concomitantly reduced emphasis on striving for gains. Thus, older adults compared to younger adults should nominate more goals that aim at avoiding losses and fewer goals directed at striving for gains. A third, *compensatory secondary control* in older adults should be identifiable in four ways: a greater flexibility to disengage from goals; a higher satisfaction with the current life situation; a greater tendency to identify with younger age groups in terms of one's subjective age status and the normative age ascribed to one's own developmental goals; and the perception that one's prime of life is at relatively higher ages.

In contrast, developmental regulation in the face of *sociohistorical challenges* presented to residents of the former GDR by German reunification should show the following two characteristics. First, in East Germans more than in West Germans *selective primary control striving* should be focused on developmental goals addressing *economic survival*. And second, there should be an *enhanced striving for primary control* in East Germans. This enhanced striving might be expressed in greater urgency for realizing goals (i.e., shorter time intervals until realization), an increased tenaciousness in pursuing the goal, a lack of satisfaction with one's present life, and the expectation that life satisfaction will improve in the future.

Moreover, one may expect sociohistorical change to affect individuals differentially at different ages. Young adults in the former GDR can be assumed to have relatively few developmental investments in the previous social system and may therefore not differ much from their West German peers. At the other end of the adult life span a functionally analogous situation may hold. Older adults have relatively little to gain or lose in the new social system, as they are no longer part of the labor force. Thus, they may enact similar developmental regulation strategies as West German elderly people. Middle-aged adults, in contrast, may face a particularly difficult developmental ecology in the former GDR. Most of them will have already invested substantial life-course time and developmental resources in the previous social system that are now at stake in the process of reunification. At the same time, because of their restricted life time, especially in terms of labor participation, middle-aged adults face relatively bad prospects for future occupational careers. Hence, one may expect the effects on developmental regulation to be stronger for middle-aged East Germans than for young and old adults.

Sample and Procedure

Data for this study on developmental regulation in East and West Berliners were collected between spring 1991 and spring 1992. The sample included 510 adults, equally divided by age (young: 20–35 years; middle-aged: 40–55 years; old: 60 years and over), place of origin (East and West Berlin), sex, and socioeconomic status (teachers, engineers, clerks, and skilled and semiskilled workers).

The questionnaire booklet given to the subjects contained the following variables relevant to developmental regulation (see also J. Heckhausen 1997). (1) Subjects were requested to write down the five "most important personal hopes, plans, and goals for the next five to ten years." (2a) For each of the named goals, subjects were also asked about: future time extension ("When, in how many years, do you think this goal will be realized?"); (2b) probability of attainment ("In your view, how likely is it that this goal will be realized?"); (2c) causality and personal control (a scheme of questions addressing the influence of self, one's personality, powerful others, and situational circumstances on goal attainment); and (2d) the normative age of goal (subjects were asked to estimate the typical age at which most other people would attain the respective goal).[2] (3) The Tenacious Goal Pursuit Scale (sample item: "When I have set my mind on something I do not get discouraged even by great difficulties") and the Flexible Goal Adjustment Scale ("Even in great misfortune I often find meaning") were also presented (TEN-FLEX, Brandtstädter & Renner 1990). They served as measures of goal engagement (selective primary control) and disengagement (compensatory secondary control). (4) Questions about life satisfaction in the past were asked ("How satisfied are you with your life when you look back to your past?"), present ("How satisfied are you with your life at present?"), and future ("How satisfied will you be with your life in the future?"). (5) A set of questions about subjective age identification were asked ("The Ages of Me," Kastenbaum et al. 1981), including five aspects of subjective age: "the age I feel like" (feel age); "the age I look like" (appearance age); "the age resembling my interests and activities" (activities age); "the age unacquainted people would ascribe to me" (strangers' perception); and "the age my friends would ascribe to me" (friends' perception). Note that another indicator of subjective age identification was gathered in terms of estimates of normative age of personal developmental goals (see 2d). (6) Subjects were asked whether the best time of their lives was past (age estimate), was now, or would be in the future (age estimate). (7) Finally, some basic sociodemographic information (age, family status, current residence, number and age of children, education, occupational training, current occupational position, etc.) was gathered.[3]

Results

The findings relating to the age differences will be reported first, and those based on East/West German differences thereafter (for more de-

---

[2] The measure of normative age of goal was added to the design as an additional, more specifically goal-related indicator of subjective age identification and assessed by mailed questionnaire four months after the main study. A total of 457 subjects returned these ratings. This sample did not differ from the original sample in terms of the design variables.

[3] In addition, a new questionnaire about action-related beliefs was included, which separately assesses means–ends beliefs and agency beliefs about important outcomes in the work domain, the family domain, and the domain of civic/community involvement (Heckhausen & Hundertmark 1995). Means–ends beliefs concern the causal link between certain causal factors (e.g., ability, influential others, socioeconomic situation) and outcomes (occupational promotion, harmony in the family). Agency beliefs regard the individual's personal access to relevant means–ends (e.g., having the required skills for one's job). This new questionnaire proved to be reliable and structurally coherent as well as invariant across the different subgroups. It was therefore put to further use in other studies (see Study 6).

Table 6.1. *Study 5: Means for young, middle-aged, and old adults: Probability of goal attainment, personal control of goal attainment, and life satisfaction*

Variable	Young	Middle-Aged	Old	Standard Error
Probability of				
goal attainment	72.29[a]	65.41	66.88	1.270
Personal control of				
goal attainment	3.92[b]	3.48[c]	3.20	.057
Life satisfaction				
in the past	3.57	3.71	3.69	.075
at present	3.46[d]	3.34	3.77	.080
in the future	3.89	3.77	3.82	.056

[a]Young versus middle-aged and old, $p < .01$.
[b]Young versus middle-aged, $p < .01$.
[c]Middle-aged versus old, $p < .01$.
[d]Young and middle-aged versus old, $p < .01$.

tails, see J. Heckhhausen, 1997). Regarding the *aging-related challenges*, the first set of hypotheses predicted an *awareness of the decreased potential for developmental growth* in older adults. Relevant results are given in Table 6.1. In accordance with this prediction, older and middle-aged adults expected to attain their goals with lesser probability than young adults. Moreover, there was a continuous decline of perceived personal control over attaining one's goals across the adult age group, with older adults reporting least personal control.

The second set of hypotheses reflected the expectation that *selective primary control* would be *focused on age-appropriate goals*. In order to investigate the developmental goals nominated by the subjects, the goals were coded with respect to six categories: (1) work-related goals (job characteristics, education, occupational training); (2) family-related goals (partner, children, parents); (3) goals directed toward civic and community issues (economy, social welfare, politics, nature and environment); (4) goals associated with personal health; (5) goals directed toward personal financial welfare; and (6) goals addressing free time and leisure.

Figure 6.1 displays the mean frequencies (and their standard errors) of goal nominations across subjects' age for those goals with significantly increasing age trajectories – that is, goals that were selected and focused upon more by older adults than by younger adults. Health-related goals exhibited a continuous increase across adulthood, with

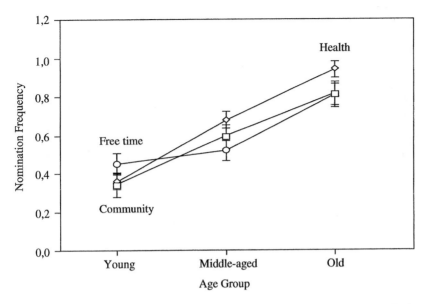

Figure 6.1. Study 5: Developmental goals with increasing age trajectories. (From J. Heck-hausen [1997]. Developmental regulation across adulthood: Primary and secondary control of age-related challenges. *Developmental Psychology, 33*, 176–187. Copyright © 1997 by the American Psychological Association. Adapted with permission.)

older adults naming more than middle-aged adults, and middle-aged adults more than young adults. Leisure-oriented goals were reported more by older than by young and middle-aged adults, and community-related goals were less frequent among the young than middle-aged and old adults.

Figure 6.2 illustrates mean age differences in goal nominations for those goals which reflected age-related decreases, thus indicating less goal engagement in older as compared to younger adults. Older adults nominated fewer work-related goals than young and middle-aged adults. Middle-aged and older adults had fewer family-related and financial goals than young adults.

In addition, it was investigated whether the goals nominated reflected an orientation toward preventing losses or striving for gains. Striving for gains was predicted to be more salient among younger adults, while preventing losses was expected to become more important in old age. Figure 6.3 illustrates the relevant findings. As predicted, there was a continuous decline in gain-oriented goals across age groups and a concomitant increase in loss-oriented goals.

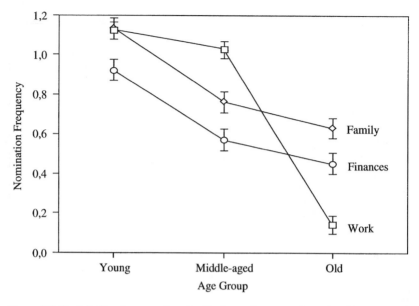

Figure 6.2. Study 5: Developmental goals with decreasing age trajectories. (From J. Heck-hausen [1997]. Developmental regulation across adulthood: Primary and secondary con-trol of age-related challenges. *Developmental Psychology, 33*, 176–187. Copyright © 1997 by the American Psychological Association. Adapted with permission.)

   The third set of hypotheses addressed the expected greater need for *compensatory secondary control* strategies at higher ages. As expected and illustrated in Figure 6.4, older adults expressed a greater flexibility of goal adjustment than middle-aged adults, and middle-aged adults, in turn, reported more flexibility than young adults. It is important to note that tenaciousness of goal pursuit remained constant across age groups. These findings support the assumption that primary control striving is essential across the life span and holds functional primacy (J. Heckhausen & Schulz, 1995). In terms of compensatory secondary con-trol, it was further found that older adults were more satisfied with their present lives than young and middle-aged adults (see Table 6.1). In addition, various indicators of self-enhancement relative to age-normative conceptions were more pronounced among older than among younger adults. With increasing age adults identified more with younger age groups on various dimensions, such as "the age I feel like" and "the age strangers ascribe to me" (see Figure 6.5). Similarly, older adults reported that the developmental goals they chose were typically pursued by people younger than themselves, while young adults per-ceived their developmental goals as more common among people older

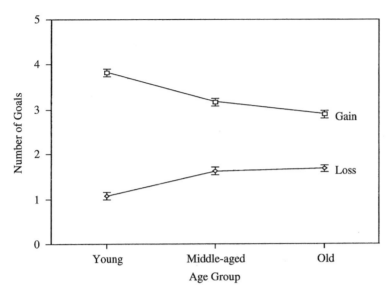

Figure 6.3. Study 5: Gain- and loss-related developmental goals in young, middle-aged, and old subjects. (From J. Heckhausen [1997]. Developmental regulation across adulthood: Primary and secondary control of age-related challenges. *Developmental Psychology*, *33*, 176–187. Copyright © 1997 by the American Psychological Association. Adapted with permission.)

than themselves. And finally, at higher age levels adults also constructed the prime of life as occuring at higher ages (see Figure 6.6).

The other challenge for developmental regulation addressed in this study is the *sociohistorical transformation* of East German society. Given the societal conditions of a recent societal collapse (the study took place in 1991, one year after German reunification and two years after the tearing down of the Berlin Wall), we expected to find *selective primary control focused on economic survival* and an enhanced striving for primary control. Regarding the former, the findings showed an increased commitment to work-related goals in East as compared to West Berliners (see Figure 6.7). Conversely, health-related goals were less frequently endorsed by East Berliners.

Enhanced striving for primary control was reflected in four indicators of goal commitment. First, East Berliners expressed a greater urgency to reach their goals by anticipating shorter time intervals for goal attainment (mean number of years = 3.73 years) than West Berliners (4.62 years). East Berliners also reported greater tenaciousness in goal pursuit and less flexibility in goal adjustment than West Berliners (see Fig-

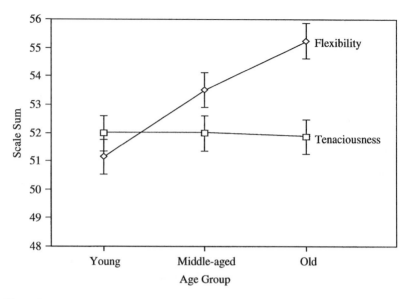

Figure 6.4. Study 5: Tenaciousness and flexibility in young, middle-aged, and old subjects. (From J. Heckhausen [1997]. Developmental regulation across adulthood: Primary and secondary control of age-related challenges. *Developmental Psychology*, *33*, 176–187. Copyright © 1997 by the American Psychological Association. Adapted with permission.)

ure 6.8). Moreover, East Berliners were less satisfied with the present and more hopeful about future life satisfaction (see Figure 6.9).

Discussion

In this study two developmental challenges were compared in their effects on individuals' developmental regulation. While both challenges were expected to present substantial threats to the individual's goal striving, aging-related challenges were conceptualized as less subject to personal control than challenges presented by a radical sociostructural transformation. This control-related conceptual distinction of the two developmental challenges was validated by the findings about perceived personal control over the attainment of developmental goals. With increasing age of subjects, perceptions of personal control declined. No such difference was found between East and West Berliners' control perceptions.

The OPS model proposed that an individual's developmental regulation should reflect the specific constraints and opportunities encountered in any given developmental ecology. For aging-related develop-

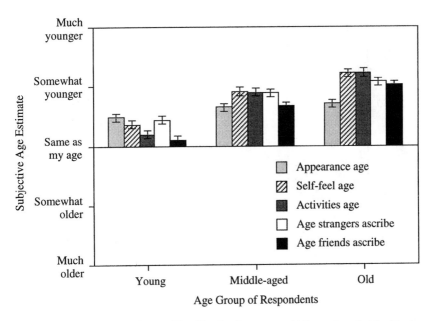

Figure 6.5. Study 5: Subjective age identification in young, middle-aged, and old subjects. (From J. Heckhausen [1997]. Developmental regulation across adulthood: Primary and secondary control of age-related challenges. *Developmental Psychology, 33*, 176–187. Copyright © 1997 by the American Psychological Association. Adapted with permission.)

mental challenges implying reduced controllability, it was predicted that the individuals would use more compensatory secondary control and that primary control would focus on age-appropriate goals. In contrast, radical sociohistorical change was expected to elicit increased striving for primary control for select goals related to economic welfare.

In the following section, the empirical findings about age differences and differences between East and West Berliners are discussed in the context of this general conceptual scheme and in view of the specific predictions raised above. Moreover, the findings are integrated into the theoretical framework of the model of "Optimization by Selection and Compensation in Primary and Secondary Control" (OPS model, J. Heckhausen & Schulz, 1993a).

Age-Related Differences. Previous research (J. Heckhausen & P. Baltes 1991) suggests that individuals are aware of aging-related threats to personal control of psychological characteristics. In this study, older adults expressed reduced perceptions of personal control and attainability of developmental goals. Thus, the study's participants construed

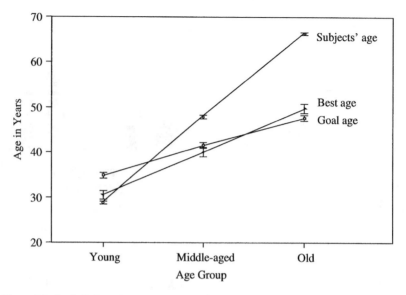

Figure 6.6. Study 5: Actual age, goal age, and best time of life in young, middle-aged, and old subjects. (From J. Heckhausen [1997]. Developmental regulation across adulthood: Primary and secondary control of age-related challenges. *Developmental Psychology, 33*, 176–187. Copyright © 1997 by the American Psychological Association. Adapted with permission.)

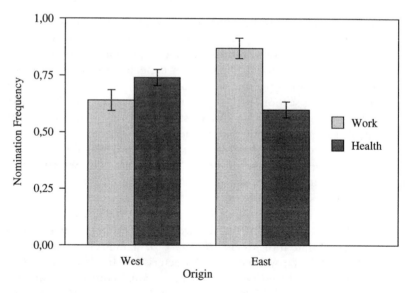

Figure 6.7. Study 5: Developmental goals of East and West German subjects. (Adapted from J. Heckhausen 1994a.)

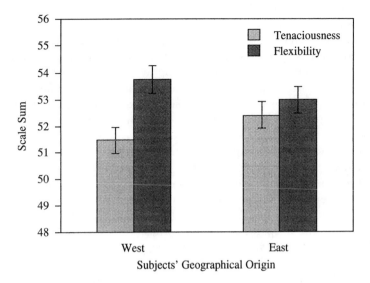

Figure 6.8. Study 5: Tenaciousness and flexibility in East and West Berlin subjects. (Adapted from J. Heckhausen 1994a.)

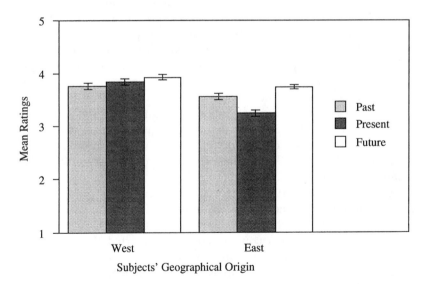

Figure 6.9. Study 5: Past, present, and future life satisfaction in East and West Berlin subjects. (Adapted from J. Heckhausen 1994a.)

the developmental challenge raised by old age as one characterized by low-control potential.

It was predicted that primary control striving in old age would be selectively focused on age-specific challenges. The findings that older adults selectively focused on age-appropriate goals support this prediction. The age trajectories of goal nominations for the domains health, community, and leisure activities follow the age-grading in opportunities and constraints. Health-related goals continually increased in salience across the adult life span, reflecting increasing medical vulnerability throughout mid-life and old age. At variance with this continual trajectory, community involvement increased only between young adulthood and mid-life, possibly reflecting increased social influence in mid-life. Leisure activities became more salient in the transition from mid-life to old age, possibly because retirement frees up a substantial amount of time to spend on such activities.

Along with the findings on decreasing goal striving in the domains of work, finances, and family, the increasing importance of health, leisure, and community concerns at older ages converges with previous research (Brandtstädter & Rothermund 1994; Nurmi 1992). An important conclusion suggested by these findings is that older adults not only focus on those goals that are still controllable or are becoming controllable in old age but also continue striving for goals that involve reduced controllability in old age, provided they are high in importance. This is the case for health-related goals that become more salient as their controllability declines. Thus, older adults do not simply adapt their choice of goals to maintain a certain level of success expectancy, but select or continue to strive for important goals even if they promise less success in old age. One may speculate whether maintenance of health represents an indispensable goal from which the individual cannot disengage, as is possible for other goals perceived as important. Health may be a basic resource of primary control that cannot be given up even in extreme adversity. This may be the reason why processes of disability often have devastating effects on motivation and emotion (Kennedy, Kalman, & Thomas 1990; Schulz, Heckhausen, & O'Brien 1994; Williamson & Schulz 1992a, 1992b).

Compensatory secondary control strategies were expected to become more important in old age for maintaining motivational resources (e.g., self-worth, self-efficacy, hopefulness) for primary control. Various indicators of compensatory secondary control supported this prediction. The older adults disengaged from obsolete goals in the life domains of work, finances, and family – all areas involving reduced primary control potential in old age.

According to the OPS model of developmental regulation, such goal disengagements, in combination with a less optimistic outlook on future control potential, need to be balanced by compensatory secondary control so as to maintain motivational resources for primary control. An important aspect of compensatory secondary control is a generalized preparedness to adjust goals flexibly when facing major obstacles or uncontrollability (see also Brandtstädter & Renner 1992, on "accommodation"). Indeed, with increasing age the adults expressed a greater tendency to adjust goals flexibly. Moreover, older adults were more satisfied with their current life situation than young and middle-aged adults. Relatively high life satisfaction implies a reduced tendency to strive for improvements in the future, and therefore exemplifies the function of compensatory secondary control.

Another realm of compensatory secondary control is the reinterpretation of the relation between the self and normative conceptions about chronological age. In contrast to the young adults, who identified with their age peers, middle-aged and especially older adults identified with younger age groups in terms of various domains of functioning. These findings are consistent with previous research (Filipp & Ferring 1989; J. Heckhausen & Krueger 1993; Montepare & Lachman 1989). The findings on the normative age timing of personal developmental goals reveal a similar pattern of compensatory age identification. The older the adults, the greater the tendency to perceive one's goals as typical of younger ages. Interestingly, the young adults saw their goals as typical of "older" ages, thus projecting developmental aspiration into midlife. It should be noted that compensatory protection of self-worth may not be the only function of identifying with younger age groups. An orientation toward younger age groups also may reflect upward social comparisons that set goals and provide models for primary control for even those goals that are typically perceived as less age-appropriate in older age. The latter function does not hold for conceptions about the prime of life, which thus represents a pure instantiation of compensatory secondary control. With increasing age of subject, the prime of life was construed to be at higher ages. Thus, life-course phases were (re)interpreted in view of and adapted to one's own actual age in such a way that one's own age appeared to be less removed from the prime of life.

Differences between East and West Berliners. It was expected that East Berliners would show enhanced striving for primary control, because the radical sociohistorical change in East Germany increases both risks for severe losses and chances for substantial gains. The findings on various indicators of selective primary control and selective secondary control strategies confirm this prediction. Primary control focused on work-related developmental goals. Concentrating on occupational issues is particularly adaptive in a situation in which previous career tracks cannot be taken for granted anymore, and consequently employment status and even basic economic resources are at stake.

Moreover, East Berliners were less committed to health-related goals, thus exhibiting selective investment in work-related goals at the expense of other important domains. This is especially noteworthy given the fact that, judging from representative statistics on life expectancy and incidence of cardiovascular disease, the state of public health in East Germany is worse than in West Germany (source: Statistisches Bundesamt, 1993). One would expect health concerns to figure more prominently under such conditions. However, a generalized, long-term, and therefore nonsalient health risk in a given community represents a chronic and uncontrollable rather than an acute, controllable issue, and might therefore have failed to evoke a distinct compensatory reaction among the East German respondents.

Further evidence for enhanced selective primary control in the East Berliners comes from the findings on tenaciousness and flexibility in goal striving. East German respondents expressed greater tenaciousness in goal pursuit and less flexibility of goal adjustment. This coping pattern is reminiscent of the "control cycles" (Elder & Caspi 1990) found for American adults confronted with the economic threats of the Great Depression.

Based on the reasoning that motivational commitment to primary control goals is particularly essential under conditions of radical societal change, it was expected that East Berliners would exhibit indicators of enhanced selective secondary control. As predicted, they anticipated goal attainment in shorter time periods, thus expressing greater urgency. Moreover, East Berliners expressed lower satisfaction with their present lives than West Berliners. Thus, they probably felt a greater need and stronger motivation for improving their current life situation. This interpretation is corroborated by the fact that East Berliners, but not West Berliners, anticipated improvement in their future lives. Lowered present and heightened future satisfaction can be interpreted as adaptive in the context of radical sociohistorical change, because low present satisfaction can become a strong incentive to improve one's life, especially when coupled with the prospect of future improvement.

Cohort-Related Differences among East Berliners.   Another aim of this study was to explore possible intercohort differences in developmental coping of East Berliners, since radical sociohistorical change may differentially affect different age/birth cohorts. Such analyses can only be exploratory and tentative, as the data set confounds age-related and birth cohort-related differences (P. Baltes, Cornelius, & Nesselroade 1979; Ryder 1965; Schaie 1965; Schaie & Baltes 1975). It may be argued, though, that on conceptual grounds one might expect intercohort differences that selectively pertain to East Germans to be more indicative of a historical event differentially affecting different birth cohorts than of aging-related change. However, in Study 5 no interactions between subject age and East/West origin were found. Thus, this study does not suggest that East Berliners used different strategies of managing the challenges presented by German reunification. This lack of East German specific intercohort differences may be due to the early timing (April 1991 to February 1992) of the data collection in the process of German reunification. During this time period, East German adults may still have been quite hopeful with regard to their future prospects, irrespective of their location within the life span. Thereafter, with increasing unemployment particularly affecting adults in later mid-life, such optimism may well have been dampened and may have given way to more realistic accounts of personal prospects for employment, occupational success, and economic welfare. Indeed, a representative survey conducted in the spring of 1993 supports this assumption, although its results have to be treated cautiously given that the subjects' age, birth cohort, and time of measurement were confounded (Schaie 1965; Schaie & Baltes 1975). This study is reported next.

Developmental Regulation in Four East German Age/Birth Cohorts (Study 6)

In the context of a representative survey on life courses of East German adults that was conducted by the Center for Sociology and the Study of the Life Course (director: Karl Ulrich Mayer), a further investigation of East Germans' control strategies during German reunification was possible. In particular, this survey allowed us to specifically target four distinct birth cohorts, those born in 1929–31, 1939–41, 1951–53, and 1959–61. In a collaborative effort with the life-course sociologists Johannes Huinink and Martin Diewald, part of the original survey sample was studied with regard to four key variables of developmental regulation: developmental goals, action-related beliefs, primary and secondary control striving, and self-esteem (Diewald, Huinink, & Heckhausen 1994; Diewald, Huinink & J. Heckhausen 1996; J. Heckhausen, Diewald, & Huinink 1994a; J. Heckhausen, Diewald, & Huinink 1996; Huinink, Diewald, & J. Heckhausen 1996).

The major focus of this research was on investigating possible differences in developmental regulation among different age/birth cohorts. The study of cohort differences has a long-standing tradition in life-span developmental psychology and in life-course sociology (P. Baltes 1968; P. Baltes & Schaie 1973; Mayer & Huinink 1990; Ryder 1965; Schaie 1965). While the proponents of cohort research stress the need to disentangle the influence of age, birth cohort, and time of measurement (e.g., Ryder 1965; Schaie 1965), it is also acknowledged that in research practice extensive data collections such as those required for untangling these three factors of influence may not be possible (Schaie & P. Baltes 1975) or even desirable (P. Baltes, Cornelius, & Nesselroade 1979). Therefore, theory-based approaches to resolve the age-cohort time of measurement puzzle may provide more promising research instruments than purely methodological paradigms (P. Baltes, Cornelius, & Nesselroade 1979; Glenn 1976). Such a conceptual approach is attempted in Study 6, which, due to reasons of pragmatic and logical research (P. Baltes, Cornelius, & Nesselroade 1979; Glenn 1976), did not include an independent measurement of age differences, birth cohort differences, and time of measurement.

Different age/birth cohorts are affected by radical societal transformation differentially for three major reasons, all of which are based on the degree of potential upward and downward social mobility and personal control over developmental chances and risks. (1) The more years of life an individual spent under the conditions of the previous and now obsolete society, the more investments he/she will have made in terms of life time and selectively optimizing abilities and life conditions to follow a certain chosen track for life-course development. Thus, sociohistorical change is expected to affect older individuals more negatively than younger individuals. (2) The impact of sociohistorical change on an individual's life course depends on the kind of developmental tasks and life-course transitions normatively expected for the respective chronological age (see also Elder 1974; Elder, King & Conger 1996). Thus, for instance, economic turmoil that affects individuals' occupational careers and employment patterns will not affect old adults, who have retired and left the labor force. (3) Finally, the consequences of sociohistorical change are also substantially mediated by their effect on future action prospects, which differ for individuals at different ages. Temporary losses are bearable if future prospects cover most of the adult life span and therefore allow for compensation. However, if the remaining life span is more restricted, as is true for individuals in mid-life, then societal change may bring about irreversible losses (e.g., unemployment in middle adulthood).

Based on these three cohort-differential characteristics of developmental challenge, the following expectations were derived. Younger adults' life courses (birth cohort 1959–61, ages 32–34 years) are least closely tailored to the previous, now obsolete social system. Therefore, younger adults face less risk of major life-course losses than older adults. At the same time, young adults hold a longer time perspective on their future life course and thus have a greater potential to adapt their developmental regulation to the West German social structure, resulting in more chances for life-course gains. This constellation of conditions in the developmental ecology of younger East German adults should motivate a greater striving for primary control in this age cohort.

Old adults (birth cohort 1929–31, ages 62–4 years), on the other hand, who have already retired or are nearing retirement, have few potential prospects, but they also do not risk much loss in terms of social mobility. Old East German adults can therefore be expected to be more invested in compensatory secondary control, such as the readiness of goal adjustment and disengagement.

In contrast to the young and the old adults, however, the middle-aged adults (birth cohorts 1939–41 and 1951–53, ages 52–54 years and 40–42 years, respectively) face a life-course developmental calamity. They can be assumed to have relatively high investments in the collapsed societal structure, both in terms of objective life-course patterns and subjective commitment. This makes compensatory secondary control, such as goal disengagement, less accessible to them. At the same time, middle-aged adults have few opportunities to reshape their future life courses because of the restricted life time remaining until retirement. This lack of controllability is likely to discourage primary control striving in middle-aged East Germans. Within the two middle-aged cohorts one might expect a particularly devastating effect for the older middle-aged cohort. Those in their early fifties have hardly any future employment prospects and yet are too young to retire.

In general, we expected these cohort-differential conditions to be reflected in differences among the four age cohorts in developmental regulation. Developmental regulation holds substantial adaptive potential, but may also fail under excessive demands in the respective life-course ecology (see conceptual discussion in Chapter 3). The particular challenge posed for the older middle-aged adults in East Germany may present such a failure-prone developmental context. Thus, while we expected to find attempts to adjust developmental regulation to the particular sociohistorical challenge in all four age/birth cohorts, it was also predicted that these efforts might fail to control the extreme threats to the middle-aged cohorts, or at least the adults in their early fifties. Specifically, a failure of control would be reflected in decreased primary and secondary control striving, lowered perceptions about controllability and personal control, and lower self-esteem.

Moreover, it was expected that the intercohort differences based on sociohistorical change would be superimposed on general age-related differences. Similarly to the predictive scheme about age-related differences outlined for Study 5, it was predicted that developmental goals would reflect age-normative developmental tasks for different age groups. In addition, developmental goals in the older age/birth cohorts should be focused on avoiding losses rather than striving for gains. Older adults should also express higher flexibility of goal adjustment. Finally, at higher ages action-related beliefs should increasingly include the role of external factors.

Sample and Procedure

The study "Developmental Regulation in Four East German Age/Birth Cohorts" was a collaborative enterprise of Martin Diewald, Johannes Huinink, and Jutta Heckhausen that took place in the context of a larger survey, "Life Courses and Historical Change in the Former GDR" (principle investigators: Karl Ulrich Mayer and Johannes Huinink). Face-to-face interviews for the main data collection for the life-course sociological survey were conducted by "Infas," a German survey institute, between September 1991 and October 1992. A total of 2,323 subjects were sampled at random from a representative master sample of 300,000 men and women born between 1929–31, 1939–41, 1951–3, and 1959–61 who lived in the territory of the former GDR in 1990 (source: central resident register of the former GDR). Life-course sociological data collected in the main survey included detailed retrospective information about education, occupational training, employment and residence history, as well as family-related information about parents, marriage, children, and so on.

In addition, a questionnaire study on psychological indicators of developmental regulation was conducted with a subsample of 1,254 subjects who had agreed to participate in additional data collection. The distribution of this subsample was roughly even across the birth cohorts 1929–31 (age: 62–64 years; men: 166, women: 169), 1939–41 (age: 52–54 years; men: 162, women: 160), 1951–53 (age: 40–42 years; men: 137, women: 174), and 1959–61 (age: 32–34 years; men: 140, women: 157). The subsample of 1,254 involved only two slight selective biases in terms of underrepresenting respondents with lower educational background and men in the youngest age/birth cohort (Diewald & Sørensen, in press).

The questionnaire study on developmental regulation took place in spring 1993. Subjects who had agreed to participate in an additional questionnaire study at the time of the initial interview were contacted and mailed a written questionnaire. This questionnaire included various items on political attitudes, evaluation of the process of German reunification, social networks, and family life.

With regard to psychological measures related to developmental regulation, four types of items were included. (1) Subjects were requested to nominate five developmental goals for the next five to ten years (same instructions as in Study 5). (2) Primary and secondary control striving were measured by the Tenacious Goal Pursuit and Flexible Goal Adjustment Scales (Brandtstädter & Renner, 1990). (3) Action-related beliefs were assessed by a short version of the Control Agency Means–end in Adulthood Questionnaire (CAMAQ; J. Heckhausen 1991b) developed by J. Heckhausen, Diewald, and Huinink (1994b). The CAMAQ Short Version comprises thirty-three items, with one item representing each CAMAQ subscale (i.e., beliefs about agency and means–ends regarding the causal factors effort, ability, luck, powerful others, and society) for the life domains of family and work. Community-related items were not included because of their potential lack of fit with the life ecologies in the former GDR and their somewhat inferior measurement qualities (see Chapter 6). (4) Subjects were also asked to fill out a German version of the Rosenberg Self-Esteem Scale (Rosenberg 1965).

Results

In order to provide the general background about age-cohort associated differences in goal striving, the findings related to developmental goal selection are considered first. The goals nominated by the subjects were coded into eight categories: (1) goals addressing the subject's own employment, (2) goals directed at financial welfare, (3) goals referring to the subject's own health, (4) goals referring to the health of family members, (5) goals referring to the subject's partnership, (6) goals addressing the education of family members, (7) goals about travel, (8) goals addressing world peace.

Figure 6.10 contains the mean frequencies (and their standard errors) of goal nominations across age/birth cohorts for those goal categories that yielded significantly increasing trajectories across cohorts.

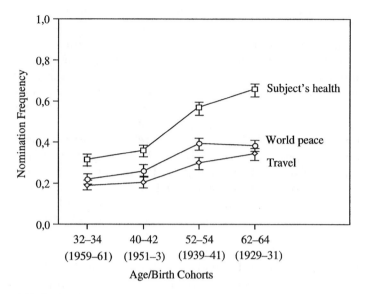

Figure 6.10. Study 6: Developmental goals with increasing age trajectories; separate for four age/birth cohorts.

Finance-related goals were reported more by the youngest adults than any other age group. Goals about the education of family members were most frequently named by adults in their early forties and least frequently by the two older cohorts. Goals addressing the health of family members were more frequent among the younger two cohorts compared to the older two cohorts. The most intriguing pattern was found for work-related goals. Not surprisingly, work-related goals were much less frequently reported by older adults than by young and middle-aged adults. But the adults aged fifty-two to fifty-four stood out by reporting more work-related goals than the younger cohorts. Thus, adults in this advanced mid-life cohort focused upon the occupational domain.

Figure 6.11 provides the relevant findings about goal nominations decreasing in frequency across the four birth/age cohorts. Goals related to personal health were most frequently reported by the oldest cohort and least frequently by the two younger cohorts. Moreover, the two older cohorts reported goals relating to travel and world peace more frequently than the two younger cohorts.

Information about the cohort-related differences with regard to the proportion of gain- and loss-oriented goals is provided in Figure 6.12. The pattern shows that, similarly to earlier findings (Study 5), gain-

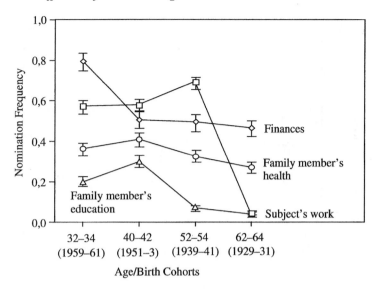

Figure 6.11. Study 6: Developmental goals with decreasing age trajectories; separate for four age/birth cohorts.

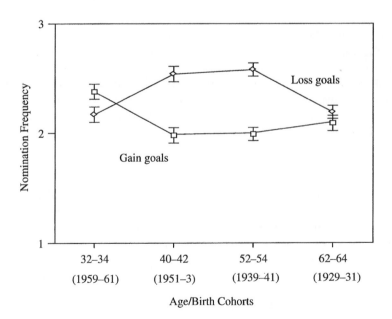

Figure 6.12. Study 6: Gain- and loss-related developmental goals; separate for four age/birth cohorts.

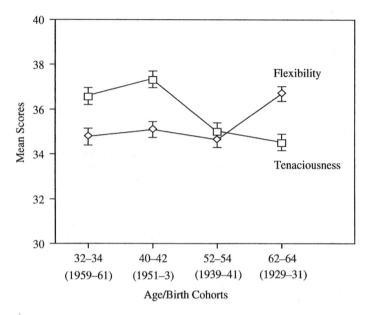

Figure 6.13. Study 6: Tenaciousness and flexibility in four subjects' age/birth cohorts.

oriented goals were more frequently reported by the young adults than by the older age cohorts. Loss-oriented goals did not show a linear increase across age groups, as found in earlier research (see Study 5). Instead, the two mid-life age groups (40–42 and 52–54 years) were more concerned with loss-oriented goals than the young and the old adults. Another striking difference between this study's findings and the findings from Study 5 was the fact that that gain-oriented goals did not predominate in this sample of East German adults. Instead, loss-oriented goals were more frequent than gain-oriented goals in the two mid-life cohorts.

In terms of birth-cohort specific effects of the sociohistorical transformation, it was expected that *primary control striving* would be highest in the young adults. Due to their comparatively unfortunate age status, we expected impoverished primary control striving in the middle-aged adults. Finally, because of the constrained developmental opportunities in old age, less primary control striving (compared to younger adults) was also expected for the old adults. Figure 6.13 illustrates differences among the four age/birth cohorts in terms of tenaciousness of goal pursuit (used as an indicator of primary control striving) and flexibility of goal adjustment (used as an indicator of secondary control striving).

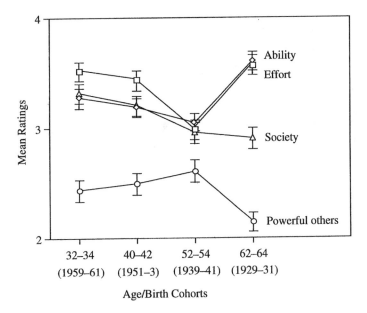

Figure 6.14. Study 6: Beliefs about means–ends in the work domain; age/birth cohort differences.

As can be seen, subjects in their early thirties and forties provided higher tenaciousness ratings than subjects belonging to the two older cohorts. Conversely, the oldest cohort expressed greater flexibility than the young and middle-aged cohorts. Thus, as expected, the young adults invested more in primary control striving, while the older adults expressed greater tendencies for compensatory secondary control. The prediction that the older middle-aged adults might be caught in between, with depressed tendencies for both primary and secondary control, was confirmed.

Next, we shall investigate how these differences between age/birth cohorts are reflected in action-related beliefs about general personal control, the effectiveness of means–ends, and personal agency. General personal control was perceived to be lower among subjects in their early fifties (mean perceived control: 2.98) compared to the other age groups (cohort 1959–61: 3.15, cohort 1951–3: 3.14; cohort 1929–31: 3.25).

The patterns of cohort differences for work-domain related beliefs about means–ends and agency and family-domain related beliefs about means–ends and agency are displayed in Figures 6.14 through 6.17.

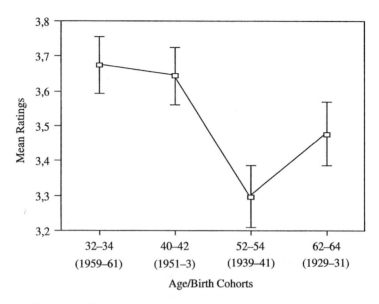

Figure 6.15. Study 6: Beliefs about agency in the work domain; age/birth cohort differences.

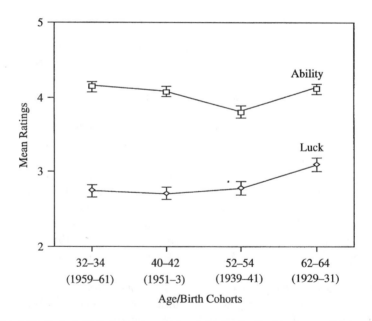

Figure 6.16. Study 6: Beliefs about means–ends in the family domain; age/birth cohort differences.

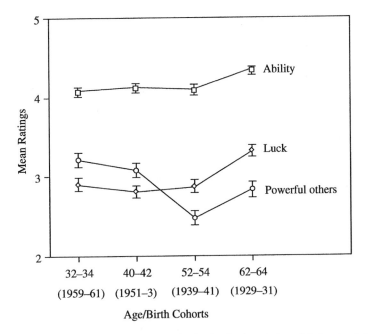

Figure 6.17. Study 6: Beliefs about agency in the family domain; age/birth cohort differences.

Overall, the findings confirm the exceptional position of the birth cohort born in 1939–41, now in their early fifties. They reported lower means–ends (Figure 6.14) and lower agency (Figure 6.15) perceptions with regard to effort for the work domain. Thus, these adults in their early fifties expressed the view that effort was less effective in the work domain and that they themselves were less prepared to invest effort in their jobs. Moreover, these middle-aged adults thought that interpersonal abilities were less helpful in solving family problems than the younger or older adults (Figure 6.16). In addition, they perceived less agency with regard to powerful others for the family domain (Figure 6.17). This means that they thought they had fewer close friends to turn to in case of a family crisis.

In addition to these differences distinguishing the adults in their early fifties from the other cohorts, there were some cohort differences that set the oldest cohort apart from the three younger cohorts. In the work domain, the oldest adults ascribed greater influence to ability and less influence to powerful others (Figure 6.14). With regard to work life, the two younger cohorts compared to the two older cohorts ascribed a greater role to societal and economic factors (Figure 6.14).

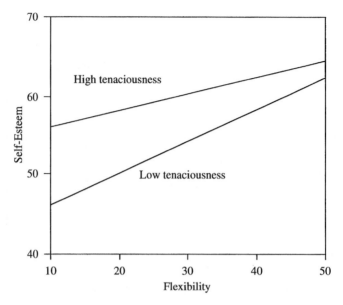

Figure 6.18. Study 6: Relationship between flexibility and self-esteem for high versus low levels of tenaciousness. (Adapted from J. Heckhausen et al. 1994a.)

Moreover, the oldest adults ascribed to luck a greater role in resolving family problems (Figure 6.16) and perceived greater agency for abilities and luck with regard to the family domain (Figure 6.17).

Finally, we need to investigate cohort differences in self-esteem as a subjective developmental outcome, as well as their possible moderation by primary and secondary control striving. As expected, the cohort in their early fifties reported lower self-esteem (mean: 56.78) than the younger cohorts (1959–61: 58.85; 1951–53: 59.08) and older cohort (1929–31: 58.54).

In order to identify the possible moderating effects of primary and secondary control striving, we investigated the predictive relations of tenaciousness (as an indicator of primary control striving) and flexibility (as an indicator of secondary control striving) to self-esteem when taking into account cohort and employment status effects. The results of these regression analyses are illustrated in Figure 6.18 (for further details see J. Heckhausen Diewald, & Huinink 1996). Both tenaciousness and flexibility contributed positively to self-esteem. Moreover, the combination of the two had an additional predictive value. Flexibility contributed more to self-esteem when tenaciousness was low than when tenaciousness was high. This was particularly true for the youngest cohort.

Discussion

This study aimed to investigate the combined impact of aging-related and sociohistorical challenges on developmental regulation in three specific age/birth cohorts of East German adults. Study 5 demonstrated differential patterns of developmental regulation for aging-related and sociohistorical challenges. Age-differential effects of the sociohistorical transformation in East Germany were not identified in Study 5. However, it was expected that such birth cohort differences within East Germans might be present at a later time of measurement, when disillusionment with German reunification might have left adults in mid-life with a life-course developmental calamity. Hence, it was expected that the differences between the four age/birth cohorts would reflect two sources of influence: changes in developmental challenge with chronological age (age-normative) and cohort-differential severity of life-course threat to the disadvantage of the adults in their early fifties (mid-life calamity). The findings for each of the variables will be discussed with respect to this overall investigative agenda. Differences related to sex will be discussed only when they invalidate the findings about age/birth cohort differences.

The pattern of intercohort differences in nomination of developmental goals mostly reflected age-graded differences in developmental tasks. Not surprisingly, retired sixty-two-to sixty-four-year-olds were less interested in employment-related goals than younger cohorts. However, with regard to employment-related goals, the mid-life calamity of those from fifty-one to fifty-three years of age also surfaced. These late mid-lifers were more concerned about their employment status than the two younger cohorts. The drop in financial goals after their early thirties probably reflected the fact that these adults were in the family-building phase and not yet in their peak earning phase. Goals related to personal health continually increased across age cohorts, in accordance with findings from previous research (e.g., J. Heckhausen 1994a, 1997; see Study 5). Travel and concern with world peace as goals followed an increasing age trajectory, possibly reflecting the increase in free time at later ages. Goals related to the health of family members were more frequent in the two younger cohorts, probably reflecting concern over the health of aging parents. Finally, goals about the education of family members peaked in the adults from forty to forty-two years of age. This peak most likely is due to their children reaching late adolescence and early adulthood, when educational attainment becomes most crucial.

When investigating developmental goals in terms of whether they reflect a striving for a gain or an avoidance of a loss, both age-normative and mid-life calamity influences emerge. The youngest adult group expressed more gain-related goals than either the middle-aged or the old adults. These findings are in accordance with the overall age decrease found for gain-related goals in Study 5. However, if only age-normative factors were decisive, one would have expected a more gradual decrease across mid-life. The findings about loss-related goals help to explain the significant drop in gain-related goals after early adulthood. Loss-related goals were nominated most by the two middle-aged cohorts. Thus, these mid-life adults seem to have felt substantial threats to their developmental future and therefore focused on loss avoidance rather than on striving for gains.

The findings pertaining to the action-related beliefs also support the special and precarious position of the late mid-life cohort. For important causal factors such as effort, they perceived little influence and also less personal access. The general pattern of action-related beliefs in these East German adults in their early fifties conveys an image of helplessness and loss of social resources. Moreover, older adults attributed less influence to powerful others and economic factors, thus potentially glorifying the past.

With regard to indicators of primary and secondary control striving at first glance only age-normative effects are obtained. An age-related drop in tenaciousness between the two younger and the two older cohorts and an age-related increase in flexibility between the three younger and the oldest cohort were found. With respect to tenaciousness, previous research has either reported stability (J. Heckhausen 1994a, 1997; J. Heckhausen 1997; Peng & Lachman 1993) or decrease (Brandtstädter & Renner 1990), but no increase across adulthood. Although other researchers in this area interpret a decline in tenaciousness as an age-related disengagement from direct or assimilative control (Brandtstädter & Renner 1990), this conclusion does not necessarily follow from the lower tenaciousness ratings found for the fifty-two- to fifty-four-year-old and sixty-two- to sixty-four-year-old East Germans. Instead, the drop in tenaciousness for the two older cohorts may be due to the radical decline in controllability associated with the sociohistorical transformation in East Germany, which probably affects older cohorts in particular. The increase in flexibility of goal adjustment found across age/birth cohorts is in accordance with previous research (Brandtstädter & Renner 1990; J. Heckhausen 1994a, 1997; Peng & Lachman 1993). However, in previous research the age-related increase was continuous throughout adulthood, whereas in this study of East Germans the increase pertained only to the oldest cohort. Taken together, the findings on tenaciousness and flexibility reveal an overall complementary pattern across age, with the exception of the fifty-two-to fifty-four-year-olds. This late mid-life cohort expressed comparatively low tenaciousness as well as low flexibility. Thus, the cohort particularly confronted with a mid-life calamity might be caught in a situation of failing control, where neither primary nor secondary control strategies function sufficiently. The findings on cohort differences in self-esteem corroborate this interpretation. The fifty-two- to fifty-four-year-olds expressed lower self-esteem than the younger and older cohorts. This indicates that the system of primary and secondary control may indeed have failed for adults in their early fifties facing a mid-life calamity in the transforming East German society.

The findings pertaining to the relationship between tenaciousness, flexibility, and age/birth cohort, on the one hand, and self-esteem, on the other, show that both primary and secondary control promoted subjective well-being. In accordance with the theoretical proposition that primary control holds functional primacy, the promotive influence on self-esteem of primary control striving (indicated by tenaciousness) as compared to secondary control tendencies (indicated by flexibility) was more pronounced. Intercohort differences for the relationships between control strategies and self-esteem were also found, although the overall pattern of relations was similar across age groups. Those differences found suggest that for the younger adults primary and secondary control can substitute for each other, while for the two older cohorts primary and secondary control need to operate in concert in order to promote self-esteem. These findings also indicate that adults aged fifty-two to fifty-four were somewhat successful in using primary and secondary control, albeit expressing lesser primary and secondary control striving and reaching lower overall levels of self-esteem. In general, these findings of the relationship between primary and secondary control striving and self-esteem have to be treated with caution. They do not warrant conclusions about causal relationships because the indicators were assessed simultaneously. Further research needs to investigate developmental challenges, control strategies, and developmental outcomes in a longitudinal sequential paradigm in order to ascertain causal relationships.

Summary

In this chapter, two life-course ecologies serve as examples of functionally different developmental challenges: aging-related change and change associated with the sociohistorical transformation in East Germany. It is argued that the two life-course ecologies differ with respect to the degree of personal control available in that aging-related change involves lower control potential than does sociohistorical transformation. It was predicted that strategies of developmental regulation reflect the different functional requirements presented by different degrees of personal control. Two studies were conducted at different points in the process of German reunification.

The first (Study 5) directly investigated aging-related differences and differences between East and West Berliners at an early point in the East German transformation process (April 1991 to February 1992). The findings revealed adaptive developmental regulation with both aging-related and sociohistorical challenges. Older adults used more compensatory secondary control than younger adults and focused their primary control striving on age-appropriate goals. East as compared to West Berliners expressed enhanced and focused primary control striving with regard to work-related goals, which are particularly at stake during the sociostructural transformation in East Germany. This selective primary control striving was supported by selective secondary control, in that goal attainment was perceived as more pressing. In this study, no evidence was found for cohort-differential strategies in managing the specific sociohistorical challenge associated with German reunification.

In the second study (Study 6), a representative sample of East Germans from four birth cohorts was investigated in spring 1993. This study aimed to identify differences among four age/birth cohorts in East Germans' developmental regulation, both in terms of aging-related and sociohistorical challenge. With regard to aging-related changes, the findings concur with those obtained in Study 5, indicating age-appropriate selection of developmental goals and an increased use of compensatory secondary control. Moreover, and in contrast to the earlier study (Study 5), Study 6 did identify differences between age/birth cohorts in developmental regulation of sociohistorical challenges. Adults in late mid-life (52 to 54 years) expressed lower levels of self-esteem, indicated by both decreased primary and secondary control, and held pessimistic beliefs about the controllability of outcomes and their own personal agency. These adults in late mid-life seemed to have run into a developmental calamity. For these middle-aged adults, life-course investments associated with the obsolete societal structure are substantial, whereas prospects for future developmental investments are severely constrained.

In sum, the findings of the two studies reported in this chapter demonstrate the adaptive resources in developmental regulation even under challenging conditions. However, they also indicate limits of control when life-course ecologies are particularly and unusually adverse.

7 Social Comparisons as Prototypical Strategies in Developmental Regulation

This chapter will discuss social comparisons as prototypical strategies in developmental regulation. The adaptive nature of strategic social comparisons has been widely studied in other areas of research (see reviews in Suls & Wills 1991; Wood 1989). I shall specifically address social comparisons in the developmental context and show that they are common, powerful, and adaptive strategies in developmental regulation. Together with other strategies, such as temporal comparison with past and future developmental states (e.g., Filipp & Buch-Bartos 1994; Ryff 1991), they help to optimize developmental regulation across the life span. First, this chapter will develop a theoretical model of social comparisons in the developmental context based on the long-standing tradition in social comparison research. Second, the model will be applied to empirical research on the similarities and dissimilarities between age-normative and self-related conceptions about development in adulthood (Study 7). Subsequently, further specific propositions about self-enhancement by social comparison under conditions of threat are derived and empirically investigated in a study on perceived problems for the self and for one's age peers (Study 8). Finally, social comparison processes will be addressed directly in a diary study and investigated in terms of their specific targets, contexts, affective consequences, and interindividual differences in primary and secondary control striving (Study 9).

Three Functions of Social Comparison

Research on social comparison has a long-standing tradition, going back to Leon Festinger's work on self-assessment and self-improvement as two basic functions of social comparison (Festinger 1954). For Festinger the main function of social comparison was *self-assessment*. Most psychological characteristics cannot be assessed objectively and therefore need social comparison as a frame of reference to validate and calibrate evaluations and assessments of the self. People compare their own standing with regard to abilities, opinions, and personality characteristics with those of other people. For such social comparisons, similar others provide the most differentiated frame of reference and are therefore preferred over those who are superior or inferior in the relevant comparison dimension (Festinger 1954). Social comparison with similar others is referred to as *lateral comparison*. Self-assessment is essential for maintaining and expanding primary control, because it informs the individual about strengths and weaknesses in his/her own capacities and thus helps to set goals for primary control. The concept of self-assessment by social comparison can be transferred to the developmental context. Age-normative conceptions about life-span development and the timing of life-course events provide a standard of reference for the self. Using age-normative conceptions the individual can derive expectations about his/her own present and future development in terms of changes anticipated for certain ages. Moreover, the individual can evaluate his/her own past development as being on-time or off-time with regard to the age-normative standard. Age-normative conceptions about age peers therefore help the individual to focus developmental regulation on age-appropriate challenges.

Extending Festinger's model, more recent research about social comparison has emphasized the role of *self-enhancement* as a major function of social comparison processes (e.g., review in Wood 1989). Self-enhancement can be attained by selecting a reference for social comparison that is inferior to the self on the relevant evaluative dimension. When compared with an inferior other, the self appears in a more positive light, and thereby self-esteem can be maintained even under conditions of threat. Such social comparisons are known as *downward comparisons* (Wills 1981). Numerous empirical studies indicate that individuals choose lower-status or less fortunate others and even actively denigrate them (or actively denigrate those who are similar) so that their own standing will appear enhanced in comparison (e.g., Diener 1984; Taylor, Wood, & Lichtman 1984; Taylor & Lobel 1989; Wills 1981). Downward social comparison is particularly likely under conditions of stress, uncertainty, and threat to the self (Wills 1981). Empirical evidence for this assumption is found in research on severe illness (Taylor & Lobel 1989; Taylor, Wood, & Lichtman 1984), disability (Schulz & Decker 1985), and crime-related victimization (Burgess & Holmstrom 1979a, 1979b). In the face of objective deprivation, subjective well-being may be maintained by strategically selecting reference groups that are at least as deprived as oneself (Diener 1984; Wills 1981).

Downward social comparisons are an important strategy of secondary control because they help to protect self-esteem and hopefulness – important resources for primary control. Moreover, downward social comparisons are a particularly adaptive strategy of secondary control because they do not affect the validity of conceptions about one's own functioning but merely manipulate the reference standard according to which the individual evaluates his/her own standing. Thus, accurate perceptions about self-functioning are not compromised, as would be the case if other strategies of illusory secondary control were used. In the context of life-span development, aging-related losses present a normative threat to the self and call for secondary control so as to protect self-esteem. Downward social comparison with age peers who suffer even greater loss may help the individual to maintain a positive self-image. It will be argued that a negative stereotypic view of old age may serve exactly this purpose and provide a suitable social reference for downward comparison (Harris & Associates 1975, 1981; O'Gorman 1980; Thomas 1981).

Finally, Festinger (1954) also postulated a "unidirectional drive upward" (p. 124), which directs individual behavior and social comparison processes toward *self-improvement.* Self-improvement is fostered when people compare themselves with other people who are superior to themselves in the comparison dimension. This type of social comparison is referred to as *upward comparison* (Wood 1989). Upward social comparisons help the individual to set goals by providing models for how to attain these goals. Therefore, upward comparisons promote an extension of primary control. In the life-span developmental context, the age-graded distribution of relatively superior or inferior developmental states across the life span is reflected in age-normative conceptions about gains and losses at various ages. Previous research has indicated that the proportion of developmental gains relative to losses decreases across adulthood (J. Heckhausen, Dixon, & Baltes 1989). At the same time, the absolute number of ongoing processes of developmental growth peaks in mid-life (J. Heckhausen, Dixon, & Baltes 1989; see insert to Figure 2.3 in Chapter 2). Thus, one would predict that upward social comparisons would exhibit the following age pattern: Young adults should be oriented toward somewhat older ("more mature") adults who are in mid-life, while older adults should also compare themselves with middle-aged adults who are, however, younger ("less aged") than themselves. Study 5 revealed a convergent pattern of findings which showed that younger adults perceived their developmental goals as typical for mid-life people, whereas middle-aged and especially older adults indicated that their personal goals were typical for younger age groups. Study 7 will further empirically investigate upward comparison processes in different adult age groups.

After having outlined the three types of social comparison – lateral, downward, and upward – the question arises: How does the individual determine when to use which? According to the context of the general life-span theory of control (J. Heckhausen & Schulz 1995), the criterion for adaptiveness of any given behavior is its functional relation to primary control. Therefore, the variable determining whether upward, downward, or lateral comparison is adaptive in a given situation is the potential for primary control available for the respective comparison dimension (e.g., a skill, a health condition, a job promotion, etc.). Downward social comparison processes that foster self-enhancement are more likely to be adaptive when controllability is relatively low – that is, when the individual commands little primary control and therefore has to resort to secondary control. A similar situation arises when primary control striving is extremely costly and therefore compromises future primary control. On the other hand, lateral and upward social comparisons that foster primary control are most adaptive when primary control potential is high and its long-term costs are not prohibitive.

In Study 9, two further situational characteristics are discussed that enhance the influence of controllability on the adaptiveness of primary versus secondary control and, accordingly, upward and lateral versus downward comparisons (Wrosch 1994; Wrosch & J. Heckhausen 1996b). *Expectations of future gains* should increase the tendency to compare upwardly or laterally, whereas expectations about *future losses* should dampen the tendency toward such comparisons and render downward comparisons more adaptive. Moreover, *high versus low importance* of the comparison dimension should also moderate the effects of controllability and future expectations.

Developmental Expectations for the Self and Most Other People (Study 7)

In this study, adults' conceptions about the development of the self are compared to age-normative conceptions about development in most other people (Heckhausen, 1991a; J. Heckhausen & Krueger 1993; Hundertmark & J. Heckhausen 1994; Krueger & Heckhausen 1993). Based on previous research (J. Heckhausen & Baltes 1991; J. Heckhausen, Dixon, & Baltes 1989), which showed that age-normative conceptions about adult development are widely shared, it was expected that such conceptions provide a normative reference system of development-related expectations against which personal developmental trajectories are evaluated. Thus, in this study the degree of congruence and the kinds of differences between self-related and age-normative (i.e., related to the generalized other) conceptions about adult development are used as a paradigm to study social comparison processes. Although separate assessments of self- and other-related beliefs do not directly represent social comparisons, they do indicate the reference frame of norms and beliefs within which the self is construed.

The study was aimed at identifying the three functions of social comparison – self-assessment, self-enhancement, and self-improvement – in adults at different ages. In the context of the life-span theory of control, self-improvement and self-assessment can be conceptualized to directly serve primary control striving, while self-enhancement serves secondary control. Moreover, it was expected that self-enhancement would become more important at later ages in adulthood while self-improvement functions would become less salient. This prediction was based on the reasoning that, because less developmental gains and more losses occur at higher ages (P. Baltes 1987; J. Heckhausen, Dixon, & Baltes 1989; Kliegl & Baltes 1987; Salthouse 1985), the individual has less scope for primary control (J. Heckhausen & Baltes 1991; Schulz, Heckhausen, & Locher 1991; J. Heckhausen & Schulz 1995) and needs to use secondary control to compensate for aging-related decline. One particularly appropriate strategy of compensatory secondary control is social comparison with age peers whom the individual can perceive as suffering from more aging-related losses. In large cross-national U.S. surveys, Harris and Associates (1975, 1981) have shown that, consistently across various life domains, older adults perceive problems of their age peers ("other old people") as substantially more serious than their own. Thus, it was predicted that, during early adulthood, when developmental change is perceived to be still controllable, priority would be given to informational (self-assessment) and motivational (self-improvement) needs. In contrast, during old age, when less can be done to avert decline, it would be most adaptive to focus on protecting self-esteem (self-enhancement). Specifically, self-assessment is reflected in congruence of self- and other-related age trajectories of gains and losses. Self-enhancement is shown in expectations of more gains and fewer losses for the self compared to the generalized other. Finally, self-improvement can be identified by investigating subjective age identification and developmental aspirations. It was expected that older adults identify with younger ages, which they construe as more desirable than their own age group.

162   DEVELOPMENTAL REGULATION IN ADULTHOOD

Sample and Procedure

A volunteer sample of 180 West Berliners took part in this study.[1] The sample was equally divided by (1) age (young adults: twenty-one to thirty-five years; middle-aged adults: forty to fifty-five years; and old adults: sixty to eighty years), (2) sex, and (3) educational background (low: German Hauptschulabschluß, i.e., nine years of schooling; medium: German Realschule, i.e., ten years of schooling; high: German Gymnasium, i.e., thirteen years of schooling).

Subjects were presented a list of a hundred adjectives describing psychological attributes according to a scheme reported by Goldberg (1973). These attributes represented five dimensions of personality: extraversion (e.g., assertive or inhibited), agreeableness (e.g., affectionate or quarrelsome), conscientiousness (e.g., dependable or irresponsible), emotional stability (e.g., self-controlled or nervous), and intellectual functioning (e.g., knowledgeable or naive). Each dimension was represented by ten desirable and ten undesirable attributes. Analyses of desirability ratings and internal consistency of the ten scales (i.e., desirable and undesirable attributes of five dimensions) identified nine nonconsistent attributes, which were not included in further analyses.

Subjects were asked to rate each attribute according to six dimensions: (1) desirability; (2) expected change (increase, decrease, or stability) in seven decades of adulthood (i.e., twenties through eighties); (3) perceived controllability; (4) self-description (i.e., "How characteristic of you is this attribute?"); (5) developmental goals (i.e., "Do you want to change this attribute?"); and (6) normative age of developmental goal (i.e., "What is the age at which people typically would hold this developmental goal?"). Ratings for expected change and perceived controllability were requested for two instructional targets: for the self and for most other people. These ratings were collected in three sessions. Moreover, one year after the initial assessment, 153 subjects of the initial sample took part in a further data collection, including assessments of subjective age identification (according to Kastenbaum et al. 1981), verbal IQ, and an age estimate for the typical age at which people pursue the developmental goals that subjects had nominated.

Retest stability for all questionnaires was assessed six months after the initial data collection. Test-retest coefficients were moderate (for perceived control for the self .45 and for most other people .66) to high (ranging between .80 and .98 for the other variables).

---

[1] This study was conducted before the Berlin Wall came down.

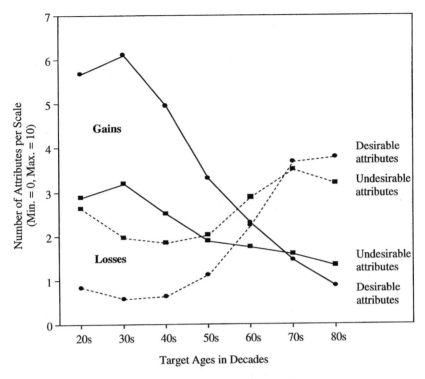

Figure 7.1. Study 7: Expected gains and losses in desirable and undesirable attributes across seven decades of the adult life span. (From J. Heckhausen & J. Krueger [1993]. Developmental expectations for the self and most other people: Age grading in three functions of social comparison. *Developmental Psychology, 29,* 539–548. Copyright © 1993 by the American Psychological Association. Adapted with permission.)

Results

Findings will be reported with regard to three aspects. First, the expected trajectories for developmental gains and losses were investigated for a descriptive account of age-normative conceptions about developmental change across adulthood. Second, the expected trajectories for self and "most other people" were compared so as to identify congruence and potential relative self-enhancement via downward social comparisons. Finally, developmental aspirations were investigated as potential indicators of upward social comparison.

In order to investigate the *expected trajectories for developmental gains and losses,* we identified two types of gains and two types of losses. Decreases in desirable attributes and increases in undesirable attributes were classified as losses, while decreases in undesirable attributes and increases in desirable attributes were classified as gains. Figure 7.1 illustrates the expected trajectories for these four types of developmental change. Across age decades, gains in desirable attributes were expected to decrease and losses in desirable attributes were expected to increase. Conversely, worsening of undesirable attributes was perceived as accelerating across age and improvements were expected to occur less often at higher ages. This reflected a shift from a predominance of gains in early adulthood toward greater risks for losses and diminishing chances for growth in advanced age.

Developmental trajectories expected for the self and for "most other people" were compared in order to determine the degree of *self–other congruence and self-enhancement.* Figure 7.2 displays separately for the three subject age groups the expected age trajectories of desirable and undesirable attributes for the self and most other people (top panel: young adults; middle panel: middle-aged adults; bottom panel: old adults). As can be seen, self- and other-related age trajectories were largely congruent. Desirable attributes were expected to increase rapidly during the twenties and thirties and thereafter to exhibit continually slowing increase across adulthood, until they began to actually decrease in the seventies and eighties. Undesirable attributes, in contrast, were expected to first decrease somewhat during the thirties and forties, and to increase at a growing rate after the age of sixty.

In spite of the overall congruence between self- and other-related trajectories, there were also discrepancies pertaining to the decades between the fifties and the eighties, when less decrease in desirable and less increase in undesirable attributes were expected for the self when compared to most other people. Thus, for higher target ages a self-enhancement pattern of downward social comparison was found.

Moreover, differences between different age groups of subjects were found in the degree of self–other difference at later target ages. In general, middle-aged and especially old adults indicated larger self–other differences with regard to older adults than did young adults. As shown in the upper panel of Figure 7.2, young adults saw almost no difference in the change trajectories of desirable attributes between the self and the generalized other. With regard to undesirable attributes, young adults perceived almost the entire adult life span, except for early adulthood, as more promising for the self than for most other people. The middle-aged adults (middle panel in Figure 7.2) expected more favorable development for the self than for others with regard to the change in desirable attributes during advanced old age, and even more pronouncedly with regard to undesirable attributes in old age. However, middle-aged adults reported less decrease during early adult-

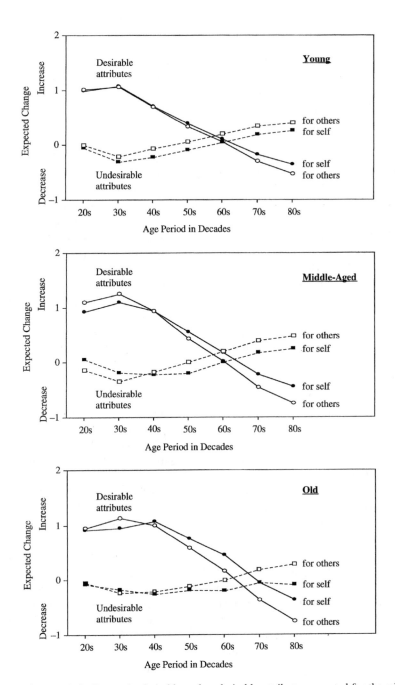

Figure 7.2. Study 7: Change in desirable and undesirable attributes expected for the self and most other people; separate for young, middle-aged, and old adults. (From J. Heckhausen & J. Krueger [1993]. Developmental expectations for the self and most other people: Age grading in three functions of social comparison. *Developmental Psychology, 29*, 539–548. Copyright © 1993 by the American Psychological Association. Adapted with permission.)

hood in undesirable attributes for the self than for other people. Finally, the old adults (lower panel in Figure 7.2) selectively viewed their late-life development as more favorable than other people's late-life development, both in terms of desirable and undesirable attributes.

Developmental aspirations were investigated as indicators of social comparisons with superior targets, which might serve the function of self-improvement. An orientation toward higher-status age groups was expected – that is, somewhat older adults would be comparison targets for young adults, and somewhat younger adults would be comparison targets for older adults. Developmental aspirations were investigated in terms of two indicators: (1) the age with which a person subjectively identifies in terms of five aspects (appearance, feels like, activities level, strangers' perceptions, and friends' perceptions), and (2) the age perceived to be normative for one's developmental goals.

Figure 7.3 shows the pattern of subjective age perceptions across the five aspects of subjective age for young, middle-aged, and old adults. Overall, old ($M = 1.889$) and middle-aged adults ($M = 2.05$) identified more with younger ages than with their own actual age, whereas young subjects ($M = 2.96$) identified with their own age group. Moreover, for young adults appearance age was perceived as relatively younger and for old adults as relatively older than other aspects of subjective age: young appearance versus other aspects. As can be seen in Figure 7.3, young adults barely deviated in their subjective age identification from their actual age, except with regard to appearance age, which they construed as more youthful. In contrast, middle-aged and old adults identified with younger age groups with regard to all aspects of subjective age identification.

The second indicator of developmental aspirations was the normative age ascribed to self-developmental goals. In order to specifically investigate the predicted age-differential overtaxing and undertaxing of developmental goals, the differences between the actual chronological age of the individual subjects and the normative ages endorsed for the developmental goals were compared across age groups. The middle-aged ($M = -12.1$ years) and especially the old ($M = -24.0$ years) adults described their own developmental goals as similar to those of people younger than themselves, whereas the young adults thought that their developmental goals were characteristic of people a little older than themselves ($M = 6.0$ years).

Discussion

The general trajectory of perceived developmental change across adulthood found in Study 7 replicates the previously found pattern of de-

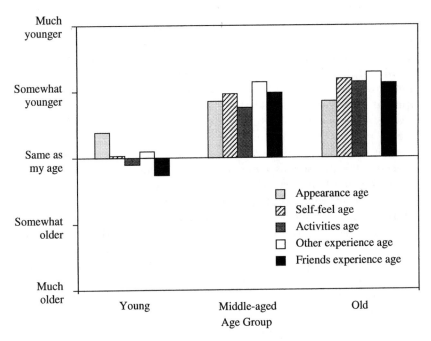

Figure 7.3. Study 7: Subjective age identification by young, middle-aged, and old adults for five aspects of subjective age. (From J. Heckhausen & J. Krueger [1993]. Developmental expectations for the self and most other people: Age grading in three functions of social comparison. *Developmental Psychology, 29*, 539–548. Copyright © 1993 by the American Psychological Association. Adapted with permission.)

creasing expected potential for growth and increasing risks for decline at higher adult ages (J. Heckhausen & Baltes 1991; J. Heckhausen, Dixon, & Baltes 1989). This finding supports the assumption that normative conceptions about development are highly consensual social constructions of reality (Berger & Luckmann 1966) that might serve as standard frames of reference for the evaluation of personal development.

Substantial congruence between age trajectories pertaining to the development of the self and most other people was found. This congruence suggests that normative conceptions about most other people have a validation function in the process of self-assessment. The fact that developmental expectations for the self were not simply biased, for instance, in terms of not expecting any decline in old age supports the notion that subjects were interested in valid self-assessments. Further analyses of this data set also indicated that adults at various age levels selected developmental goals that reflected the age-normative expectations about developmental gains in young adulthood and developmental losses in advanced adulthood (Hundertmark 1990; Hundertmark & J. Heckhausen 1994). Moreover, it was found that age peers as a social reference group might allow a more stable self-assessment throughout adulthood, in that they provide a reference scale that undergoes age-normative developmental shifts shared with one's own personal development (Krueger & J. Heckhausen 1993).

Clear evidence was also found for the widespread comparison practice of perceiving the generalized other as inferior or less fortunate than oneself. More potential for gains and less risks for losses were expected for the self as compared to the generalized other. A self-enhancing tendency was also found in ratings of controllability. Personal controllability was judged to be higher ($M = 5.94$) than controllability for most other people ($M = 5.53$).

Characteristically, the self-enhancement for perceived developmental trajectories almost exclusively pertained to advanced age, when developmental prospects are threatened by aging-related losses. Moreover, self-enhancement with regard to old age was particularly pronounced in the older subjects. Thus, those age groups most imminently threatened by late-life developmental losses seem to experience a greater need to use social comparison strategies that allow for self-enhancement, especially with regard to old age, when most developmental losses are anticipated.

With regard to the self-improvement function of social comparison, two indicators of developmental aspirations were used. Subjective age identification reflected an orientation toward younger age groups for middle-aged, and especially for old adults. Moreover, normative ages ascribed to one's own developmental goals indicated an orientation toward higher-status age groups for all three adult age groups. The young adults strove for goals they thought were typical of people somewhat older than themselves. Middle-aged and old adults, in contrast, pursued developmental goals that were conceived of as typical for younger adults. Using the data set of Study 7 it is difficult to ascertain whether the age differences found for normative goal ages reflect a distorted interpretation of one's own goals with regard to age timing or the fact that the present culture of old age (P. Baltes 1991) does not provide sufficient unique developmental goals. However, the similar pattern of age-group differential age ascriptions found in Study 6, in which substantial age differences in reported developmental goals were also obtained, suggests that the age difference in normative ages ascribed to developmental goals may be due to a distorted age ascription of one's own goals.

To conclude, the findings of Study 7 indicate that age-normative conceptions provide the opportunity for three functions and modes of social comparison: self-assessment by lateral comparisons, self-enhancement by downward comparisons, and self-improvement by upward comparisons. Whereas self-assessment and self-improvement were salient in all three age groups, the use of self-enhancement was age-differential. Although self-enhancement was present in all three age groups, it became more salient at higher ages, when aging-related losses confront the individual with a developmental threat, and thus compensatory secondary control is needed. Study 8 investigates more closely the way in which developmental threat motivates the individual to downgrade the social reference group.

Self and Other at Mid-Life: Self-Enhancement by Social Downgrading (Study 8)

Age-normative conceptions and negative stereotypes about aging in particular might serve as a backdrop for social downgrading when the individual feels threatened by aging-related losses. A number of studies about self- and other-related conceptions have provided support for this assumption. In two large representative surveys, Harris and Associates (1975, 1981) showed that the images about old age held by U.S. Americans are substantially more negative than the perceptions old adults hold about themselves. A large discrepancy emerges from a comparison of the elderly respondents' problem ratings for themselves with those pertaining to most other old people. Older adults believe that they themselves have many fewer problems in important life domains, such as health, finances, and social contacts, than do others their age. Similar findings were obtained in other studies (Borges & Dutton 1976; Bultena & Powers 1976; Schulz & Fritz 1988). Borges and Dutton (1976) showed, moreover, that at increasing ages the self-enhancing discrepancy between self- and other-related conceptions broadens. Thomas (1981) has explained this apparent paradox, the "expectation gap," in the framework of reference-group theory. The expectation gap between self- and other-related conceptions is a product of an age-graded anticipatory lowering of aspirations, which exceeds its goal. Because one has aged, one expects less than before (see also P. Baltes 1989a, 1989b; P. Baltes & M. Baltes 1989). Given these lowered aspirations, it is easy for the individual to excel in his/her own age-graded standards. In this way, one might argue, negative aging stereotypes might serve an adaptive function in promoting the self-esteem of older adults.

A reanalysis of the Harris survey data by O'Gorman (1980) is particularly revealing with regard to the motivational foundation of the social downgrading based on aging stereotypes. O'Gorman demonstrated that older adults who personally experienced problems in a certain domain ascribed particularly serious problems in this domain to most other elderly people. Thus, experiencing a threat in a particular life domain had a domain-specific effect on the social downgrading of one's own age group. Similarly, for the domain of personality, Hakmiller (1966) demonstrated that individuals who perceive a threat to a given personality dimension select comparison targets out of an array of different persons so that the target person is inferior to themselves with regard to the personality dimension under threat. Analogous findings are reported for threats to self-esteem. In a study using experimentally induced threats to self-esteem, Crocker and colleagues (Crocker et al. 1987) showed that subjects who perceive a threat to their self-esteem are more likely to engage in prejudice-based downward social comparisons. Thus, downward social comparisons appear to be used domain-differentially, in that they focus on a domain perceived to be under threat.

The study on "Self and Other at Midlife" (J. Heckhausen & Brim, 1997) was aimed at investigating the prevalence of similar phenomena of social downgrading in a broader age range across the adult life span. Negative stereotypes about age groups pertain not only to old age but also to middle adulthood. The belief in a mid-life crisis is widespread, but it is based on little or no empirical support. Although adults at mid-life face a variety of developmental demands in terms of juggling priorities and adjusting aspirations, time schedules, and frames of reference, they also may be particularly well equipped to face these challenges because of accumulated resources in terms of finances, power, and, not least, personal experience in life management (Brim 1992).

One of the major compensatory secondary control strategies for the particular developmental challenges at mid-life may be social downgrading of one's age peers so as to construct oneself as a favorable exception to one's own age group. Therefore, it was predicted that self/other discrepancies would be found not only for elderly respondents but also for individuals at mid-life. Moreover, it was predicted that social downgrading would be particularly pronounced for those domains in which an individual perceives problems in his/her own life.

Sample and Procedure

The 2,022 adults who participated in this telephone survey comprised a U.S. cross-national probability sample of 1,006 women and 1,016 men aged 18 years and over. The distribution of subjects across age groups was as follows: 242 subjects aged 18–24; 509 subjects aged 25–34; 520 subjects aged 35–44; 312 subjects aged 45–54; 208 subjects aged 55–64; and 197 subjects aged 65 and over. Moreover, subjects were sampled representatively from different regions of the United States and from metropolitan ($n = 1,565$) and nonmetropolitan ($n = 457$) areas. In addition, the sample included representative proportions of white ($n = 1,688$), black ($n = 157$), Hispanic ($n = 141$), and Asian ($n = 24$) adults. However, because initial analyses revealed various interactions with subject's race/ethnicity, and because the nonwhite minority members were insufficient in number to allow separate analyses, further analyses had to be restricted to white subjects only.

The telephone interviews were conducted in the context of a consumer survey using the Opinion Research Corporation's computer-assisted telephone interviewing system (CATI). Subjects were asked to provide some basic demographic information about area of residence, sex, age, education, occupation, income, family status, and number of people living in the household. Regarding the specific purpose of the study "Self and Other at Midlife," subjects were asked to rate the seriousness of problems in the following twelve domains on a five-point scale ranging from "very serious" to "not serious at all": (1) not having enough money to live a good life, (2) poor health, (3) not having friends to rely on, (4) having trouble in one's marriage, (5) too much stress, (6) feeling there is no meaning in life, (7) not having enough sex, (8) feeling physically unattractive, (9) having a boring job, (10) feeling disappointed with how one's children have turned out, (11) not having enough time for leisure activities, and (12) poor physical fitness. The ratings of problem seriousness were requested for two instructional targets: the self ("you personally") and most people of the subject's age ("most people your age").

Results

Results will be reported with regard to the two major aims of this study: to explore the prevalence of social downgrading in different age groups and different life domains and to investigate whether social downgrading is a function of feeling personally threatened in a given domain (Heckhausen & Brim, 1997). With regard to the *prevalence of social downgrading*, it was found that problem ratings for the self were lower than those ascribed to "most other people my age" for each of the twelve domains. This is illustrated in Figure 7.4.

For eight out of the twelve domains differences between age groups

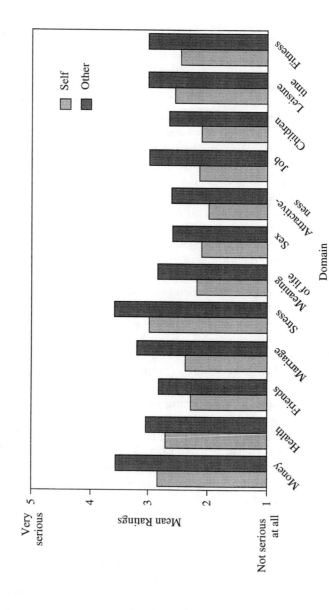

Figure 7.4. Study 8: Ratings of problem seriousness for self and other in twelve domains of functioning.

were found, four of which were homogeneous across self- and other-related ratings. Table 7.1 shows means and standard deviations for significant age differences and age by self/other interactions. Health-related problems increased in seriousness across subjects' age, while stress- and job-related problems, as well as problems related to a lack of leisure time, were stable well into mid-life but decreased thereafter.[2]

For the domains of money, marriage, attractiveness, children, and fitness the pattern of age differences was different for self- and other-related ratings (see means for significant interactions in Table 7.1). Overall, problem ratings for the self are remarkably stable, except for the domain of money, which has lowered problem ratings at ages fifty-five to fifty-nine and age sixty-five and older.

For *money-related problems*, both self- and other-related problem ratings were relatively stable across age groups but converged during the age range of 35–54 years. *Marriage-related problems* were perceived as increasing for most other people until mid-life and as decreasing after age fifty, which meant that self- and other-related problem perceptions for this domain diverged between ages twenty-nine and forty-nine. With regard to *attractiveness*, the ratings for the generalized other reflect an image of decreasing problem proneness across adulthood, with large discrepancies between self- and other-related ratings during young adulthood and middle adulthood up to the age of fifty and convergence thereafter. Problems with the way one's *children* have turned out were perceived as increasingly serious for the generalized other, peaking during mid-life (age range: 35–59), and dropping thereafter. The self/other discrepancies were greatest during the age range of 35–59 and converged both in early and late adulthood. Finally, problem perceptions about *physical fitness* for the generalized other peaked and diverged most from self-conceptions between the ages of forty-five and forty-nine and at age sixty and older.

The other major aim of Study 8 was to identify *social downgrading as a function of perceived personal threat* in a given domain. Multiple regression analyses revealed that, based on a subject's self-related problem rating for a particular domain, other-related problem ratings could be predicted. In fact, self-related problem ratings accounted for the major share of the variance (between 10 and 24 percent) in the other-related

---

[2] Only few main effects of sex and educational attainment were found. Money-related problems were perceived as more serious by females ($M = 3.26$) than males ($M = 3.12$), and sex-related problems were perceived as more serious by males ($M = 2.46$) than females ($M = 2.11$). Moreover, subjects with lower educational attainment ($M = 3.18$) perceived money and health-related problems as more serious than subjects with higher educational attainment ($M = 2.93$).

Table 7.1. *Means and standard deviations for significant age effects and age by self/other interactions on perceived problem ratings in twelve life domains*

		18–24	25–29	30–34	35–39	40–44	45–49	50–54	55–59	60–64	65+	Age	Age x Self/Other
Money													
Self:	x̄	3,08	2,87	2,77	2,98	2,95	2,95	3,02	2,48	2,94	2,41	*	*
	SD	1,40	1,34	1,35	1,37	1,43	1,45	1,41	1,49	1,65	1,42		
Other:	x̄	3,65	3,73	3,52	3,55	3,58	3,42	3,34	3,26	3,55	3,62		
	SD	1,19	1,03	1,17	1,11	1,04	1,26	1,13	1,25	1,30	1,19		
Health													
Self:	x̄	2,71	2,48	2,42	2,61	2,62	2,78	3,06	2,68	2,75	3,10	*	
	SD	1,68	1,69	1,61	1,57	1,69	1,68	1,69	1,68	1,67	1,63		
Other:	x̄	2,71	2,62	2,68	2,91	3,08	3,24	3,29	3,21	3,59	3,75		
	SD	1,38	1,33	1,35	1,31	1,26	1,35	1,36	1,34	1,24	1,21		
Marriage													
Self:	x̄	2,57	2,50	2,37	2,37	2,34	2,43	2,49	2,16	2,14	2,12	*	*
	SD	1,69	1,63	1,69	1,62	1,66	1,69	1,71	1,61	1,68	1,63		
Other:	x̄	2,91	3,41	3,39	3,53	3,50	3,38	3,05	2,97	2,60	2,69		
	SD	1,44	1,22	1,19	1,06	1,19	1,22	1,34	1,35	1,33	1,44		
Stress													
Self:	x̄	3,13	3,17	3,01	3,22	3,09	3,05	3,07	2,83	2,80	2,39	*	
	SD	1,38	1,31	1,45	1,32	1,39	1,48	1,45	1,40	1,74	1,46		
Other:	x̄	3,46	3,51	3,60	3,85	3,86	3,79	3,54	3,44	3,40	3,00		
	SD	1,24	1,89	1,15	1,09	1,04	1,09	1,10	1,22	1,42	1,29		

Attractiveness											
Self:	x̄	2,17	2,01	2,00	1,96	1,95	2,08	2,07	1,80	1,91	1,78 *
	SD	1,24	1,20	1,22	1,20	1,24	1,26	1,28	1,20	1,37	1,11
Other:	x̄	3,05	2,72	2,56	2,69	2,78	2,80	2,51	2,06	2,42	2,14
	SD	1,34	1,33	1,20	1,18	1,18	1,18	1,24	1,09	1,34	1,22
Job											
Self:	x̄	2,61	2,18	2,15	2,20	2,03	2,16	2,18	1,98	1,92	1,70 *
	SD	1,54	1,35	1,42	1,39	1,31	1,42	1,39	1,25	1,42	1,27
Other:	x̄	3,39	3,27	3,14	3,15	3,12	3,15	2,85	2,62	2,44	2,14
	SD	1,28	1,20	1,56	1,06	1,13	1,23	1,20	1,24	1,33	1,40
Child											
Self:	x̄	2,17	2,02	1,98	2,04	2,14	2,16	2,31	2,06	2,16	1,97 *
	SD	1,50	1,43	1,42	1,42	1,42	1,46	1,50	1,32	1,41	1,38
Other:	x̄	2,03	2,30	2,42	2,85	3,05	2,98	2,86	2,88	2,66	2,72
	SD	1,30	1,31	1,25	1,26	1,21	1,26	1,24	1,31	1,37	1,34
Leisure											
Self:	x̄	2,81	2,72	2,85	2,80	2,69	2,70	2,50	2,10	1,99	1,77 *
	SD	1,33	1,24	1,36	1,25	1,24	1,31	1,25	1,12	1,34	1,18
Other:	x̄	3,12	3,14	3,24	3,28	3,38	3,33	2,87	2,70	2,47	2,03
	SD	1,34	1,18	1,20	1,10	1,04	1,12	1,11	1,12	1,29	1,23
Fitness											
Self:	x̄	2,41	2,46	2,36	2,47	2,50	2,55	2,60	2,41	2,47	2,43
	SD	1,40	1,36	1,38	1,35	1,34	1,36	1,39	1,45	1,54	1,43
Other:	x̄	2,82	2,77	2,78	3,01	3,12	3,32	3,00	2,95	3,28	3,20
	SD	1,26	1,33	1,20	1,14	1,24	1,12	1,14	1,24	1,30	1,25

Note: * indicates significant effects at $p < .01$.

problem ratings in all domains. Thus, subjects who perceived more serious problems for themselves personally in a given domain also thought that most other people their age had more serious problems in the same domain. Moreover, subject's age predicted other-related problem ratings positively for the domains of health, children, and fitness. This implies that at higher ages more serious problems with health, the development of children, and physical fitness were attributed to most other people. Subject's age negatively predicted other-related problem ratings for the domains of marriage, stress, attractiveness, job, and leisure. This means that at higher ages less serious problems were ascribed to the generalized other for these domains.

Finally, the degree of covariance between self- and other-ratings varied across subjects' age for the domains of health, marriage, stress, job, and leisure. An investigation of regression lines for the three age groups in these problem domains revealed that, for older adults, self- and other-related problem ratings were more closely related (for more details, see Heckhausen & Brim, 1997). Thus, though adults of all ages gave higher problem ratings for most other people their age when they themselves perceived problems in the respective domain, for most domains this tendency was most pronounced in the old adults.

Discussion

The first main expectation addressed in Study 8 was that self/other discrepancies in terms of social downgrading of age peers would not only occur for old adults but also for adults in mid-life. This prediction was confirmed. Adults at all ages expressed the belief that they themselves experienced less serious problems in various domains of life than most other people their age.

Moreover, age increases in problems perceived personally were only found for the health domain. This finding is remarkable, because many of the domains investigated might well have involved age increases in proneness to the problems. For example, with regard to the issue of how one's children have turned out, increases between early adulthood and mid-life can be strongly expected simply because of life-timing pragmatic constraints to problems in early adulthood. A similar argument can be made for problems about physical fitness. It is very surprising that subjects did not identify more serious problems with physical fitness in later mid-life, or at least in old age.

One way to interpret this absence of age increases in problem ratings for the self is simply to accept this as evidence that there are no age changes in objective challenges in these domains. However, this seems implausible when one considers the domains in particular. Another possible explanation for this absence of age-related declines is that self-related problem ratings should be viewed in the context of age-normative conceptions about which problems to expect at certain ages. According to this perspective, individuals construct conceptions about what a problem is for themselves in the framework of what can be typically expected at their age. Thus, experiencing moderate problems in an area of functioning that one perceives as a trouble spot for one's age group in general might feel less threatening. In this way, age-normative conceptions about problem proneness of certain domains can serve as a reference for social downgrading and thereby allow self-enhancement. As a result, personal problems in the respective domain might appear less serious.

The second expectation addressed by Study 8 was that other-related problem perceptions reflect a self-enhancement need that is motivated by a perceived personal threat. It was expected that social downgrading would be particularly pronounced when the individual perceives a personal threat in the respective domain. This prediction was confirmed for all domains and all age groups. The more serious one personally perceived a problem to be, the more serious were the problems attributed to other people of one's age. This self-enhancement tendency under threat was particularly pronounced in older adults. Because of impending decline in various domains, older adults might feel a particular need to compensate for problem experiences by way of social downgrading. Moreover, negative aging stereotypes provide older adults with a social frame of reference that is particularly well-suited to social downgrading of age peers. And finally, by way of accumulated life-course experience, older adults might have become more proficient in using social comparison as a strategy of compensatory secondary control.

Thus, in sum, Study 8 shows that downward comparison with age peers is not only used by the elderly but is commonly employed across adulthood. Self/other discrepancies are construed particularly when a given age group is normatively expected to go through a problem phase. And, most importantly, social downgrading is focused specifically on those domains in which individuals feel most seriously affected by problems themselves. These findings indicate that select downward social comparison is an important and well-tailored strategy to compensate for the potentially negative effects of experienced losses on motivational resources for primary control. While all age groups use downward social comparison with age peers, older adults appear to be particularly well equipped to make adaptive use of this strategy of compensatory secondary control.

Everyday Use of Downward, Upward, and Lateral Social Comparisons (Study 9)

The two previously reported studies showed that the generalized other (i.e., "most other people") can be flexibly used as a social frame of reference for the upward or downward comparison needs of the individual. Conceptions of the generalized other reflect the age-graded and idiosyncratic needs of the individual to compensate for a perceived threat in a given domain of functioning (downward comparison) or to model and direct the striving for primary control (upward comparison). Study 9 aimed at three major purposes: investigating actual social comparison processes used with regard to their directionality (upward, downward, and lateral); studying the affective consequences of upward, downward, and lateral comparisons; and identifying interindividual differences (preferences for primary or secondary control) in using upward and downward comparisons.[3]

The first purpose of Study 9 was to investigate the employment of upward, downward, and lateral comparisons in different groups of subjects and with regard to different target persons for social comparison, life domains, and comparison dimensions (J. Heckhausen & Wrosch 1998). It was expected, for instance, that older adults would use fewer upward comparisons and more downward comparisons, because they are likely to experience developmental losses in various domains of functioning that are not readily controllable. Direct evidence of everyday social comparison processes is not available from previous research. However, the frequency of downward comparisons given in free-format, self-descriptive statements supports the prediction that older adults use more downward social comparisons (Filipp & Buch-Bartos 1994).

The second purpose of Study 9 was to investigate the affective consequences of social comparisons (J. Heckhausen & Wrosch 1998). In general, it was expected that downward comparisons would lead to positive changes in affective state and upward comparisons would produce negative changes in affective state. Moreover, it should be explored for whom (e.g., males or females, East Germans or West Germans) and

---

[3]   Another purpose of this study was to provide basic descriptive information about the targets, comparison dimensions, and contexts as well as general differences between groups of different age, gender, and educational background. Relevant findings are reported in Heckhausen and Wrosch (1998).

under which conditions (e.g., with close or distant target persons) affective consequences of downward and upward comparisons are enhanced.

The third purpose of Study 9 was to explore potential interindividual differences in the employment of upward and downward comparisons for subjects differing in striving for primary and secondary control (Wrosch, 1994; Wrosch & J. Heckhausen 1996b). In general, it was expected that upward comparisons would be more important for subjects with high primary control striving, whereas downward comparisons would be more important for subjects with high secondary control striving. This interindividual difference in emphasis on downward or upward comparisons should be reflected in selective adaptiveness of downward or upward comparisons. Specifically, it was expected that subjects with high striving for primary control would adapt their use of upward comparisons more closely to situational conditions. Subjects with high striving for secondary control were expected to adapt their downward comparisons more closely to situational conditions. The rationale for defining adaptiveness of upward and downward comparisons is given below.

Our theory would predict that upward social comparisons are chosen when the individual perceives substantial primary control potential over the comparison dimension. Conversely, when perceived personal control is low, the need for compensatory secondary control increases, and therefore downward social comparison is more adaptive.

In addition to the dimension of controllability, two other aspects should play a major role in determining whether the individual aims at primary control or secondary control and adjusts his/her social comparisons accordingly. Major, Testa, and Bylsma (1991) propose that social comparisons should be influenced by two dimensions: the relevance of the comparison dimension for self-esteem and the degree of perceived control. Similarly, Wood and Taylor (1991) argue that social comparisons in self-relevant domains should have a greater impact on subjective well-being than non-self-relevant comparisons. Thus, we predicted that social comparisons of dimensions judged to be important should be more carefully tailored to the functional requirements of the situation in terms of primary and secondary control. Thus, important social comparisons should be more consistently and pronouncedly upward under conditions of high personal control and more saliently downward under conditions of low personal control. The other aspect expected to have a determining impact on the direction of social comparison is the expectation for future change in the comparison dimension. Positive expected change should lead to a focus on primary control and thus to the tendency to upwardly compare with other people in this dimension. Conversely, negative expected change should prompt the individual to engage in compensatory secondary control and therefore select inferior others for downward comparisons.

Thus, in sum, upward comparisons are assumed to be most adaptive when perceived personal control and importance of the comparison dimension is high and future expectations are positive. Conversely, downward comparisons are conceptualized as most adaptive when perceived personal control is low, importance is high, and future expectations are negative. Specifically, we expect that subjects who exhibit a high striving for both primary and secondary control would exhibit a pattern of highly adaptive comparisons in both the upward and the downward directions. Subjects with only high striving for primary control should display high adaptiveness for upward comparisons, while subjects with only high striving for secondary control should show high adaptiveness for downward comparisons.

Sample and Procedure

A total of 158 subjects participated in the study. The sample design was balanced with regard to the following dimensions: sex, East and West Berliners, age (young: twenty to thirty-five years; middle-aged: forty to fifty-five years; old: sixty to eighty-one years), and educational attainment (low: German Haupt- and Realschule, i.e., maximum of ten years of schooling; high: university degree).

Data collection was conducted in two parts. First, in a group session at the Max Planck Institute the following questionnaires were used: Rosenberg Self-Esteem Scale (Rosenberg 1965), the CES-D-Scale on depression, the Tenaciousness of Goal Pursuit and Flexibility of Goal Adjustment Scales (Brandtstädter & Renner 1992), subjective age identification (Kastenbaum et al. 1981), and a question on the five personal developmental goals (J. Heckhausen 1997). Moreover, some information about the demographic characteristics of the subjects was gathered (marital status, occupational position, etc.). In addition, in the second part of the data collection the subjects were instructed about social comparisons. What is meant by social comparisons was explained in terms of examples that represented the topical scope (e.g., physical characteristics, possessions, traits, abilities), situational contexts (e.g., in direct contact, in a telephone conversation, in thought), and different directions (upward, downward, lateral) of social comparisons.

The second part of data collection covered a period of fourteen days and was performed by the subjects at home. Subjects were given a small notebook with a time schedule covering the time period from 7:00 A.M. to 11:00 P.M. and were asked to note briefly each occasion of a social comparison during the day at the respective time slot. In the evenings of each day during the fourteen-day period, subjects were to go through these notes and fill out a questionnaire on social comparisons ("Social Comparison Form") for each instance of a social comparison that occurred during the day. The "Social Comparison Form" (SCF, J. Heckhausen & Wrosch 1998) is an adaptation and extension of the "Rochester Social Comparison Record" used by Wheeler and Miyake (1992). For each social comparison, the subject gives ratings on the following dimensions: (1) the type of target person in terms of the relationship to the subject (e.g., close friend, parent, colleague, imagined person); (2) the sex of the target person; (3) the age of the target person (i.e., younger, same age, or older than subject); (4) the geographical origin of the target person (East or West Germany); (5) social context of comparison (e.g., direct contact, telephone contact, imagined person); (6) domain of life involved (e.g., work, family, standard of living); (7) dimension involved (e.g., ability, personality trait, opinion); (8) open-ended question on comparison dimension; (9) similarity of self and comparison target (better, same, or worse than target); (10) expectations for future change in comparison dimension (positive, stable, negative); (11) importance of comparison dimension; (12) personal control over comparison dimension; (13) intention to change with regard to comparison dimension; (14) rating of mood state (i.e., down and blue vs. happy, discouraged vs. encouraged) before social comparison occurred; (15) rating of mood state after social comparison occurred. Subjects mailed the completed forms back to the Max Planck Institute.

Results

Results will be reported in three sections. First, the employment of upward, downward, and lateral social comparisons is considered in terms of differences between subject groups and three key characteristics of the comparison dimension (personal control, importance, expected future change). Second, results about the affective consequences of social comparisons are considered. And third, findings pertaining to the differential adaptiveness in employing upward and downward comparisons in subject groups differing in primary (tenaciousness) and secondary (flexibility) control striving will be reported.

The overall frequency of social comparison events reported by the subjects indicated that social comparisons were common and relatively

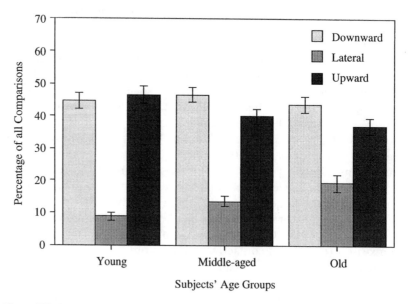

Figure 7.5. Study 9: Mean frequencies of upward, lateral, and downward comparisons; separate for subjects' age groups.

frequent. Across the fourteen days of diary data collection on daily social comparisons, the 158 subjects reported a total of 4,587 social comparison instances. The distribution of social comparisons across the fourteen days was stable, with the mean number of 2.04 per day. An investigation in the frequency of different levels (1, 2, or 3) of upward, downward, and lateral comparisons indicated that all levels were used at comparable frequency, with the intermediate levels ($+2$ and -2) of upward and downward comparison used most frequently.

Figure 7.5 displays the percentages of *upward, downward, and lateral comparisons* reported by young, middle-aged, and old adults. Old adults reported fewer upward comparisons than young adults and more lateral comparisons than young and middle-aged adults. No differential effects for comparison direction were found when considering comparison targets differing by gender, age, or social context.

With regard to the type of target person, analyses of variance revealed a significant main effect of target type. Comparisons with strangers ($M = -.12$) were more likely to be downward comparisons than comparisons with either of the other target types ($M = .60$).

In comparison to targets, who were not classified as either East or West Germans, the old adults ($M = -.72$) perceived themselves as

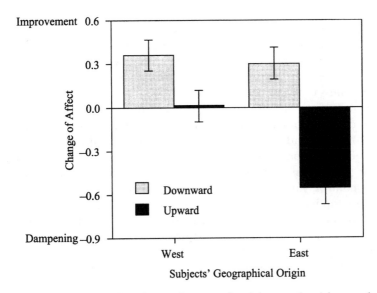

Figure 7.6. Study 9: Mean affect change after upward and downward social comparisons; separate for East and West Berlin subjects.

more superior than the young ($M = .33$) and middle-aged adults ($M = -.06$). Moreover, East Germans ($M = -.49$) were more apt than West Germans ($M = .17$) to perceive themselves as superior to these geographically unclassified comparison targets. Furthermore, subjects perceived themselves as more superior in the health domain ($M = -.40$) than in other life domains ($M = .02$). Social comparisons addressing social skills ($M = -.47$), personality traits ($M = -.38$), and attitudes ($M = -.69$) involved more social downgrading than those directed at abilities ($M = .38$), physical attractiveness ($M = .22$), and life-style ($M = -.01$).

For the analysis of *affective consequences* of social comparisons the two indicators of mood state (happy/down, encouraged/discouraged) were averaged, and mood ratings after the social comparison were subtracted from mood state before social comparison. As expected, subjects reported improved moods after downward comparisons ($M = .35$), and depressed moods after upward comparisons ($M = -.27$). Figure 7.6 shows that both East and West Berliners expressed improved moods after downward comparisons, but for upward comparisons only the East Berliners reported depressed moods. However, further investigation of specific domains revealed that, at least in two of the three major domains, work and health (but not in the family domain), West Berliners also reported mood depression after upward comparisons.

Finally, *interindividual differences in adaptiveness of upward and downward comparisons* were investigated. In accordance with the predictive scheme developed earlier (see section on rationale of study), indices of adaptiveness were calculated based on the ratings of perceived personal control, importance, and future expectations for the dimension addressed in the comparison (see Wrosch 1994; Wrosch & J. Heckhausen 1996b). These indices represent mathematical models of the adaptiveness of upward and downward comparisons, which reflect our theory-based predictions. For upward comparisons, ratings of perceived personal control, importance, and future expectations are averaged and then multiplied with the rating of directionality of social comparison (upward/downward). For downward comparisons, ratings of perceived personal control and expected future change are multiplied by -1, then averaged with the rating of importance, and then multiplied with the rating of directionality of the social comparison. In this way, indices of adaptiveness were computed for each person and each comparison episode.

Subjects were classified into high or low in primary and secondary control striving by performing a median split on the ratings of tenaciousness in goal pursuit (primary control striving) and flexibility of goal adjustment (secondary control striving). This classification was not confused with demographic characteristics of the subjects (age, sex, geographical origin, educational attainment).

Subjects with higher striving in both primary and secondary control yielded higher adaptiveness for social comparisons. In order to determine selective adaptiveness for subjects with either high primary or high secondary control striving, separate analyses of variance were conducted for upward and downward comparisons. Figure 7.7 shows the differences in adaptiveness of upward (left panel) and downward (right panel) comparisons for the groups of subjects differing in primary and secondary control striving. As can be seen in Figure 7.7, subjects showing a high striving for both primary and secondary control exhibited higher adaptiveness for both downward and upward comparisons when compared to subjects with low striving for primary and secondary control. Subjects with only high striving for primary control showed superior adaptiveness for their upward comparisons when compared to subjects with low striving for either control strategy. Finally, subjects with only high striving for secondary control exhibited superior adaptiveness of their downward comparisons compared to subjects with low striving for primary and secondary control.

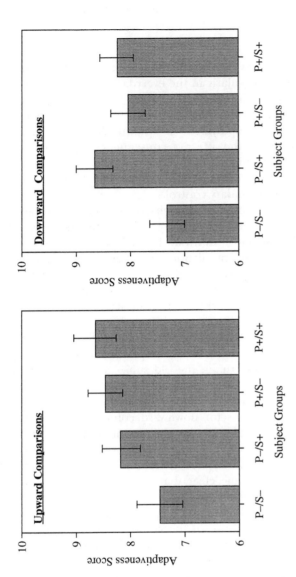

Figure 7.7. Study 9: Mean adaptiveness of upward (*left panel*) and downward (*right panel*) social comparisons; separate for subject groups with high versus low primary and secondary control striving. (Adapted from Wrosch & Heckhausen 1996b.)

Discussion

The findings of this study demonstrate that social comparison processes occur commonly and regularly in the everyday life of men and women at various ages and in different social strata. The following section discusses the findings of Study 9 with regard to the three major purposes of this study: (1) the employment of upward, downward, and lateral social comparisons, (2) the affective consequences of social comparisons, and (3) interindividual differences in the selective adaptiveness of upward and downward comparisons in adults who differ in their striving for primary and secondary control.

It was predicted that, because of their greater need to use secondary control strategies to compensate for age-related threats to self-esteem, old adults would use more downward social comparisons and fewer upward comparisons. This prediction was partly confirmed. Old adults used fewer upward comparisons and more lateral comparisons but did not differ in the frequency of downward comparisons. Thus, the older subjects exhibited a decreased tendency for self-improvement in their social comparison processes but maintained a commitment to self-assessment, which is best served by lateral comparisons. The fact that no age-related increase in downward comparisons was found may have various reasons. For one thing, the old subjects in Study 9 may have been a positive selection of their age group, who as yet perceive little aging-related decline. Moreover, older adults may be more constrained in selecting target persons for downward comparisons because their reduced social roles and restricted mobility confine them to their closer social network, which is presumably mostly comprised of younger family members and other acquaintances. When discussing further age differences below, it will become clear that the old adults did readily use opportunities, when available, to compare downwardly.

In general, adults of all ages used opportunities for downward social comparisons when the nature of the comparison target placed fewer constraints on their comparative evaluations. With regard to strangers, whose specific standing on a comparison dimension is either unknown or can be constructed by freely selecting the target person, more downward comparisons were reported. Moreover, downward comparisons were used more frequently with regard to comparison dimensions that are not easily diagnosable and thus are subject to more arbitrary evaluations, such as social skills, personality traits, and attitudes. Characteristically, this was not the case for the comparison dimensions of abilities, physical attractiveness, and life-style, which are public, more easily diagnosed, and involve more consensual evaluations. A similar reasoning may be applicable to interpret the finding that health-related comparisons involved more social downgrading, because for a layperson relative health status may not be easily discernible.

The findings showing more social downgrading by the East Berliners can be interpreted in the same context. East Berliners were found to use more downward social comparisons with target persons unclassified as East or West Germans. Persons unclassified as East or West Germans are most likely foreign immigrants.[4] Because they are unknown and often particularly low in social status, such persons lend themselves more easily to downward comparisons. In their current life ecologies, many East Germans may be confronted with more opportunities to compare upwardly than to compare downwardly. Therefore, foreign immigrants may provide a welcome opportunity to compare downwardly. Interestingly, old adults exhibited a similar tendency to socially downgrade persons unclassified as East or West Germans. Possibly, the reduced opportunities of older adults for downward comparisons in their immediate social context prompted them to search out more suitable targets for downward comparisons in the non-German population.

As predicted with regard to the affective consequences of social comparisons, improved mood state was found after downward comparisons in all groups of subjects. For upward comparisons, however, only East Berliners reported depressed moods. For the West Berliners, upward comparisons only prompted depressed moods when the work or the health domain was involved. Possibly, inferior performance in other domains was perceived as less threatening by the West Berliners and therefore did not affect their emotions negatively. Thus, overall, the prediction that downward comparisons enhance positive mood while upward comparisons may negatively affect mood state was confirmed.

Moreover, the findings of more generalized negative emotional effects of upward comparisons in the East Berliners suggest that individuals under threat, such as the threat presented by the radical sociohistorical change in East Germany, are more vulnerable to depressing effects of perceiving oneself as inferior to others. These findings converge with previous research, which showed that upward comparisons have particularly negative consequences for affect when individuals feel threatened with regard to the comparison dimension (Buunk et al. 1990).

Finally, it was proposed that individuals with a strong striving for

---

[4] Persons unclassified as East or West Germans could also be strangers. However, for downward comparisons with strangers no significant differences between subject groups of different geographical origin or different age were found.

primary control should adapt their upward comparisons carefully to situational conditions with regard to perceived personal control, importance, and future expectations. Conversely, individuals with a strong secondary control tendency should focus more on adapting downward comparisons to situational conditions. This predictive scheme was supported by the findings of Study 9. Subjects with high primary and secondary control striving showed superior adaptation of both upward and downward comparisons when compared to subjects with low striving in either control strategy. Individuals with strong primary control striving exhibited superior adaptation of their upward comparisons, whereas individuals with strong secondary control striving optimized their downward comparisons in a more adaptive manner than those low in either control striving. These findings were not due to confounding self-esteem or even depression. On the contrary, if anything, the relationships between preference for primary and secondary control were more pronounced when controlling for the effect of depression.

The findings imply that individuals with high striving in both primary and secondary control are best equipped to optimize their social comparison behavior in various situational contexts. They use upward social comparisons when they see the potential for personal control and positive future change. Under inverse situational constraints, however, when personal control and future change are perceived as unpromising, these individuals also readily employ downward social comparisons, and thus protect their long-term resources for primary control. Individuals with high striving for only primary or for only secondary control appear to be more specialized in their social comparison behavior. In the case of individuals predominantly oriented to primary control, they either make the most use of upward comparisons or, in the case of a stronger orientation to secondary control, optimize the use of downward comparisons. Those exhibiting neither high primary nor high secondary control striving can make the least use of opportunities for strategic social comparisons, in that they do not take appropriate account of the degree of personal control, future expectations, and importance when deciding whether to compare with inferior or superior others.

Thus, in sum, Study 9 demonstrates that social comparisons are a common phenomenon in the everyday life of adults. The target persons, contexts, and content domains selected for upward and downward social comparison reflect the adults' most pressing concerns. While downward comparisons improve mood state, upward comparisons lead to depressed affect in most subjects and in various important life domains. Finally, adults differing in striving for primary and secondary control exhibited concomitant differences in selective adaptedness in their upward and downward comparisons.

Summary

In this chapter, social comparison strategies are introduced as prototypical mechanisms in developmental regulation. Social comparisons can serve three major functions: (1) self-assessment by comparing with similar others, (2) self-improvement by comparing with superior others, and (3) self-enhancement by comparing with inferior others. Whereas self-assessment and particularly self-improvement serve to promote primary control, self-enhancement is associated with secondary control.

In Study 7, age-normative and self-related conceptions about developmental change throughout adulthood were juxtaposed. The substantial congruence of self- and other-related expected developmental trajectories indicated that self-assessment is served by normative conceptions about age-related change. Self-enhancement was found in conceptions about development in old age, in that expectations for the self were more optimistic than expectations for other people. Self-enhancement tendencies were more pronounced in old as compared to young subjects. Striving for self-improvement was identified in developmental aspirations pertaining to subjective identifications with higher-status age groups and with regard to perceived age-timing of personal developmental goals.

Study 8 specifically investigated the social downgrading of age peers as a means of compensatory secondary control used by individuals who experience a developmental threat. The findings indicate that downward comparisons with age peers are common throughout adulthood. Self/other discrepancies are especially pronounced when a given age group is normatively expected to go through a phase of challenge or loss. Individuals who experience a particular threat to themselves are most likely to downgrade their age peers socially with regard to the domain at stake. This tendency was particularly common among the older adults. Thus, downward social comparisons with age peers seem to be an important compensatory secondary control strategy to protect motivational resources for primary control in the face of developmental threat.

Finally, Study 9 investigated social comparison processes directly in their everyday occurrence. This diary study demonstrated that adults at different ages and in various social strata commonly and regularly use social comparisons in their everyday life. Upward comparisons became less prominent at higher ages. Downward comparisons focused on targets and content domains that lend themselves more easily to social downgrading and were more pronounced in adults experiencing a threat to primary control (older adults and East Berliners). The affective consequences of upward and downward comparisons were inverse. Upward comparisons led to positive changes in mood, while downward comparisons resulted in depressed moods in various domains and for large portions of the sample. Finally, adults with high primary and high secondary control striving were particularly well equipped to adapt their upward and downward comparisons to the situational conditions, whereas adults with either high primary or high secondary control striving appeared to be more specialized in their employment of upward and downward comparisons, respectively. The least adaptive employment of upward and downward social comparison was exhibited by adults who had both low primary and low secondary control striving.

Thus, in sum, the studies reported in this chapter indicate that strategic social comparisons are commonly and regularly used by adults at different ages. Strategic social comparison provides a flexible and adaptive instrument for developmental regulation in terms of both primary and secondary control.

8   Conclusions and Prospects
for Future Research

This final chapter will briefly review the conclusions that can be drawn from the theory and empirical research presented in the previous chapters. Because of the nature of this research program, the theory is much larger in scope than the empirical studies reported. Therefore, the tasks and questions set for empirical research, which follow from the life-span theory of control and its model of developmental regulation, are extensive. Some selected prospects for future research in each of the areas covered will be developed in the following section. Because of the wide scope of phenomena involved in developmental regulation across the life course, the discussion of research prospects needs to be selective and focused on areas of particular intellectual promise.

The great variability and relative dearth of biologically based determination in human behavior pose two basic challenges to human behavioral regulation: the management of *selectivity* and *failure compensation* (J. Heckhausen & Schulz 1995). The individual needs to choose certain action goals out of many alternatives and then focus the investment of resources for primary control on the goal selected. Moreover, the individual has to compensate for the frustration and threat to self-esteem that may result from regular failure experiences. In the context of ontogenetic change across the life course, both selectivity and failure compensation become even more pressing and more essential.

The individual's action and the regulation of behavioral selectivity and failure compensation occur in the context of the life course. The *life course comprises structural constraints* that are based on chronological age and sequential patterns of life transitions. These external constraints can be conceived of as adaptive challenges because they provide a scaffold for the individual's developmental regulation and set up age-graded challenges for development. Such external constraints of development across the life span are based on biological maturation and aging, the social structure of the life course, and age-normative conceptions commonly shared in a given social community. Particular empha-

191

sis has been placed on age-normative conceptions as adaptive constraints to developmental regulation, because these are inherently psychological as well as social.

Future research may focus on three questions. First, normative conceptions about age-sequential constraints have so far received little empirical attention. However, when the individual aims at optimizing developmental processes across her lifetime, long-term trade-offs within and also across domains need to be taken into account. This can only be achieved on the basis of knowledge about the sequential constraints of a given chosen path.

Second, one might also investigate the effects of intercultural differences in the degree of certainty, consensus, and social sanctions associated with age-normative constraints. For instance, in a society that particularly relies on the predictability of life-course patterns and discourages cross-path shifts after early adulthood, such long-term developmental planning and a common and firm framework of age-normative conceptions are more essential than under more flexible conditions. Moreover, the relationship between external (i.e., sociostructural) and internal (i.e., internalized age norms) constraints should be further explored, both conceptually and empirically. When comparing societies with different divisions of labor, one might find that internal and external constraints mutually compensate for each other. When external constraints to life-course patterns are pronounced, internal constraints need not be elaborate. It may be expected, for instance, that in preindustrial societies with rigid age-grading systems marked by socially prescribed *rites des passages*, individuals do not develop personal goals for their life courses and development. Conversely, in Western industrialized societies with looser institutional constraints for age-related timing of events, age-normative conceptions as they are internalized by the individual become more influential in determining individuals' developmental behavior.

Third, the potential protective effects of age-normative conceptions about developmental losses should be investigated. Strategies of secondary control, such as goal disengagement, are probably more easily invoked for normative than nonnormative losses. Normatively expected losses confront the individual with predictable challenges for compensation and therefore permit and facilitate anticipatory post hoc secondary control. Nonnormative and therefore unexpected losses, in contrast, provide an opportunity only for post hoc secondary control, which has to be developed under the emotional impact of the loss. Secondary control of nonnormative losses may therefore be delayed and less effective in preventing or minimizing negative effects for the control system.

The individual can rely on two types of control for developmental regulation and behavioral optimization in general. *Primary control* is directed at affecting changes in the external world, while secondary control addresses the internal world of the individual. Primary control holds functional primacy over secondary control. *Secondary control* serves primary control in terms of the two basic challenges to behavioral regulation: selectivity and failure compensation. It also supports the motivational commitment for selected action goals and compensates for the negative effects of losses in primary control on the emotional and motivational resources for future primary control.

On a general level, two major questions might prove most productive for future conceptual and empirical work on the control system. First, the role played by emotion in the control system (Schulz & J. Heckhausen 1997). The assumption of the primacy of primary control leads to a conception that emotions might function as mediators of primary and secondary control striving. The fact that increases in control do not lead to persistent positive affect and a decrease of primary control striving but, on the contrary, motivate increases in aspiration levels indicates that emotional systems might have evolved to maximize primary control striving rather than to optimize emotional experiences (Schulz & J. Heckhausen 1997; see also discussion in Chapter 3). Second, comparative work both across species and across cultures might yield insights into the evolution of the regulatory processes involved in control-related behavior. Phenomena such as the preference for behavior–event contingencies or for moderate discrepancies could be conceptualized as preadapted modules (Fodor 1987) that provide the proximal mechanisms for primary control striving. Moreover, basic phenomena of motivational regulation, such as stalking prey and submission in intraspecies aggression, may be interpreted as basic modules for secondary control. Both types of modules could drive primary and secondary control behavior in humans yet be accessible to conscious intervention and strategic usage (Rozin 1976), as is conceptualized as optimization in the model of developmental regulation (see Chapter 4).

Opportunities for primary control change considerably across the human life span. They increase rapidly in early life, plateau during most of mid-life, and then decline in old age. The demands placed on secondary control shift accordingly. Young children have almost no capacity for secondary control and therefore rely on their caretaker for failure compensation. Very little is known about the developmental origin and acquisition of secondary control strategies in childhood. When in early childhood do secondary control processes first occur? There is some initial and sketchy evidence that the acquisition of secondary control strategies may be contingent on the evolution of cognitive operations (Band & Weisz 1990; Nolen-Hoeksema, Girgus, & Seligman 1992). The relationship between cognitive development and the acquisition of secondary control strategies needs to be investigated more systematically. The same holds for the development of motivation. The life-span theory of control would predict that the use of secondary control becomes critical when the child has developed the concept of his own competence, because then self-esteem becomes vulnerable to failure experiences. This prediction should be empirically investigated. Moreover, no empirical research is available on the role of caretakers in the process of developing secondary control. Are secondary control processes self-generated in response to failure experiences, or are they modeled or even directly taught by adult caretakers?

By early adulthood various secondary control strategies have evolved, and some further growth in this regard may occur throughout mid-life and in old age. The further growth and transformations of secondary control strategies during middle adulthood and old age is a promising area for future research. Can one identify increased variability of strategies across age, or do individuals specialize in using certain strategies at the expense of strategy diversity?

Secondary control becomes increasingly important during old age, when aging-related declines severely restrict the primary control potential of the individual. The control system may fail when the individual is deprived of even basic levels of primary control and there is no hope for future improvement. This is often the case at the end of life, and particularly in the case of sudden, unexpected, and severe illness. Future research should longitudinally track the changes in control behavior under conditions of severe health threats. How does the individual manage the balance between primary and secondary control striving when primary control potential decreases? Which secondary control strategies are used under conditions of low versus high prospects for future regeneration of primary control? Under which conditions and for which secondary control strategies is future potential for primary control fostered or compromised? The biological consequences of control-related behavior (e.g., immune and endocrine functioning) may also be of particular interest for future research. The life-span theory of control suggests that the biological effects of losses in primary control could only be observed if secondary control also failed to serve as a second line of defense.

A *life-span model of developmental regulation (the OPS model)* was developed to conceptualize how individuals use primary and secondary control to master the challenges of selectivity and failure compensation throughout the life course (J. Heckhausen & Schulz 1993a; Schulz & J. Heckhausen 1996). A two-dimensional model involving the dimensions primary and secondary control, on the one hand, and selectivity and failure compensation, on the other, comprises four types of strategies in developmental regulation: selective primary, compensatory primary, selective secondary, and compensatory secondary control. The adaptive use of these four types of strategies is regulated by a higher-order process of optimization. The criterion for the adaptiveness of optimization in developmental regulation is the extent to which it promotes and maintains the potential for primary control across the life span. One of the major functions of optimization is to regulate primary and secondary control when there is a conflict between short-term and long-term primary control. However, such conflicts are often resolved by external and proximal constraints, such as developmental deadlines, that take most of the regulatory load off the individual's shoulders.

Future research should systematically investigate individual's regulatory behavior in life-course settings that are rich in such long-term/short-term or interdomain conflicts. Examples of long-term/short-term conflicts are decisions made about occupational careers that juxtapose the option of immediate gainful employment with the option of further education. An example of an interdomain conflict is the situation of career women who also have to care for their children.

A promising area for future research would be the study of developmental regulation in individuals who lead exceptional lives. Nonnormative successful life courses have to be realized without, and often in opposition to, the scaffolding of sociostructural and age-normative opportunities and constraints. These exceptional individuals have to rely almost entirely on individual regulation and resources to attain successful development. This should require greatly enhanced selectivity in resource investment and particularly powerful secondary control strategies in order to volitionally support this selective investment.

The individual's developmental regulation is organized around *developmental goals*. Developmental goals are long-term action units in developmental regulation. As an extension of previously related concepts, the concept of developmental goals emphasizes the life-course context and the role of the individual as an agent in her own development and applies an action-theoretical model that involves multiple action phases. In their pursuit of developmental goals, individuals have to take into account developmental deadlines, which set ultimate timing constraints on the attainability of their goals (J. Heckhausen & Fleeson 1993). When approaching a developmental deadline the individual experiences urgency and can be expected to increase resource investment in the deadline-related goal. Once the deadline is passed, the individual needs to disengage from the respective goal because primary control of goal attainment is no longer available, and thus resource investment is futile and harmful to future primary control striving.

Developmental regulation around developmental deadlines provides an extensive and intellectually challenging area for future research. At this point, almost nothing is known about the proposed urgency/disengagement shift when moving from predeadline to postdeadline processing. Research into potential shifts in cognitive processing before and after passing the deadline might be particularly fruitful. Predeadline processing should be selectively focused on the relevant goal in terms of attention, recognition, and memory, whereas processing after failing to meet a deadline should be diverse and focused on a search for substitute goals. Another important topic in this context is premature compensatory secondary control. Individuals might choose to disengage from a goal anticipatorily when the respective deadline comes close and goal attainment is unlikely. In this way, the individual can protect herself from the extreme negative affect that would ensue if she missed the deadline after having striven for it with great urgency. Such a failure might be very harmful to long-term motivational resources for primary control. Therefore, giving up primary control on goal attainment even before the deadline might ultimately be adaptive in view of the life-span encompassing potential for primary control. However, this also highlights a dangerous setting in developmental regulation. Anticipatory secondary control is impossible if opportunities for action unexpectedly and suddenly vanish. The developmental ecology of East Germans who are in their early fifties may represent exactly this situation, where developmental regulation may fail.

Developmental regulation was investigated specifically in the context of *two different developmental challenges: aging-related and sociohistorical change.* While aging-related change involves relatively little personal control, radical sociohistorical transformations, such as in the former GDR after German reunification, call for enhanced striving for primary control. Unfortunately, measurement instruments specifically addressing primary and secondary control strategies in developmental regulation were not yet developed at the time of these studies. However, we were able to use existing measurement instruments and characteristics of goal striving as tentative indicators of such strategies. The findings suggest that, in convergence with the theoretical assumptions of the life-span theory of control, older as compared to younger adults use more compensatory secondary control strategies, and they focus their primary control striving on age-appropriate goals. As expected, East compared to West Berliners exhibited enhanced selective primary and selective secondary control with regard to goals that were at stake during socioeconomic transformation. In another study involving East Germans, intercohort differences in developmental regulation were identified. The members of the birth/age cohort from fifty-two to fifty-four years, who were confronted with particularly severe restrictions in primary control, seemed to have run into a developmental calamity. Various indicators of primary and secondary control behavior among these individuals in their early fifties suggested that their control systems were stretched beyond their limits and therefore failed to protect them from losses in self-esteem. Taken together, Studies 6 and 7 demonstrate the adaptive resources of developmental regulation even under challenging conditions. However, limits to primary and secondary control under extreme and unusually adverse conditions also became apparent.

However, two major caveats have to be stated when considering the empirical research presented here. The measurement instruments used in these studies were not developed to test the conceptual assumptions of the life-span theory of control. This was due to the synchronous and mutually stimulating development of theory and empirical studies. Future studies should employ instruments that are specifically developed to assess strategies of developmental optimization and of selective primary, compensatory primary, selective secondary, and compensatory secondary control. Such work is currently under way (J. Heckhausen, Schulz, & Wrosch 1998).

The second caveat relates to the cross-sectional nature of the studies reported. Cross-sectional comparisons do not allow for investigating the sequential, let alone causal, relations among developmental challenges, strategies of developmental regulation, and developmental outcomes. Future research should focus on specific developmental challenges and the way in which individuals try to regulate their development when facing these challenges. The employment of specific strategies of developmental regulation and their effectiveness should be studied in a microsequential manner across a relevant longitudinal span (e.g., adaptation to a disability). Moreover, cohort differences in the developmental regulation of sociohistorical challenges are best studied by using cohort sequential designs, which allow for disentangling age and time of measurement effects. A longitudinal follow-up to the East German study (Study 6) will provide such cohort sequential comparisons (Diewald & Mayer 1996).

The investigation of the variability, frequency of use, and employment pattern of specific primary and secondary control strategies over the life course should be a rich field for future research. Moreover, almost nothing is known about the adaptive value of specific control strategies for specific developmental challenges. It may be useful to carry out a conceptual cost/benefit analysis of specific primary and secondary control strategies for certain developmental challenges and subsequently to investigate their validity empirically. For example, relinquishing primary control and using secondary control strategies might be most appropriate when the controllability of goal attainment is low or the long-term costs of primary control striving outweigh their short-term benefits. Such an approach might be particularly useful when investigating the transition from primary to secondary control in developmental regulation around age-related deadlines. Again, such research must involve longitudinal designs so as to track the mutual influences among developmental challenges, regulatory processes, and developmental outcomes.

Social comparisons are prototypical strategies in developmental regulation. They serve three major functions: self-assessment by comparing oneself to similar others, self-improvement by comparing oneself to superior others, and self-enhancement by comparing oneself to inferior others. Whereas self-assessment and self-improvement are important means for promoting primary control, self-enhancement serves secondary control purposes. Study 7 showed that age-normative conceptions about development in adulthood provide a framework for self-assessment of developmental status, self-enhancement in comparison to negative stereotypes of aging, and self-improvement in terms of developmental aspirations. The self-enhancement function was particularly salient in the old adults. Study 8 revealed that individuals at all adult ages use social downgrading of age peers as a means of compensatory secondary control. When the individual perceived a personal threat in a given domain of functioning, social downgrading was particularly salient and focused on the domain at stake. Again, social downgrading of age peers was particularly pronounced in old adults. Finally, Study 9 demonstrated that social comparisons are used commonly and regularly in the everyday life of adults at various ages. The target persons, social contexts, contents, and direction selected for social comparisons reflect the individual's characteristics, life-course position, and social roles, as well as the availability of comparison targets in personal social networks. Again, old adults differed in their social comparison behavior from younger adults, in that they used less upward and more lateral comparisons. Moreover, the situational adaptiveness of upward and downward comparisons was differential across individuals who differed in primary and secondary control striving.

Future research may focus on the combination of informational (primary) and evaluational (secondary) functions of social comparisons. As suggested by Taylor and others (Taylor & Lobel 1989; Taylor, Buunk, & Aspinwall 1990), for example, upward contacts and downward comparisons with regard to a specific domain of functioning are not exclusive but may complement each other. In the context of the life-span theory of control, upward contacts provide models for primary control, while downward comparisons serve secondary control because they promote optimism, perceived control, and self-esteem – all important motivational resources for primary control. It appears that both functions are essential to adaptive behavior (Aspinwall & Taylor 1992; Taylor & Gollwitzer 1995; Taylor, Kemeney, & Aspinwall 1992) and may be pursued simultaneously, especially when primary control is at stake. Another challenging task for future research is to explore the relation and potential mutual compensation between social comparisons and temporal intraindividual comparisons across different times in the life course.

In sum, the theoretical model of developmental regulation proposed in this research provides a useful framework for the empirical investigation of various phenomena related to developmental regulation under different societal and life-course conditions. The empirical studies show the power and adaptiveness of human developmental regulation, even when faced with substantial challenges. The individual's developmental regulation is scaffolded by external constraints, which provide structure and predictability to developmental challenges. The life-span theory of control and its model of developmental regulation provide a rich field for future research.

References

Abramson, L. Y.; Seligman, M. E. P.; & Teasdale, J. D. (1978). Learned helplessness in humans: Critique and reformulation. *Journal of Abnormal Psychology, 87,* 49–74.

Ahammer, I. M., & Baltes, P. B. (1972). Objective versus perceived age differences in personality: How do adolescents, adults, and older people view themselves and each other? *Journal of Gerontology, 27,* 46–51.

Aisenberg, R. (1964). What happens to old psychologists? A preliminary report. In R. Kastenbaum (Ed.), *New thoughts on old age.* New York: Springer.

Alloy, L. B., & Abramson, L. Y. (1979). Judgement of contingency in depressed and non-depressed students: Sadder but wiser? *Journal of Experimental Psychology, 108,* 441–485.

Altshuler, J. L., & Ruble, D. N. (1989). Developmental changes in children's awareness of strategies for coping with uncontrollable stress. *Child Development, 60,* 1337–1349.

Aspinwall, L. G., & Taylor, S. E. (1992). Modeling cognitive adaptation: A longitudinal investigation of the impact of individual differences and coping on college adjustment and performance. *Journal of Personality and Social Psychology, 63,* 989–1003.

Atkinson, J. W. (1957). Motivational determinants of risk-taking behavior. *Psychological Review, 64,* 359–72.

Azuma, H. (1984). Secondary control as a heterogeneous category. *American Psychologist, 39,* 970–971.

Bäckman, L., & Dixon, R. A. (1992). Psychological compensation: A theoretical framework. *Psychological Bulletin, 112,* 259–283.

Baltes, M. M. (1987). Erfolgreiches Altern als Ausdruck von Verhaltenskompetenz und Umweltqualität [Successful aging as a product of behavioral competence and quality of environment]. In C. Niemitz (Ed.), *Der Mensch im Zusammenspiel von Anlage und Umwelt* (pp. 353–376). Frankfurt: Suhrkamp.

(1995). Dependencies in old age: Gains and losses. *Current Directions in Psychological Science, 4,* 14–19.

(1996). *The many faces of dependency in old age.* New York: Cambridge University Press.

Baltes, M. M., & Carstensen, L. L. (1996). The process of successful aging. *Ageing and Society, 16,* 397–422.

Baltes, M. M.; Kühl, K.-P.; & Sowarka, D. (1992). Testing for limits of cognitive reserve capacity: A promising strategy for early diagnosis of dementia? *Journal of Gerontology: Psychological Sciences, 47,* 165–167.

Baltes, M. M., & Reisenzein, R. (1986). The social world in long term care institutions: Psychological control toward dependency? In M. M. Baltes & P. B. Baltes (Eds.), *The psychology of control and aging* (pp. 315–343). Hillsdale, NJ: Erlbaum.

Baltes, M. M., & Silverberg, S. B. (1994). The dynamics between dependency and autonomy: Illustrations across the life span. In D. L. Featherman, R. M. Lerner, & M. Perlmutter (Eds.), *Life-span development and behavior,* Vol. 12 (pp. 42–91). Hillsdale, NJ: Erlbaum.

Baltes, P. B. (1968). Longitudinal and cross-sectional sequences in the study of age and generation effects. *Human Development, 11,* 145–171.

(1983). Life-span developmental psychology: Observations on history and theory revisited. In R. M. Lerner (Ed.), *Developmental psychology: Historical and philosophical perspectives* (pp. 79–111). Hillsdale, NJ: Erlbaum.

(1987). Theoretical propositions of life-span developmental psychology: On the dynamics between growth and decline. *Developmental Psychology, 23,* 611–626.

(1989a). Das Doppelgesicht des Alterns [The dual face of aging]. In Max-Planck-Gesellschaft (Ed.), *Max-Planck-Gesellschaft Jahrbuch* (pp. 41–60). Göttingen: Vandenhoeck/Ruprecht.

(1989b). The dynamics between growth and decline. *Contemporary Psychology, 34,* 983–984.

(1991). The many faces of human aging: Toward a psychological culture of old age. *Psychological Medicine, 21,* 837–854.

(1993). The aging mind: Potential and limits. *Gerontologist, 33,* 580–594.

Baltes, P. B., & Baltes, M. M. (1980). Plasticity and variability in psychological aging: Methodological and theoretical issues. In G. E. Gurski (Ed.), *Determining the effects of aging on the central nervous system* (pp. 41–66). Berlin: Schering.

(1989). Optimierung durch Selektion und Kompensation: Ein psychologisches Modell erfolgreichen Alterns [Optimization by selection and compensation: A psychological model of successful aging]. *Zeitschrift für Pädagogik, 35,* 85–105.

(1990). Psychological perspectives on successful aging: The model of selective optimization with compensation. In P. B. Baltes & M. M. Baltes (Eds.), *Successful aging: Perspectives from the behavioral sciences* (pp. 1–34). New York: Cambridge University Press.

Baltes, P. B.; Cornelius, S. W.; & Nesselroade, J. R. (1979). Cohort effects in developmental psychology. In J. R. Nesselroade & P. B. Baltes (Eds.), *Longitudinal research in the study of behavior and development* (pp. 61–87). New York: Academic Press.

Baltes, P. B.; Dittmann-Kohli, F.; & Dixon, R. A. (1984). New perspectives on the development of intelligence in adulthood: Toward a dual-process conception. In P. B. Baltes & O. G. Brim, Jr. (Eds.), *Life-span development and behavior,* Vol. 6 (pp. 33–76). New York: Academic Press.

Baltes, P. B.; Dittmann-Kohli, F.; & Kliegl, R. (1986). Reserve capacity of the elderly in aging-sensitive tests of fluid intelligence: Replication and extension. *Psychology and Aging, 1,* 172–177.

Baltes, P. B., & Graf, P. (1996). Psychological aspects of aging: Facts and frontiers. In D. Magnusson et al. (Eds.), *The life-span development of individuals:*

Behavioural, neurobiological and psychosocial perspectives (pp. 427–459). Cambridge: Cambridge University Press.

Baltes, P.; Lindenberger, U.; & Staudinger, U. (1998). Life-span theory in developmental psychology. *Theoretical models of human development.* 5th ed. (pp. 1029–1143). New York: Wiley. In W. Damon (Ed.), *Handbook of child Psychology:* vol. 1.

Baltes, P. B.; Reese, H. W.; & Lipsitt, L. P. (1980). Life-span developmental psychology. *Annual Review of Psychology, 31,* 65–110.

Baltes, P. B., & Schaie, K. W. (1973). On life-span developmental research paradigms: Retrospects and prospects. In P. B. Baltes & K. W. Schaie (Eds.), *Life-span developmental psychology: Personality and socialization* (pp. 365–395). New York: Academic Press.

(1976). On the plasticity of intelligence in adulthood and old age: Where Horn and Donaldson fail. *American Psychologist, 31,* 720–725.

Band, E. B., & Weisz, J. R. (1988). How to feel better when it feels bad: Children's perspectives on coping with everyday stress. *Developmental Psychology, 24,* 247–253.

(1990). Developmental differences in primary and secondary control coping and adjustment to juvenile diabetes. *Journal of Clinical Child Psychology, 19,* 150–158.

Bandura, A. (1977). Self-efficacy: Toward a unifying theory of behavioral change. *Psychological Review, 84,* 191–215.

(1982a). Self-efficacy mechanisms in human agency. *American Psychologist, 37,* 122–147.

(1982b). The psychology of chance encounters and life paths. *American Psychologist, 37,* 747–755.

(1986). *Social foundations of thought and action: A social cognitive theory.* Englewood Cliffs, NJ: Prentice-Hall.

(1988). Self-regulation of motivation and action through goal systems. In V. Hamilton, G. H. Bower, & N. H. Frijda (Eds.), *Cognitive perspectives on emotion and motivation* (pp. 37–61). Dordrecht: Kluwer Academic.

(1992) Exercise of personal agency through the self-efficacy mechanism. In R. Schwarzer (Ed.), *Self-efficacy: Thought control of action* (pp. 3–38). Washington, DC: Hemisphere.

Bandura, A., & Cervone, D. (1983). Self-evaluation and self-efficacy mechanisms governing the motivational effects of goal systems. *Journal of Personality and Social Psychology, 45,* 1017–1028.

Banziger, G., & Drevenstedt, J. (1982). Achievement attributions by young and old judges as a function of perceived age of stimulus person. *Journal of Gerontology, 37,* 468–474.

Beckmann, J., & Gollwitzer, P. M. (1987). Deliberative and implemental states of mind: The issue of impartiality in predecisional and postdecisional information processing. *Social Cognition (Special Issue: Cognition and Action), 5,* 259–279.

Beisecker, A. E. (1988). Aging and the desire for information and input in medical decisions: Patient consumerism in medical encounters. *Gerontologist, 28,* 330–335.

Bell, B. D., & Stanfield, G. G. (1973). Chronological age in relation to attitudinal judgments: An experimental analysis. *Journal of Gerontology, 28,* 491–496.

Berger, P., & Luckmann, T. (1966). *The social construction of reality.* New York: Doubleday.

Berlyne, D. E. (1960). *Conflict, arousal, and curiosity.* New York: McGraw-Hill.

(1971). *Aesthetics and psychobiology.* New York: Appleton-Century-Crofts.

Birren, J. E. (1988). A contribution to the theory of the psychology of aging: As a counterpart of development. In J. E. Birren & V. L. Bengtson (Eds.), *Emergent theories of aging* (pp. 153–176). New York: Springer.

(1995). Editorial: New models of aging: Comment on need and creative effort. *Canadian Journal on Aging, 14,* 1–7.

Bjorklund, D. F., & Green, B. L. (1992). The adaptive nature of cognitive immaturity. *American Psychologist, 47,* 46–50.

Blanchard-Fields, R., & Irion, J. C. (1988). The relation between locus of control and coping in two contexts: Age as a moderator variable. *Psychology and Aging, 3,* 197–203.

Blank, T. O. (1987). Attributions as dynamic elements in a life-span social psychology. In R. Abeles (Ed.), *Life-span perspectives and social psychology* (pp. 61–84). Hillsdale, NJ: Erlbaum.

Blau, Z. S. (1956). Changes in status and age identification. *American Sociological Review, 21,* 198–203.

Blossfeld, H.-P. (1987). Labor market entry and the sexual segregation of careers in the Federal Republic of Germany. *American Journal of Sociology, 93,* 89–118.

(1988). Sensible Phasen im Bildungsverlauf—Eine Längsschnittanalyse über die Prägung von Bildungskarrieren durch den gesellschaftlichen Wandel [Critical phases in educational careers: A longitudinal analysis about the impact of societal change on educational careers]. *Zeitschrift für Pädagogik, 34,* 45–63.

Blossfeld, H.-P., & Mayer, K. U. (1988). Labor market segmentation in the Federal Republic of Germany: An empirical study of segmentation theories from a life course perspective. *European Sociological Review, 4,* 123–140.

Borges, M. A., & Dutton, L. J. (1976). Attitudes toward aging: Increasing optimism found with age. *The Gerontologist, 16,* 220–224.

Bowsher, J. E., & Gerlach, M. J. (1990). Personal control and other determinants of psychological well-being in nursing home elders. *Scholarly Inquiry for Nursing Practice, 4,* 91–102.

Braithwaite, V. A. (1986). Old age stereotypes: Reconciling contradictions. *Journal of Gerontology, 41,* 353–360.

Braithwaite, V. A.; Gibson, D.; & Holman, J. (1985–1986). Age stereotyping: Are we oversimplifying the phenomenon? *International Journal of Aging and Human Development, 22,* 315–325.

Brandtstädter, J. (1984). Personal and social control over development: Some implications of an action perspective in life-span developmental psychology. In P. B. Baltes & O. G. Brim, Jr. (Eds.), *Life-span development and behavior,* Vol. 6 (pp. 1–32). New York: Academic Press.

(1986). Personale Entwicklungskontrolle und entwicklungsregulatives Handeln: Ueberlegungen und Befunde zu einem vernachlässigten Forschungsthema [Personal control and regulative action in development: Thoughts and findings on an underrated issue of research]. *Zeitschrift für Entwicklungspsychologie und Pädagogische Psychologie, 18,* 316–334.

(1989). Personal self-regulation of development: Cross-sequential analyses of development-related control beliefs and emotions. *Developmental Psychology,* 25, 96–108.

(1990). Entwicklung im Lebenslauf: Ansätze und Probleme der Lebensspannen-Entwicklungspsychologie [Life-span development: Approaches and problems of life-span developmental psychology]. *Kölner Zeitschrift für Soziologie und Sozialpsychologie, 31,* 322–350.

Brandtstädter, J., & Greve, W. (1992). Das Selbst im Alter: adaptive und protektive Mechanismen [The self in old age: Adaptive and protective mechanisms]. *Zeitschrift für Entwicklungspsychologie und Pädagogische Psychologie, 24,* 269–297.

(1994). The aging self: Stabilizing and protective processes. *Developmental Review, 14,* 52–80.

Brandtstädter, J.; Krampen, G.; & Greve, W. (1987). Personal control over development: Effects on the perception and emotional evaluation of personal development in adulthood. *International Journal of Behavioral Development, 10,* 99–120.

Brandtstädter, J., & Renner, G. (1990). Tenacious goal pursuit and flexible goal adjustment: Explication and age-related analysis of assimilative and accommodative strategies of coping. *Psychology and Aging, 5,* 58–67.

(1992). Coping with discrepancies between aspirations and achievements in adult development: A dual-process model. In L. Montada, S.-H. Filipp, & R. M. Lerner (Eds.), *Life crises and experiences of loss in adulthood* (pp. 301–319). Hillsdale, NJ: Erlbaum.

Brandtstädter, J., & Rothermund, K. (1994). Self-percepts of control in middle and later adulthood: Buffering losses by rescaling goals. *Psychology and Aging, 9,* 265–273.

Brandtstädter, J.; Wentura, D.; & Greve, W. (1993). Adaptive resources of the aging self: Outlines of an emergent perspective. *International Journal of Behavioral Development, 16,* 323–349.

Brim, O. G., Jr., (1992). *Ambition: How we manage success and failure throughout our lives.* New York: Basic Books.

Brim, O. G., Jr., & Ryff, C. D. (1980). On the properties of life events. In P. B. Baltes & O. G. Brim, Jr. (Eds.), *Life-span development and behavior,* Vol. 3 (pp. 367–388). New York: Academic Press.

Brim, O. G., Jr., & Wheeler, S. (1966). *Socialization after childhood: Two essays.* New York: Wiley.

Brock, D. B.; Guralnick, J. M.; & Brody, J. A. (1990). Demography and epidemiology of aging in the United States. In E. L. Schneider & J. W. Rowe (Eds.), *Handbook of the biology of aging,* 3d ed. (pp. 3–23). New York: Academic Press.

Brown, A. (1982). Learning and development: The problem of compatibility, access, and induction. *Human Development, 25,* 89–115.

Brubaker, T. H., & Powers, E. A. (1976). The stereotype of "old": A review and alternative approach. *Journal of Gerontology, 31,* 441–447.

Brunstein, J. C. (1993). Personal goals and subjective well-being: A longitudinal study. *Journal of Personality and Social Psychology, 65,* 1061–1070.

(1995). Persönliche Anliegen und subjektives Wohlbefinden [Personal goals and subjective well-being]. In K. Pawlik (Ed.), *Bericht über den 39. Kongreß der Deutschen Gesellschaft für Psychologie in Hamburg.* Göttingen: Hogrefe.

Bühler, C. (1933). *Der menschliche Lebenslauf als psychologisches Problem* [The human life course as a topic of psychology]. Leipzig: Hirzel.
   (1953). The curve of life as studied in biographies. *Journal of Applied Psychology,
   19*, 405–409.
   (1962). Genetic aspects of the self. *Annals of the New York Academy of Sciences.
   96*, 730–764.
Bühler, K. (1919). *Abriß der geistigen Entwicklung des Kindes* [Sketch of the mental
development of the child]. Leipzig: Quelle & Meyer.
Bultena, G., & Powers, E. (1976). Effects of age-grade comparisons on adjustment in later life. In J. Gubrium (Ed.), *Time, roles and self in old age*
(pp. 165–178). New York: Behavioral Publications.
Burgess, A. W., & Holmstrom, L. L. (1979a). *Rape: Crisis and recovery*. Bowie, MD:
Brady.
Burgess, J. M., & Holmstrom, L. L. (1979b). Adaptive strategies and recovery
from rape. *American Journal of Psychiatry, 136*, 1278–1282.
Buunk, B. P.; Collins, R. L.; Taylor, S. E.; VanYperen, N. W.; & Dakof, G. A.
(1990). The affective consequences of social comparison: Either direction
has its ups and downs. *Journal of personality and social psychology, 59*, 1238–
1249.
Cairns, R. B. (1991). Multiple metaphors for a singular idea. *Developmental Psychology, 27*, 23–26.
Cameron, P. (1969). Age parameters of young adult, middle-aged, old, and
aged. *Journal of Gerontology, 24*, 201–202.
Cantor, N., & Fleeson, W. (1991). Life tasks and self-regulatory processes. In
M. L. Maehr & P. R. Pintrich (Eds.), *Advances in motivation and achievement,*
Vol. 7 (pp. 327–369). Greenwich, CT: JAI.
   (1994). Social intelligence and intelligent goal pursuit: A cognitive slice of
   motivation. In W. Spaulding (Ed.), *Nebraska symposium on motivation*, Vol.
   41 (pp. 125–179). Lincoln: University of Nebraska Press.
Cantor, N., & Kihlstrom, J. F. (1987). *Personality and social intelligence*. Englewood
Cliffs, NJ: Prentice-Hall.
Cantor, N.; Markus, H.; Niedenthal, P.; & Nurius, P. (1986). On motivation and
the self concept. In R. M. Sorrentino & E. T. Higgins (Eds.), *Handbook of
motivation and cognition* (pp. 65–96). Chichester: Wiley.
Cantor, N.; Norem, J. K.; Langston, C.; Zirkel, S.; Fleeson, W.; & Cook-
Flannagan, C. (1991). Life tasks and daily life experience. *Journal of Person-
ality, 59*, 425–451.
Cantor, N.; Norem, J. K.; Niedenthal, P. M.; Langston, C. A.; & Brower, A. M.
(1987). Life tasks, self-concept ideals, and cognitive strategies in a life transition. *Journal of Personality and Social Psychology, 53*, 1178–1191.
Carstensen, L. L. (1993). Motivation for social contact across the life-span: A
theory of socioemotional selectivity. In J. Jacobs (Ed.), *Nebraska symposium
on motivation*, Vol. 40 (pp. 205–254). Lincoln: University of Nebraska Press.
Carstensen, L. L., & Fredrickson, B. L. (1992). *Aging, illness and social preferences.*
Paper presented at the International Congress of Psychology, Brussels, July
1992.
Carus, F. A. (1808). *Psychologie. Zweiter Teil: Specialpsychologie* [Psychology. Part
two: Special psychology]. Leipzig: Barth & Kummer.
Caspi, A., & Elder, G. H. (1986). Life satisfaction in old age: Linking social
psychology and history. *Psychology and Aging, 1*, 18–26.

Charlesworth, B. (1990). Natural selection and life history patterns. In D. E. Harrison (Ed.), *Genetic Effects on Aging II.* Caldwell, NJ: Telford Press.

Chiriboga, D. A. (1978). Evaluated time: A life course perspective. *Journal of Gerontology, 33,* 388–393.

Claessens, D. (1968). *Instinkt, Psyche, Geltung: Bestimmungsfaktoren menschlichen Verhaltens. Eine soziologische Anthropologie* [Instinct, psyche, status – determining factors in human behavior: A sociological anthropology]. Cologne and Opladen: Westdeutscher Verlag.

Clausen, J. A. (1986). *The life course: A sociological perspective.* Englewood Cliffs, NJ: Prentice-Hall.

Compas, B. E. (1987). Coping with stress during childhood and adolescence. *Psychological Bulletin, 101,* 393–403.

Compas, B. E.; Banez, G. A.; Malcarne, V.; & Worsham, N. (1991a). Perceived control and coping with stress: A developmental perspective. *Journal of Social Issues, 47,* 23–34.

(1991b). *Perceived control, coping with stress, and depressive symptoms in school-age children.* Burlington: University of Vermont.

Compas, B. E., & Worsham, N. (1991). *When mom or dad has cancer: Developmental differences in children's coping with family stress.* Society for Research in Child Development meeting, Seattle, WA, April 1991.

Connor, C. L., & Walsh, R. P. (1980). Attitudes toward the older job applicant: Just as competent, but more likely to fail. *Journal of Gerontology, 35,* 920–927.

Connor, C. L.; Walsh, R. P.; Litzelman, D. K.; & Alvarez, M. G. (1978). Evaluation of job applicants: The effects of age versus success. *Journal of Gerontology, 33,* 246–252.

Crews, D. E. (1993). Biological anthropology and human aging: Some current directions in aging research. *American Review of Anthropology, 22,* 395–423.

Crocker, J.; Thompson, L. L.; McGraw, K. M.; & Ingerman, C. (1987). Downward comparison, prejudice, and evaluations of others: Effects of self-esteem and threat. *Journal of Personality and Social Psychology, 52,* 907–916.

Crockett, W. H.; Press, A. N.; & Osterkamp, M. (1979). The effect of deviation from stereotyped expectations upon attitudes toward older persons. *Journal of Gerontology, 34,* 368–374.

Cross, S., & Markus, H. (1991). Possible selves across the life span. *Human Development, 34,* 230–255.

Csikszentmihalyi, M. (1975). *Beyond boredom and anxiety.* San Francisco, CA: Jossey-Bass.

(1985). Emergent motivation and the evolution of the self. In M. Maehr (Ed.), *Advances in motivation and achievement* (pp. 93–119). Greenwich, CT: JAI.

Curry, S. L., & Russ, S. W. (1985). Identifying coping strategies in children. *Journal of Clinical Child Psychology, 14,* 61–69.

Dannefer, D. (1987). Aging as intracohort differentiation: Accentuation, the Matthew effect, and the life course. *Sociological Forum, 2,* 211–236.

(1988). Differential gerontology and the stratified life course: Conceptual and methodological issues. *Annual Review of Gerontology and Geriatrics, 8,* 3–36.

(1989). Human action and its place in theories of aging. *Journal of Aging Studies, 3,* 1–20.

Dannefer, D., & Sell, R. R. (1988). Age structure, the life course and "aged heterogeneity": Prospects for research and theory. *Comprehensive Gerontology, 2,* 1–10.

Danner, D. B., & Schröder, H. C. (1992). Biologie des Alterns: Ontogenese und Evolution [Biology of aging: Ontogenesis and evolution]. In P. B. Baltes & J. Mittelstraß (Eds.), *Zukunft des Alterns und gesellschaftliche Entwicklung* (pp. 95–123). Berlin: de Gruyter.

Diener, E. (1984). Subjective well-being. *Psychological Bulletin, 95,* 542–575.

Diewald, M.; Huinink, J.; & Heckhausen, J. (1994). *Zusammenhang von Kontrollüberzeugungen und Kontrollstrategien ostdeutscher Erwachsener mit deren Lebensläufen und Wendeerfahrungen* [Relationship between East Germans' control beliefs and control strategies and their life courses and experiences in societal transformation]. Poster presented at the 39. Kongreß, Deutsche Gesellschaft für Psychologie, Hamburg, September 1994.

(1996). Lebensverläufe und individuelle Entwicklung im gesellschaftlichen Umbruch: Kohortenschicksale und Kontrollverhalten in Ostdeutschland nach der Wende [Life courses and individual development during societal transformation: Cohort differences and control behavior in East Germany after reunification]. *Kölner Zeitschrift für Soziologie und Sozialpsychologie, 48,* 219–248.

Diewald M., & Mayer, K. U. (Eds.). (1996). Zwischenbilanz der Wiedervereinigung [State of affairs in German reunification]. Opladen: Leske & Budrich.

Diewald, M., & Sørensen, A. (in press). Lebensform und Familienverlauf als Determinanten sozialer Ungleichheit [Family patterns and their change as determinants of social inequality]. In U. Gerhardt, S. Hradil, D. Lucke, & B. Nauck (Eds.), *Familie der Zukunft. Lebensbedingungen und Lebensformen.* Opladen: Leske & Budrich.

Dinkel, R. H. (1992). Demographische Alterung: Ein Ueberblick unter besonderer Berücksichtigung der Mortalitätsentwicklung [Demographic aging: A review with a focus on the development of mortality]. In P. B. Baltes & J. Mittelstraß (Eds.), *Zukunft des Alterns und gesellschaftliche Entwicklung* (pp. 62–93). Berlin: de Gruyter.

Dittmann-Kohli, F. (1991). Meaning and personality change from early to late adulthood. *European Journal of Gerontology, 1,* 98–103.

(1995). *Das persönliche Sinnsystem: Ein Vergleich zwischen frühem und spätem Erwachsenenalter* [The system of personal meaning: A comparison between early and late adulthood]. Göttingen: Hogrefe.

Dohrenwend, B. S., & Dohrenwend, B. P. (1974). *Stressful life events: Their nature and effects.* New York: Wiley.

Douglas, M. (1986). *How institutions think.* Syracuse, NY: Syracuse University Press.

Dowd, J. J. (1987). The reification of age: Age stratification theory and the passing of the autonomous subject. *Journal of Aging Studies, 1,* 317–335.

Drevenstedt, J. (1976). Perception of onsets of young adulthood, middle age, and old age. *Journal of Gerontology, 31,* 53–57.

Durham, W. H. (1991). *Coevolution: Genes, culture, and human diversity.* Stanford, CA: Stanford University Press.

Dweck, C. S., & Leggett, E. L. (1988). A social-cognitive approach to motivation and personality. *Psychological Review, 95,* 256–273.

Dweck, C. S., & Reppucci, N. D. (1973). Learned helplessness and reinforcement responsibility in children. *Journal of Personality and Social Psychology, 25,* 109–116.

Elder, G. H., Jr. (1974). *Children of the great depression*. Chicago: University of Chicago Press.

——— (1979). Historical change in life patterns. In P. B. Baltes & O. G. Brim, Jr. (Eds.), *Life-span development and behavior*, Vol. 2 (pp. 117–159). New York: Academic Press.

——— (1985). *Life course dynamics: Trajectories and transitions, 1968–1980*. Ithaca, NY: Cornell University Press.

——— (1986). Military times and turning points in men's lives. *Developmental Psychology, 22*, 233–245.

Elder, G. H., Jr., & Caspi, A. (1990). Studying lives in a changing society: Sociological and personological explorations. In A. Rabin, R. Zucker, R. Emmons, & S. Frank (Eds.), *Studying persons and lives* (pp. 201–247). New York: Springer.

Elder, G. H., Jr., King, V.; & Conger, R. D. (1996). Intergenerational continuity and change in rural lives: Historical and developmental insights. *International Journal for Behavioral Development, 19*, 433–455.

Elias, N. (1969). *Ueber den Prozess der Zivilisation: Soziogenetische und psychogenetische Untersuchungen* [On the process of civilization: Sociogenetic and psychogenetic investigations]. Bern: Francke Verlag.

Elster, J. (1983). *Sour grapes: Studies in the subversion of rationality*. Cambridge: Cambridge University Press.

Emmons, R. A. (1986). Personal strivings: An approach to personality and subjective well-being. *Journal of Personality and Social Psychology, 51*, 1058–1068.

——— (1989). The personal striving approach to personality. In L. A. Pervin (Ed.), *Good concepts in personality and social psychology* (pp. 87–126). Hillsdale, NJ: Erlbaum.

——— (1991). Personal strivings, daily life events, and psychological and physical well-being. *Journal of Personality, 59*, 453–472.

——— (1992a). Abstract versus concrete goals: Personal striving level, physical illness, and psychological well-being. *Journal of Personality and Social Psychology, 62*, 292–300.

——— (1992b). Striving and feeling: Personal goals and subjective well-being. In P. M. Gollwitzer & J. A. Bargh (Eds.), *The psychology of action: Linking motivation to cognition and behavior*. New York: Guilford Press.

Emmons, R. A., & Diener, E. (1986). A goal-affect analysis of everyday situational choices. *Journal of Research in Personality, 20*, 309–326.

Emmons, R. A., & King, L. A. (1988). Conflict among personal strivings: Immediate and long-term implications for psychological and physical well-being. *Journal of Personality and Social Psychology, 54*, 1040–1048.

Ericsson, K. A. (1990). Peak performance and age: An examination of peak performance in sports. In P. B. Baltes & M. M. Baltes (Eds.), *Successful aging: Perspectives from the behavioral sciences*. (pp. 164–196). New York: Cambridge University Press.

Ericsson, K. A.; Krampe, R. T.; & Tesch-Römer, C. (1993). The role of deliberate practice in the acquisition of expert performance. *Psychological Review, 100*, 363–406.

Erikson, E. H. (1959). *Identity and the life cycle. Psychological Issues Monograph 1*. New York: International University Press.

——— (1963). *Childhood and society* (2d ed.). New York: Norton.

Essau, C. (1992). *Primary-secondary control and coping. A cross-cultural comparison*. Regensburg: Roderer.

Essau, C., & Trommsdorff, G. (1993). Kontrollorientierung von Jugendlichen im Kulturvergleich [A cross-cultural perspective of control orientation in adolescents]. *Zeitschrift für Sozialisationsforschung und Erziehungssoziologie, 13,* 311–325.

Esser, H. (1993). *Soziologie.* Frankfurt: Campus Verlag.

Fallo-Mitchell, L., & Ryff, C. D. (1982). Preferred timing of female life events. *Research on Aging, 4,* 249–267.

Featherman, D. L. (1983). The life-span perspective in social science research. In P. B. Baltes & O. G. Brim, Jr. (Eds.), *Life-span development and behavior,* Vol. 5 (pp. 1–59). New York: Academic Press.

Featherman, D. L., & Lerner, R. M. (1985). Ontogenesis and sociogenesis: Problematics for theory and research about development and socialization across the life span. *American Sociological Review, 50,* 659–679.

Festinger, L. (1954). A theory of social comparison processes. *Human Relations, 7,* 117–140.

Filipp, S.-H. (1987). Das mittlere und höhere Erwachsenenalter [Middle adulthood and old age]. In R. Oerter & L. Montada (Eds.), *Entwicklungspsychologie. Ein Lehrbuch* (pp. 375–410). Munich: Psychologie Verlags Union.

Filipp, S.-H. (Ed.). (1981). *Kritische Lebensereignisse* [Critical life events]. Munich: Urban & Schwarzenberg.

Filipp, S.-H., & Buch-Bartos, K. (1994). Vergleichsprozesse und Lebenszufriedenheit im Alter: Ergebnisse einer Pilotstudie [Comparison processes and life satisfaction with age: Results of a pilot study]. *Zeitschrift für Entwicklungspsychologie und Pädagogische Psychologie, 26,* 22–34.

Filipp, S.-H., & Ferring, D. (1989). Zur alters- und Bereichsspezifität subjektiven Alterserlebens [The relationship between objective and subjective age and the domain specifity of subjective age]. *Zeitschrift für Entwicklungspsychologie und Pädagogische Psychologie, 21,* 279–293.

Filipp, S.-H., & Gräser, H. (1982). Psychologische Prävention im Umfeld kritischer Lebensereignisse [Psychological prevention in the context of critical life events]. In J. Brandtstädter & A. von Eye (Eds.), *Psychologische Prävention. Grundlagen, Programme, Methoden* (pp. 155–196). Bern: Huber.

Filipp, S.-H.; Klauer, T.; Freudenberg, E.; & Ferring, D. (1990). The regulation of subjective well-being in cancer patients: An analysis of coping effectiveness. *Psychology and Health, 4,* 305–317.

Filipp, S.-H., & Olbrich, E. (1986). Human development across the life span: Overview and highlights of the psychological perspective. In A. B. Sørensen, F. E. Weinert, & L. R. Sherrod (Eds.). *Human development and the life course: Multidisciplinary perspectives* (pp. 343–375). Hillsdale, NJ: Erlbaum.

Finch, C. E. (1986). Issues in the analysis of interrelationships between the individual and the environment during aging. In A. B. Sørensen, F. E. Weinert, & L. R. Sherrod (Eds.), *Human development and the life course: Multidisciplinary perspectives* (pp. 17–29). Hillsdale, NJ: Erlbaum.

——— (1990). *Longevity, senescence, and the genome.* Chicago, IL: University of Chicago Press.

Fisseni, H. J. (1985). Perceived unchangeability of life and some biographical correlates. In J. M. A. Munnichs, E. Olbrich, P. Mussen, & P. Coleman (Eds.), *Life span and change in a gerontological perspective* (pp. 103–131). Orlando, FL: Academic Press.

Flammer, A. (1988). *Entwicklungstheorien: Psychologische Theorien der menschlichen*

Entwicklung [Developmental theories: Psychological theories on human development]. Bern: Huber.

(1990). *Erfahrung der eigenen Wirksamkeit: Einführung in die Psychologie der Kontrollmeinung* [Experiencing one's own efficacy: Introduction to the psychology of control beliefs]. Bern: Huber.

Flammer, A.; Züblin, C.; & Grob, A. (1988). Sekundäre Kontrolle bei Jugendlichen [Secondary control in adolescents]. *Zeitschrift für Entwicklungspsychologie und Pädagogische Psychologie, 20*, 239–262.

Fodor, J. A. (1987). *The modularity of mind.* Cambridge, MA: MIT Press.

Folkman, S.; Lazarus, R. S.; Dunkel-Schetter, C.; DeLongis, A.; & Gruen, R. (1986). The dynamics of stressful encounter: Cognitive appraisal, coping, and encounter outcomes. *Journal of Personality and Social Psychology, 50*, 992–1003.

Folkman, S.; Lazarus, R. S.; Pimley, S.; & Novacek, J. (1987). Age differences in stress and coping processes. *Psychology and Aging, 2*, 171–184.

Ford, D. H., & Lerner, R. M. (1992). *Developmental systems theory: An integrative approach.* London: Sage.

Fredrickson, B. L., & Carstensen, L. L. (1990). Choosing social partners: How old age and anticipated endings make us more selective. *Psychology and Aging, 5*, 335–347.

Fries, J. F. (1980). Aging, natural death, and the compression of morbidity. *New England Journal of Medicine, 303*, 130–135.

Frieze, I. H. (1984). Causal attributions for the performances of the elderly: Comments from an attributional theorist. *Basic and Applied Social Psychology, 5*, 127–130.

Frijda, N. H. (1988). The laws of emotion. *American Psychologist, 43*, 349–358.

Fry, C. L. (1976). The ages of adulthood: A question of numbers. *Journal of Gerontology, 31*, 170–177.

(1980). Cultural dimensions of age: A multidimensional scaling analysis. In C. L. Fry (Ed.), *Aging in culture and society: Comparative viewpoints and strategies* (pp. 43–64). New York: Praeger.

Gehlen, A. (1958). *Der Mensch. Seine Natur und seine Stellung in der Welt* [The human being: His nature and status in the world]. Bonn: Athenäum.

Geppert, U., & Heckhausen, H. (1990). Ontogenese der Emotion [Ontogenesis of emotion]. In K. R. Scherer (Ed.), *Enzyklopädie der Psychologie, Vol. C/IV/3, Psychologie der Emotionen* (pp. 115–213). Göttingen: Hogrefe.

Geppert, U., & Küster, U. (1983). The emergence of 'Wanting to do it oneself': A precursor of achievement motivation. *International Journal of Behavioral Development, 3*, 355–369.

Geulen, D. (1981). Zur Konzeptionalisierung sozialisationstheoretischer Entwicklungsmodelle [Conceptualizing developmental models in socialization theory]. In J. Matthes (Ed.), *Lebenswelt und soziale Probleme. Verhandlungen des 20. Deutschen Soziologentages* (pp. 537–556). Frankfurt am Main: Campus.

Glenn, N. D. (1976). Cohort analysts' futile quest: Statistical attempts to separate age, period and cohort effects. *American Sociological Review, 41*, 900–904.

Goldberg, L. R. (1973). *Normative data on 1710 trait adjectives.* Unpublished manuscript, Oregon Research Institute.

Golde, P., & Kogan, N. (1959). A sentence completion procedure for assessing attitudes toward old people. *Journal of Gerontology, 14*, 355–363.

Gollwitzer, P. M. (1986). The implementation of identity intentions: A motivational-volitional perspective on symbolic self-completion. In F. Halisch & J. Kuhl (Eds.), *Motivation, intention, and volition* (pp. 349–369). Heidelberg: Springer.

(1987). Suchen, Finden und Festigen der eigenen Identität: Unstillbare Zielintentionen [Searching, finding, and consolidating of one's own identity: Unsaturatable goal intentions]. In H. Heckhausen, P. M. Gollwitzer, & F. E. Weinert (Eds.), *Jenseits des Rubikon: Der Wille in den Humanwissenschaften* (pp. 176–189). Berlin: Springer.

(1990). Action phases and mind-sets. In E. T. Higgins & R. M. Sorrentino (Eds.), *Handbook of motivation and cognition: Foundations of social behavior,* Vol. 2 (pp. 53–92). New York: Guilford Press.

(1993). Goal achievement: The role of intentions. *European Review of Social Psychology, 4,* 141–185.

Gollwitzer, P. M.; Heckhausen, H.; & Ratajczak, H. (1990). From weighing to willing: Approaching a change decision through pre- and post-decisional mentations. *Organizational Behavior and Human Decision Process, 45,* 41–65.

Gollwitzer, P. M.; Heckhausen, H.; & Steller, B. (1990). Deliberative and implemental mind-sets: Cognitive tuning toward congruous thoughts and information. *Journal of Personality and Social Psychology, 59,* 1119–1127.

Gollwitzer, P. M., & Kinney, R. F. (1989). Defects of deliberative and implemental mind-sets on illusion of control. *Journal of Personality and Social Psychology, 56,* 531–542.

Gollwitzer, P. M.; Stephenson, B.; & Wicklund, R. A. (1982). *Self-symbolizing and self-reflection.* Unpublished manuscript, University of Texas at Austin.

Gollwitzer, P. M., & Wicklund, R. A. (1985). The pursuit of self-defining goals. In J. Kuhl & J. Beckmann (Eds.), *Action control: From cognition to behavior* (pp. 61–85). Berlin: Springer.

Gottlieb, G. (1991). Experiential canalization of behavioral development: Theory. *Developmental Psychology, 27,* 4–13.

Gould, S. J. (1977). *Ontogeny and Phylogeny.* Cambridge, MA: Belknap Press of Harvard University Press.

Gould, S. J., & Lewontin, R. C. (1979). The spandrels of San Marco and the Panglossian paradigm: A critique of the adaptionist programme. *Proceedings of the Royal Society of London, B 205,* 581–598.

Gould, S. J., & Vrba, E. S. (1982). Exaptation – a missing term in the science of form. *Paleobiology, 8,* 4–15.

Green, S. K. (1979). *Stereotyping, behavioral expectancies, and age as a causal variable.* Paper presented at the American Psychological Association Convention, New York, 1979.

(1981). Attitudes and perceptions about the elderly: Current and future perspectives. *Journal of Aging and Human Development, 13,* 99–119.

(1984). Senility versus wisdom: The meaning of old age as a cause for behavior. *Basic and Applied Social Psychology, 5,* 105–110.

Greve, W. (1990). Stabilisierung und Modifikation des Selbstkonzeptes im Erwachsenenalter: Strategien der Immunisierung [Stabilization and modification of the self concept in adulthood: Strategies of immunization]. *Sprache und Kognition, 4,* 218–230.

Groffmann, K. I. (1970). Life-span developmental psychology in Europe. In

L. R. Goulet & P. B. Baltes (Eds.), *Life-span developmental psychology: Research and theory* (pp. 54–68). New York: Academic Press.

Grover, D. R., & Hertzog, C. (1991). Relationships between intellectual control beliefs and psychometric intelligence in adulthood. *Journal of Gerontology, 46,* 109–115.

Hagestad, G. O. (1990). Social perspectives on the life course. In R. Binstock & L. George (Eds.), *Handbook of aging and the social sciences,* 3d ed (pp. 151–168). New York: Academic Press.

Hagestad, G. O., & Neugarten, B. L. (1985). Age and the life course. In R. H. Binstock & E. Shanas (Eds.), *Handbook of aging and the social sciences* (pp. 35–61). New York: Van Nostrand Reinhold.

Hakmiller, K. L. (1966). Threat as a determinant of downward comparison. *Journal of Experimental Social Psychology, 2,* 32–39.

Harris, L., & Associates (1975). *The myth and reality of aging in America.* Washington, DC: National Council on the Aging.

(1981). *Aging in the eighties: America in transition.* Washington, DC: National Council on the Aging.

Harter, S. (1974). Pleasure derived from cognitive challenge and mastery. *Child Development, 45,* 661–669.

Havighurst, R. J. (1952). *Developmental tasks and education.* New York: McKay.

(1953). *Human development and education.* London: Longmans.

(1973). History of developmental psychology: Socialization and personality development through the life span. In P. B. Baltes & Schaie, K. W. (Eds.), *Life-span developmental psychology: Personality and socialization* (pp. 3–24). New York: Academic Press.

Hebb, D. O. (1955). Drives and the C.N.S. (conceptual nervous system). *Psychological Review, 53,* 243–254.

Heckhausen, H. (1965). Leistungsmotivation [Achievement motivation]. In H. Thomae (Ed.), *Handbuch der Psychologie,* Vol. 2 (pp. 602–702). Göttingen: Hogrefe.

(1974). *Motivationsanalysen* [Analyses of motivation]. Berlin: Springer.

(1980). *Motivation und Handeln* [Motivation and action]. Berlin: Springer.

(1982). The development of achievement motivation. In W. W. Hartup (Ed.), *Review of child development research,* Vol. 6 (pp. 600–668). Chicago: University of Chicago Press.

(1984). Emergent achievement behavior: Some early developments. In J. Nicholls (Ed.), *The development of achievement motivation,* Vol. 3 (pp. 1–32). Greenwich, CT: JAI Press.

(1987a). Causal attribution patterns for achievement outcomes: Individual differences, possible types, and their origins. In F. E. Weinert & R. H. Kluwe (Eds.), *Metacognition, motivation, and understanding* (pp. 143–184). Hillsdale, NJ: Erlbaum.

(1987b). *Bruchstücke für eine vorläufige Intentions- und Volitionstheorie* [Fragments towards a preliminary theory of intention and volition]. Unpublished manuscript, Max-Planck-Institut für psychologische Forschung, Munich.

(1987c). Wünschen, Wählen, Wollen [Fragments towards a preliminary theory of intention and volition]. In H. Heckhausen & P. M. Gollwitzer (Eds.), *Jenseits des Rubikon: Der Wille in den Humanwissenschaften* (pp. 3–9). Berlin: Springer.

214   *References*

(1989). *Motivation und Handeln* [Motivation and action] (2nd ed.). Berlin: Springer.

(1991). *Motivation and action.* New York: Springer.

Heckhausen, H., & Gollwitzer, P. M. (1986). Information processing before and after the formation of an intent. In F. Klix & H. Hagendorf (Eds.), *In memoriam Hermann Ebbinghaus: Symposium on the structure and function of human memory* (pp. 1071–1082). Amsterdam: Elsevier.

(1987). Thought contents and cognitive functioning in motivational and volitional states of mind. *Motivation and Emotion, 11,* 101–120.

Heckhausen, H., & Kuhl, J. (1985). From wishes to action: The dead ends and short cuts on the long way to action. In M. Frese & J. Sabini (Eds.), *Goal-directed behavior: The concept of action in psychology* (pp. 134–159). Hillsdale, NJ: Erlbaum.

Heckhausen, J. (1988). Becoming aware of one's competence in the second year: Developmental progression within the mother–child dyad. *International Journal of Behavioral Development, 11,* 305–326.

(1989). Normatives Entwicklungswissen als Bezugsrahmen zur (Re)Konstruktion der eigenen Biographie [Normative conceptions about development as a frame of reference for (re)constructing one's own biography]. In P. Alheit & E. Hoerning (Eds.), *Biographisches Wissen: Beiträge zu einer Theorie lebensgeschichtlicher Erfahrung* (pp. 202–282). Frankfurt: Campus.

(1990a). Erwerb und Funktion normativer Vorstellungen über den Lebenslauf: Ein entwicklungspsychologischer Beitrag zur sozio-psychischen Konstruktion von Biographien [Acquisition and function of normative conceptions about the life course: A developmental psychology approach to the socio-psychological construction of biographies]. *Kölner Zeitschrift für Soziologie und Sozialpsychologie, 31,* 351–373.

(1990b). Entwicklung im Erwachsenenalter aus der Sicht junger, mittelalter und alter Erwachsener [Development in adulthood as perceived by young, middle-aged, and old adults]. *Zeitschrift für Entwicklungspsychologie und Pädagogische Psychologie, 22,* 1–21.

(1991a). Adults' expectancies about development and its controllability: Enhancing self-efficacy by social comparison. In R. Schwarzer (Ed.), *Self-efficacy: Thought control of action* (pp. 107–126). Washington, DC: Hemisphere.

(1991b). *CAMAQ, Control Agency Means-ends in Adulthood Questionnaire.* Berlin: Max Planck Institute for Human Development and Education.

(1993). The development of mastery and its perception within caretaker–child dyads. In D. Messer (Ed.), *Mastery motivation in early childhood: Development, measurement and social processes* (pp. 55–79). New York: Routledge.

(1994a). Entwicklungsziele und Kontrollüberzeugungen Ost- und Westberliner Erwachsener [Developmental goals and control beliefs in East and West Berlin adults]. In G. Trommsdorff (Ed.), *Psychologische Aspekte des soziopolitischen Wandels in Ostdeutschland* (pp. 124–133). Berlin: DeGruyter.

(1994b). Life-span development. In T. Husen & T. N. Postlethwaite (Eds.), *The international encyclopedia of education,* 2nd. ed., Vol. 6 (pp. 3425–3428). Oxford: Pergamon.

(1996). Being on-time or off-time: Developmental deadlines for regulating one's own development. Paper presented at the International Conference "Mind and Time," Neuchâtel, Switzerland, September 1996.

(1997). Developmental regulation in East and West Berliners: Primary and secondary control of aging-related and socio-historical challenges. *Developmental Psychology, 33,* 176–187.

Heckhausen, J., & Baltes, P. B. (1991). Perceived controllability of expected psychological change across adulthood and old age. *Journal of Gerontology: Psychological Sciences, 46,* 165–173.

Heckhausen, J., & Brim, O. G., Jr. (1997). Perceived problems for self and other: Self-protection by social downgrading throughout adulthood. *Psychology and Aging, 12,* 125–136.

Heckhausen, J.; Diewald, M.; & Huinink, J. (1994a). *Kontrollstrategien, Entwicklungsziele und Selbstwert ostdeutscher Erwachsener* [Control strategies, developmental goals, and self-esteem in East German adults]. Paper presented at the 39. Kongreß, Deutsche Gesellschaft für Psychologie, Hamburg, September 1994.

(1994b). *Control agency means–ends in adulthood questionnaire – short version.* Unpublished questionnaire, Max Planck Institute for Human Development, Berlin.

(1996). *East German cohort differences in developmental regulation: Maintaining and losing control under radical socio-historical change.* Unpublished manuscript, Max Planck Institute for Human Development, Berlin.

Heckhausen, J.; Dixon, R. A.; & Baltes, P. B. (1989). Gains and losses in development throughout adulthood as perceived by different adult age groups. *Developmental Psychology, 25,* 109–121.

Heckhausen, J., & Fleeson, W. (1993). *Primary-secondary control shifts in developmental regulation around age deadlines for developmental tasks: Actional and postactional functioning with impending versus passed action opportunities.* Unpublished manuscript, Max Planck Institute for Human Development, Berlin.

Heckhausen, J., & Hosenfeld, B. (1988). *Lebensspannenentwicklung von normativen Vorstellungen über Lebensspannenentwicklung* [Life-span development of normative conceptions about life-span development]. Paper presented at the 36. Kongreß, Deutsche Gesellschaft für Psychologie, Berlin, October 1988.

Heckhausen, J., & Hundertmark, J. (1995). *Action-related beliefs in adulthood: Measurement of perceived agency, means-ends relations, and personal control in three adult life domains.* Unpublished manuscript, Max Planck Institute for Human Development, Berlin.

Heckhausen, J., & Krueger, J. (1993). Developmental expectations for the self and most other people: Age grading in three functions of social comparison. *Developmental Psychology, 29,* 539–548.

Heckhausen, J., & Lang, F. R. (1996). Social construction in old age: Normative conceptions and interpersonal processes. In G. R. Semin & K. Fiedler (Eds.), *Applied social psychology* (pp. 374–398). London: Sage.

Heckhausen, J., & Mayr, U. (1998). Entwicklung im Erwachsenenalter: Entwicklungsregulation durch primäre und sekundäre Kontrolle [Development in adulthood: Developmental regulation via primary and secondary control]. In H. Keller (Ed.), *Lehrbuch für Entwicklungspsychologie.* Bern: Huber.

Heckhausen, J., & Schulz, R. (1993a). Optimisation by selection and compensation: Balancing primary and secondary control in life-span development. *International Journal of Behavioral Development, 16,* 287–303.

(1993b). *An Analysis of "Good" Stress and Coping in Adulthood.* 60th Meeting of the Society for Research in Child Development, New Orleans.

(1994). *Primacy of primary control as a universal feature of human behavior.* Paper presented at the 13th Biennial Meetings of the International Society for the Study of Behavioral Development, Amsterdam, June–July 1994.

(1995). A life-span theory of control. *Psychological Review, 102,* 284–304.

(1998). Developmental regulation in adulthood: Selection and compensation via primary and secondary control. In J. Heckhausen & C. S. Dweck (Eds.), *Life-span perspectives on motivation and control* (pp. 50–77). New York: Cambridge University Press.

Heckhausen, J.; Schulz, R.; & Wrosch, C. (1998). *Developmental regulation in adulthood: Optimization in primary and secondary control.* Manuscript submitted for publication, Max Planck Institute for Human Development, Berlin.

Heckhausen, J., & Wrosch, C. (1998). *Social comparison as a strategy of developmental regulation in adulthood.* Manuscript in preparation, Max Planck Institute for Human Development Berlin.

Held, T. (1986). Institutionalization and deinstitutionalization of the life course. *Human Development, 29,* 157–162.

Helmchen, H.; Baltes, M. M.; Geiselmann, B.; Kanowski, S.; Linden, M.; Reischies, F.; & Wilms, H.-U. (1996). Psychische Erkrankungen im Alter. In K. U. Mayer & P. B. Baltes (Eds.), *Die Berliner Altersstudie,* (pp. 185–219).

Helson, H. (1948). Adaptation level as a basis for a quantitative theory of frames of reference. *Psychological Review, 55,* 297–313.

Henretta, J. C., & Campbell, R. T. (1976). Status attainment and status maintenance: A study of stratification in old age. *American Sociological Review, 41,* 981–992.

Herzog, A. R.; House, J. S.; & Morgan, J. N. (1991). Relation of work and retirement to health and well-being in older age. *Psychology and Aging, 6,* 202–211.

Hogan, D. (1981). *Transitions and the life course.* New York: Academic Press.

Holahan, C. J., & Moos, R. H. (1987). Personal and contextual determinants of coping strategies. *Journal of Personality and Social Psychology, 52,* 946–955.

Hollingworth, H. L. (1927). *Mental growth and decline: A survey of developmental psychology.* New York: Appleton.

Hosenfeld, B. (1988). *Persönlichkeitsveränderungen im Erwachsenenalter aus der Sicht Jugendlicher* [Personality change in adulthood as perceived by adolescents]. Unpublished master's thesis, Institut für Psychologie, Freie Universität Berlin.

Huinink, J. (1993). *Warum noch Familie? Zur Attraktivität von Partnerschaft und Elternschaft in unserer Gesellschaft* [Why family today? On the attractiveness of partnership and parenthood in our society]. Habilitation thesis, Fachbereich Philosophie und Sozialwissenschaften I, Freie Universität Berlin.

Huinink, J.; Diewald, M.; & Heckhausen, J. (1996). Veränderungen im Erwerbsverlauf nach 1989 und ihr Zusammenhang mit Kontrollüberzeugungen und Kontrollstrategien [Changes in employment patterns after 1989 and their relation to control beliefs and control strategies]. In M. Diewald & K. U. Mayer (Eds.), *Zwischenbilanz der Wiedervereinigung: Mobilität im Transformationsprozeß* (pp. 251–267). Leverkusen: Leske & Budrich.

Hultsch, D. F., & Plemons, J. K. (1979). Life events and life-span development. In P. B. Baltes & O. G. Brim, Jr. (Eds.), *Life-span development and behavior,* Vol. 2 (pp. 1–37). New York: Academic Press.

Hummert, M. L. (1990). Multiple stereotypes of elderly and young adults: A comparison of structure and evaluation. *Psychology and Aging, 5*, 182–193.

——— (1993). Age and typicality judgments of stereotypes of the elderly: Perceptions of elderly vs. young adults. *International Journal of Aging and Human Development, 37*, 217–226.

Hummert, M. L.; Garstka, T. A.; Shaner, J. L.; & Strahm, S. (1994). Stereotypes of the elderly held by young, middle-aged, and old adults. *Journal of Gerontology: Psychological Sciences, 49*, 240–249.

Hundertmark, J. (1990). Entwicklungsbezogene Intentionen im Lebenslauf: Selbstbild und normative Entwicklungsvorstellungen als Einflußfaktoren [Development-related intentions across the life span: The role of self-related and age-normative conceptions]. Unpublished master's thesis, Fachbereich II, Gesellschafts-und Planungswissenschaften, Technische Universität Berlin.

——— (1995). *Primäre und Sekundäre Kontrollstrategien zur Entwicklungsregulation im Erwachsenenalter* [Primary and secondary control strategies in developmental regulation throughout adulthood]. Manuscript in preparation, Max Planck Institute for Human Development and Education, Berlin.

Hundertmark, J., & Heckhausen, J. (1994). Entwicklungsziele junger, mittelalter und alter Erwachsener [Developmental goals of young, middle-aged, and old adults]. *Zeitschrift für Entwicklungspsychologie und Pädagogische Psychologie, 26*, 197–217.

Janos, O., & Papousek, H. (1977). Acquisition of appetition and palpebral conditioned reflexes by the same infants. *Early Human Development, 1*, 91–97.

Jencks, C. (1992). *Rethinking social policy: Race, poverty, and the underclass.* Cambridge, MA: Harvard University Press.

Kastenbaum, R.; Derbin, V.; Sabatini, P.; & Artt, S. (1981). "The ages of me": Toward personal and interpersonal definitions of functional aging. In R. Kastenbaum (Ed.), *Old age and the new scene* (pp. 48–67). New York: Springer.

Keller, M. L.; Leventhal, H.; & Prohaska, T. R. (1989). Beliefs about aging and illness in a community sample. *Research in Nursing and Health, 12*, 247–255.

Kelley, H. H. (1967). Attribution theory in social psychology. In D. Levine (Ed.), *Nebraska symposium on motivation* (pp. 192–238). Lincoln: University of Nebraska Press.

Kennedy, G. J.; Kelman, J. R.; & Thomas, C. (1990). The emergence of depressive symptoms in late life: The importance of declining health and increasing disability. *Journal of Community Health, 15*, 93–104.

Kliegl, R., & Baltes, P. B. (1987). Theory-guided analysis of mechanisms of development and aging through testing-the-limits and research on expertise. In C. Schooler & K. W. Schaie (Eds.), *Cognitive functioning and social structure over the life course* (pp. 95–119). Norwood, NJ: Ablex.

Kliegl, R.; Smith, J.; & Baltes, P. B. (1990). On the locus and process of magnification of age differences during mnemonic training. *Developmental Psychology, 26*, 894–904.

Klinger, E. (1975). Consequences of commitment and disengagement from incentives. *Psychological Review, 82*, 1–25.

——— (1977). *Meaning and void. Inner experience and the incentives in people's lives.* Minneapolis: University of Minnesota Press.

Klinger, E.; Barta, S. G.; & Maxeiner, M. E. (1980). Motivational correlates of thought content frequency and commitment. *Journal of Personality and Social Psychology, 39,* 1222–1237.

Koenig, H. G.; George, L. K.; & Siegler, I. C. (1988). The use of religion and other emotion-regulating coping strategies among older adults. *The Gerontologist, 28,* 303–310.

Kogan, N. (1961). Attitudes toward old people: The development of a scale and an examination of correlates. *Journal of Abnormal Psychology, 62,* 44–54.

———. (1975). Judgments of chronological age: Adult age and sex differences. *Developmental Psychology, 11,* 107.

———. (1979). A study of age categorization. *Journal of Gerontology, 34,* 358–367.

Kogan, N., & Shelton, F. C. (1962). Images of "old people" and "people in general" in an older sample. *The Journal of Genetic Psychology, 100,* 3–21.

Kohli, M. (1981). Zur Theorie der biographischen Selbst-und Fremdthematisierung [Theory of biographical accounts of the self and others]. In J. Matthes (Ed.), *Lebenswelt und soziale Probleme: Verhandlungen des 20. Deutschen Soziologentages* (pp. 502–520). Frankfurt am Main: Campus.

Kohli, M., & Meyer, J. W. (1986). Social structure and social construction of life stages. *Human Development, 29,* 145–180.

Kohn, M. L., & Schooler, C. (1982). Job conditions and personality: A longitudinal assessment of their reciprocal effects. *American Journal of Sociology, 87,* 1257–1286.

Krampen, G. (1987). Entwicklung von Kontrollüberzeugungen: Thesen zu Forschungsstand und Perspektiven [Development of control beliefs: Propositions about state of the art and research perspectives]. *Zeitschrift für Entwicklungspsychologie und Pädagogische Psychologie, 19,* 195–227.

———. (1989). *Diagnostic von Attributionen und Kontrollüberzeugungen* [Measurement of attributions and control beliefs]. Göttingen: Hogrefe.

Krause, N., & Baker, E. (1992). Financial strain, economic values, and somatic symptoms in later life. *Psychology and Aging, 7,* 4–14.

Krause, N.; Jay, G.; & Liang, J. (1991). Financial strain and psychological well-being among the American and Japanese elderly. *Psychology and Aging, 8,* 170–181.

Krueger, J., & Heckhausen, J. (1993). Personality development across the adult life span: Subjective conceptions versus cross-sectional contrasts. *Journal of Gerontology: Psychological Sciences, 48,* 100–108.

Krueger, J.; Heckhausen, J.; & Hundertmark, J. (1995). Perceiving middle-aged adults: Effects of stereotype-congruent and incongruent information. *Journal of Gerontology: Psychological Sciences, 50B,* 82–93.

Kruse, A., & Lehr, U. (1989). Longitudinal analysis of the developmental process in chronically ill and healthy elderly persons. *International Psychogeriatrics, 1,* 73–85.

Kühl, K.-P., & Baltes, M. M. (1989). Dementielle Erkrankung im Alter: Früherkennung mit Hilfe des "Testing-the-Limits"-Ansatzes [Senile dementia of the Alzheimer type: Early diagnosis by testing-the-limits]. In M. M. Baltes, M. Kohli, & K. Sames (Eds.), *Erfolgreiches Altern. Bedingungen und Variationen* (pp. 289–293). Bern: Huber.

Kuhl, J. (1983). *Motivation, Konflikt und Handlungskontrolle* [Motivation, conflict, and action control]. Berlin: Springer.

(1984). Motivational aspects of achievement motivation and learned helplessness: Toward a comprehensive theory of action control. In B. A. Maher & W. B. Maher (Eds.), *Progress in experimental personality research,* Vol. 13 (pp. 99–171). New York: Academic Press.

Lachman, M. E. (1986a). Locus of control in aging research: A case for multidimensional and domain-specific assessment. *Psychology and Aging, 1,* 34–40.

(1986b). Personal control in later life: Stability, change and cognitive correlates. In M. M. Baltes & P. B. Baltes (Eds.), *The psychology of control and aging* (pp. 207–236). Hillsdale, NJ: Erlbaum.

(1991). Perceived control over memory aging: Developmental and intervention perspectives. *Journal of Social Issues, 47,* 159–175.

Lachman, M. E., & Leff, R. (1989). Perceived control and intellectual functioning in the elderly: A 5-year longitudinal study. *Developmental Psychology, 25,* 722–728.

Lakatta, E. G. (1990). Heart and circulation. In E. L. Schneider & J. W. Rowe (Eds.), *Handbook of the biology of aging,* 3d ed. (pp. 181–216). New York: Academic Press.

Lang, F. R., & Carstensen, L. L. (1994). Close emotional relationships in late life: Further support for proactive aging in the social domain. *Psychology and Aging, 9,* 315–324.

Lang, F. R.; Görlitz, D.; & Seiwert, M. (1992). Altersposition und Beurteilungsperspektive als Faktoren laienpsychologischer Urteile über Entwicklung [Age status and evaluative perspective as determinants of lay psychological perceptions of development]. *Zeitschrift für Entwicklungspsychologie und Pädagogische Psychologie, 14,* 298–316.

Lang, F. R.; Marsiske, M.; Baltes, M. M.; & Baltes, P. B. (1994). *Selective optimization with compensation: Different facets of control.* Paper presented at the 13th Biennial Meetings of the International Society for the Study of Behavioral Development, Amsterdam, June–July 1994.

Lang, F. R.; Staudinger, U. M.; & Carstensen, L. L. (1995). *Socioemotional selectivity in late life: How personality does (and does not) make a difference.* Manuscript submitted for publication.

Langer, E. J., & Rodin, J. (1976). The effects of choice and enhanced personal responsibility for the aged: A field experiment in an institutional setting. *Journal of Personality and Social Psychology, 34,* 191–198.

Lehman, H. C. (1953). *Age and achievement.* Princeton, NJ: Princeton University Press.

Lehr, U. (1982). Social-psychological correlates of longevity. *Annual Review of Gerontology and Geriatrics, 3,* 102–147.

(1984). *Psychologie des Alterns* [Psychology of aging] (5th ed.). Heidelberg: Quelle & Meyer.

Lehr, U., & Thomae, H. (1987). *Formen seelischen Alterns. Ergebnisse der Bonner Gerontologischen Längsschnittstudie (BOLSA)* [Forms of psychological aging. Results of the Bonn longitudinal study of aging]. Stuttgart: Enke.

Lerner, R. M. (1984). *On the nature of human plasticity.* New York: Cambridge University Press.

(1989). Developmental contextualism and the life-span view of person–context interaction. In M. Bornstein & J. S. Bruner (Eds.), *Interaction in human development* (pp. 217–239). Hillsdale, NJ: Erlbaum.

Lerner, R. M., & Busch-Rossnagel, N. A. (Eds.). (1981). *Individuals as producers of their development: A life-span perspective.* New York: Academic Press.

Lerner, R. M., & Kauffman, M. B. (1985). The concept of development in contextualism. *Developmental Review, 5,* 309–333.

Lewin, K.; Dembo, T.; Festinger, L.; & Sears, P. S. (1944). Level of aspiration. In J. McHunt (Ed.), *Personality and the behavior disorders,* Vol. 1 (pp. 333–378). New York: Ronald Press.

Lewinsohn, P. M.; Mischel, W.; Chaplin, W.; & Barton, R. (1980). Social competence and depression: The role of illusory self-perceptions. *Journal of Abnormal Psychology, 89,* 203–212.

Little, B. R. (1983). Personal projects. A rationale and method for investigation. *Environment and Behavior, 15,* 273–309.

 (1989). Personal projects analysis: Trivial pursuits, magnificent obsessions, and the search for coherence. In D. M. Buss & N. Cantor (Eds.), *Personality psychology: Recent trends and emerging directions* (pp. 15–31). New York: Springer.

Lowenthal, M. F.; Thurnher, M.; & Chiriboga, D. (1977). *Four stages of life; A comparative study of women and men facing transition* (3d ed.). San Francisco, CA: Jossey-Bass.

Lutsky, N. S. (1980). Attitudes toward old age and elderly persons. In C. Eisdorfer (Ed.), *Annual Review of Gerontology and Geriatrics,* Vol. 1 (pp. 287–336). New York: Springer.

Maddox, G. L., & Douglas, E. (1974). Aging and individual differences: A longitudinal analysis of social, psychological, and physiological indicators. *Journal of Gerontology, 29,* 555–563.

Major, B.; Testa, M.; & Bylsma, W. H. (1991). Responses to upward and downward social comparisons: The impact of esteem-relevance and perceived control. In J. Suls & T. A. Wills (Eds.), *Social comparisons: Contemporary theory and research* (pp. 237–259). Hillsdale, NJ: Erlbaum.

Marini, M. M. (1984). Age and sequencing norms in the transition to adulthood. *Social Forces, 63,* 229–244.

Markus, H., & Nurius, P. (1986). Possible selves. *American Psychologist, 41,* 954–969.

Markus, H., & Wurf, E. (1987). The dynamic self-concept: A social psychological perspective. *Annual Review of Psychology, 38,* 299–337.

Marsh, H. W.; Balla, J. R.; & McDonald, R. P. (1988). Goodness-of-fit indexes in confirmatory factor analysis: The effect of sample size. *Psychological Bulletin, 103,* 391–410.

Marsiske, M.; Lang, F. R.; Baltes, P. B.; & Baltes, M. M. (1995). Selective optimization with compensation: Life-span perspectives on successful human development. In R. A. Dixon & L. Bäckman (Eds.), *Compensating for psychological deficits and declines: Managing losses and promoting gains* (pp. 35–79). Mahwah, NJ: Erlbaum.

Mayer, K. U. (1986). Structural constraints on the life course. *Human Development, 29,* 163–170.

 (1987). Lebenslaufforschung [Life course research]. In W. Voges (Ed.), *Methoden der Biographie-und Lebenslaufforschung* (pp. 51–73). Opladen: Leske & Budrich.

Mayer, K. U.; Allmendinger, J.; & Huinink, J. (1991). *Vom Regen in die Traufe: Frauen zwischen Beruf und Familie* [Out of the frying pan into the fire: Women between occupation and family]. Frankfurt: Campus.

Mayer, K. U., & Carroll, G. R. (1987). Jobs and classes: Structural constraints on career mobility. *European Sociological Review, 3,* 14–38.

Mayer, K. U., & Huinink, J. (1990). Age, period, and cohort in the study of the life course: A comparison of classical A-P-C-analysis with event history analysis or Farewell to Lexis? In D. Magnusson & L. R. Bergman (Eds.), *Data quality in longitudinal research* (pp. 211–232). Cambridge: Cambridge University Press.

Mayer, K. U., & Müller. W. (1986). The state and the structure of the life course. In A. B. Sørensen, F. E. Weinert, & L. R. Sherrod (Eds.), *Human development and the life course: Multidisciplinary perspectives* (pp. 217–245). Hillsdale, NJ: Erlbaum.

McCall, R. B. (1979). Individual differences in the pattern of habituation at 5 and 10 months of age. *Developmental Psychology, 15,* 558–568.

McClelland, D. C. (1985). How motives, skills, and values determine what people do. *American Psychologist, 40,* 812–825.

McClelland, D. C.; Atkinson, J. W.; Clark, R. A.; & Lowell, E. L. (1953). *The achievement motive.* New York: Appleton-Century-Crofts.

McTavish, D. G. (1971). Perceptions of old people: A review of research methodologies and findings. *The Gerontologist, 11,* 90–101.

Merton, R. K. (1968). The Matthew effect in science: The reward and communication systems of science. *Science, 199,* 55–63.

(1973). *The sociology of science: Theoretical and empirical investigations.* Chicago: University of Chicago Press.

Miller, R. A. (1990). Aging and the immune response. In E. L. Schneider & J. W. Rowe (Eds.), *Handbook of the biology of aging,* 3rd ed. (pp. 157–180). New York: Academic Press.

Milligan, W. L.; Powell, D. A.; Harley, C.; & Furchtgott, E. (1985). Physical health correlates of attitudes toward aging in the elderly. *Experimental Aging Research, 11,* 75–80.

Mischel, W.; Shoda, Y.; & Rodriguez, M. L. (1989). Delay of gratification in children. *Science, 244,* 933–938.

Modell, J. (1980). Normative aspects of American marriage timing since World War II. *Journal of Family History, 5,* 210–234.

Modell, J.; Furstenberg, F. F., Jr.; & Hershberg, T. (1976). Social change and transitions to adulthood in historical perspective. *Journal of Family History, 1,* 7–32.

Modell, J.; Furstenberg, F. F.; & Strong, D. (1978). The timing of marriage in the transition to adulthood: Continuity and change, 1860–1975. *American Journal of Sociology, 84,* 120–150.

Molenaar, P. C. M.; Boomsma, D. I.; & Dolan, D. V. (1993). A third source of developmental differences. *Behavior Genetics, 23,* 519–524.

Montepare, J. M., & Lachman, M. E. (1989). "You're only as old as you feel": Self-perceptions of age, fears of aging, and life satisfaction from adolescence to old age. *Psychology and Aging, 4,* 73–78.

Mueller, J. H.; Wonderlich, S.; & Dugan, K. (1986). Self-referent processing of age-specific material. *Psychology and Aging, 1,* 293–299.

Murray, H. A. (1938). *Exploration in personality.* New York: Oxford University Press.

(1951). Toward a classification of interaction. In T. Parsons & E. A. Shils (Eds.), *Toward a general theory of action* (pp. 434–464). Cambridge, MA: Harvard University Press.

Nardi, A. H. (1973). Person-perception research and the perception of life-span development. In A. B. Sørensen, F. E. Weinert, & L. R. Sherrod (Eds.), *Human development and the life course: Multidisciplinary perspectives* (pp. 285–301). Hillsdale, NJ: Erlbaum.

Nelson, A. E., & Dannefer, D. (1992). Aged heterogeneity: Fact or fiction? The fate of diversity in gerontological research. *Gerontologist, 32*, 17–23.

Neugarten, B. L. (1979). Time, age, and the life cycle. *American Journal of Psychiatry, 136*, 887–894.

Neugarten, B. L.; Moore, J. W.; & Lowe, J. C. (1965). Age norms, age constraints, and adult socialization. *American Journal of Sociology, 70*, 710–717.

Neugarten, B. L., & Peterson, W. A. (1957). A study of the American age-grade system. *Proceedings of the Fourth Congress of the International Association of Gerontology, 144*, 497–502.

Nolen-Hoeksema, S.; Girgus, J. S.; & Seligman, M. E. P. (1992). Predictors and consequences of childhood symptoms: A 5-year longitudinal study. *Journal of Abnormal Psychology, 101*, 405–422.

Norem, J. K., & Cantor, N. (1986a). Defensive pessimism: Harnessing anxiety as motivation. *Journal of Personality and Social Psychology, 51*, 1208–1217.

(1986b). Anticipatory and post hoc cushioning strategies: Optimism and defensive pessimism in "risky" situations. *Cognitive Therapy and Research, 10*, 347–362.

Nurmi, J.-E. (1989a). Adolescents' orientation to the future. *Commentationes Scientiarum Socialium, 39*.

(1989b). Development of orientation to the future during early adolescence: A four-year longitudinal study and two cross-sectional comparisons. *International Journal of Psychology, 24*, 195–214.

(1991). How do adolescents see their future? A review of the development of future orientation and planning. *Developmental Review, 11*, 1–59.

(1992). Age differences in adult life goals, concerns, and their temporal extension: A life course approach to future-oriented motivation. *International Journal of Behavioral Development, 15*, 487–508.

(1993). Adolescent development in an age-graded context: The role of personal beliefs, goals, and strategies in the tackling of developmental tasks and standards. *International Journal of Behavioral Development, 16*, 169–189.

Nurmi, J.-E.; Pulliainen, H.; & Salmela-Aro, K. (1992). Age differences in adults' control beliefs related to life goals and concerns. *Psychology and Aging, 7*, 194–196.

Oerter, R. (1978). Zur Dynamik von Entwicklungsaufgaben im menschlichen Lebenslauf [The dynamic of developmental tasks across the human life span]. In R. Oerter (Ed.), *Entwicklung als lebenslanger Prozess* (pp. 66–110). Hamburg: Hoffmann & Campe.

(1986). Developmental tasks through the life span: A new approach to an old concept. In P. B. Baltes, D. L. Featherman, & R. M. Lerner (Eds.), *Life-span development and behavior*, Vol.7 (pp. 233–269). Hillsdale, NJ: Erlbaum.

O'Gorman, H. J. (1980). False consciousness of kind: Pluralistic ignorance among the aged. *Research on Aging, 2*, 105–128.

Olbrich, E. (1981). Normative Uebergänge im menschlichen Lebenslauf: Entwicklungskrisen oder Herausforderungen [Normative transitions in the human life course: Developmental crises of developmental challenges]. In

S.-H. Filipp (Ed.), *Kritische Lebensereignisse* (pp. 128–138). Munich: Urban & Schwarzenberg.

(1985). Coping and development in the later years: A process-oriented approach to personality and development. In J. M. A. Munnichs, P. Mussen, E. Olbrich, & P. Coleman (Eds.), *Life span and change in a gerontological perspective* (pp. 42–62). Orlando, FL: Academic Press.

Olbrich, E., & Thomae, H. (1978). Empirical findings to a cognitive theory of aging. *International Journal of Behavioral Development, 1*, 67–82.

Palmore, E. (1977). Facts on aging: A short quiz. *The Gerontologist, 17*, 315–320.

Palys, T. S., & Little, B. R. (1983). Perceived life satisfaction and the organization of personal project systems. *Journal of Personality and Social Psychology, 44*, 1221–1230.

Papousek, H. (1967). Experimental studies of appetitional behavior in human newborns and infants. In H. W. Stevenson, E. H. Hess, & H. L. Rheingold (Eds.), *Early behavior: Comparative developmental approaches* (pp. 249–277). New York: Wiley & Sons.

Parsons, T. (1951). *The social system.* London: Routledge & Kegan Paul.

Passuth, P. M., & Maines, D. R. (1981). *Transformations in age norms and age constraints: Evidence bearing on the age-irrelevancy hypothesis.* Paper presented at the World Congress on Gerontology, Hamburg.

Peng, Y. (1993). Primary and secondary control in American and Chinese-American adults: Cross-cultural and life-span developmental perspectives. Unpublished doctoral dissertation, Brandeis University, Waltham, MA.

Peng, Y., & Lachman, M. E. (1993). *Primary and secondary control: Age and cultural differences.* 101st annual Convention of the American Psychological Association, Toronto.

Piaget, J. (1967). *Biologie und Erkenntnis: Ueber die Beziehung zwischen organischen Regulationen und kognitiven Prozessen* [Biology and insight: On the relationship between organic regulation and cognitive processes]. Tübingen: Fischer.

Pincus, A.; Wood, V.; & Kondrat, R. (1974). *Perceptions of age appropriate activities and roles.* Paper presented at the 27th annual meeting of the Gerontological Society, Portland, OR.

Plath, D. W., & Ikeda, K. (1975). After coming of age: Adult awareness of age norms. In T. R. Williams (Ed.), *Socialization and communication in primary groups* (pp. 107–123). The Hague: Mouton.

Plomin, R. (1986). *Development, genetics, and psychology.* Hillsdale, NJ: Erlbaum.

Quetelet, A. (1835). *Sur l'homme et de développement de ses facultés* [On the human being and the development of his abilities]. Paris: Bachelier.

Rapkin, B. D., & Fischer, K. (1992a). Framing the construct of life satisfaction in terms of older adults' personal goals. *Psychology and Aging, 7*, 138–149.

(1992b). Personal goals of older adults: Issues in assessment and prediction. *Psychology and Aging, 7*, 127–137.

Reese, H. W., & Overton, W. F. (1970). Models of development and theories of development. In L. R. Goulet & P. B. Baltes (Eds.), *Life-span developmental psychology: Research and theory* (pp. 115–145). New York: Academic Press.

Reich, J. W., & Zautra, A. J. (1989). A perceived control intervention for at-risk older adults. *Psychology and Aging, 4*, 415–425.

Reinert, G. (1979). Prolegomena to a history of life-span developmental psychology. In P. B. Baltes & O. G. Brim, Jr. (Eds.), *Life-span development and behavior*, Vol. 2 (pp. 205–254). New York: Academic Press.

Reker, G. T.; Peacock, E. J.; & Wong, P. T. P. (1987). Meaning and purpose in life and well-being: A life-span perspective. *Journal of Gerontology, 42*, 44–49.

Reno, R. (1979). Attribution for success and failure as a function of perceived age. *Journal of Gerontology, 34*, 709–715.

Riley, M. W. (1985). Age strata in social systems. In R. H. Binstock & E. Shanas (Eds.), *Handbook of aging and the social sciences*, 2d ed (pp. 369–411). New York: Van Nostrand Reinhold.

(1986). Overview and highlights of a sociological perspective. In A. Sørensen, F. Weinert, & L. Sherrod (Eds.), *Human development and the life course: Multidisciplinary perspectives* (pp. 153–175). Hillsdale, NJ: Erlbaum.

Riley, M. W.; Johnson, M. E.; & Foner, A. (Eds.). (1972). *Aging and society: A sociology of age stratification*, Vol. 3. New York: Russell Sage Foundation.

Rindfuss, R. R.; Swicegood, C. G.; & Rosenfeld, R. A. (1987). Disorder in the life course: How common and does it matter? *American Sociological Review, 52*, 785–801.

Rodin, J. (1986). Health, control, and aging. In M. M. Baltes & P. B. Baltes (Eds.), *The psychology of control and aging* (pp. 139–165). Hillsdale, NJ: Erlbaum.

Rodin, J., & Langer, E. J. (1978). Long term effects of a control-relevant intervention with the institutionalized aged. *Journal of Personality and Social Psychology, 35*, 897–902.

(1980). Aging labels: The decline of control and the fall of self-esteem. *Journal of Social Issues, 36*, 12–29.

Rose, M. (1991). *Evolutionary biology of aging*. New York: Oxford University Press.

Rosenbaum, J. E. (1984). *Career mobility in a corporate hierarchy*. New York: Academic Press.

Rosenberg, M. (1965). *Society and the adolescent self-image*. Princeton, NJ: Princeton University Press.

Roth, J. A. (1963). *Timetables; Structuring the passage of time in hospital treatment and other careers*. Indianapolis, IN: Bobbs-Merrill.

Rothbaum, F. (1983). Aging and age stereotypes. *Social Cognition, 2*, 171–184.

Rothbaum, F.; Weisz, J. R.; & Snyder, S. S. (1982). Changing the world and changing the self: A two-process model of perceived control. *Journal of Personality and Social Psychology, 42*, 5–37.

Rotter, J. B. (1966). Generalized expectancies for internal versus external control of reinforcement. *Psychological Monographs, 80*.

Rowe, J. W., & Kahn, R. L. (1987). Human aging: Usual and successful. *Science, 237*, 143–149.

Rozin, P. (1976). The evolution of intelligence and access to the cognitive unconscious. In J. A. Sprague & A. N. Epstein (Eds.), *Progress in Psychobiology and Physiological Psychology*, Vol. 6 (pp. 245–280). New York: Academic Press.

Rudinger, G., & Thomae, H. (1990). The Bonn longitudinal study of aging: Coping, life adjustment, and life satisfaction. In P. B. Baltes & M. M. Baltes (Eds.), *Successful aging: Perspectives from the behavioral sciences* (pp. 265–295). New York: Cambridge University Press.

Ruehlman, L. S., & Wolchik, S. A. (1988). Personal goals and interpersonal support and hindrance as factors in psychological distress and well-being. *Journal of Personality and Social Psychology, 55*, 293–301.

Ryder, N. B. (1965). The cohort as a concept in the study of social change. *American Sociological Review, 30,* 843–861.

Ryff, C. D. (1984). Personality development from the inside: The subjective experience of change in adulthood and aging. In P. B. Baltes, & O. G. Brim, Jr. (Eds.), *Life-span development and behavior,* Vol. 6 (pp. 243–279). New York: Academic Press.

(1985). The subjective experience of life-span transitions. In A. S. Rossi (Ed.), *Gender and the life course* (pp. 97–113). Hawthorne, NY: Aldine.

(1991). Possible selves in adulthood and old age: A tale of shifting horizons. *Psychology and Aging, 6,* 286–295.

Ryff, C. D., & Heincke, S. G. (1983). Subjective organization of personality in adulthood and aging. *Journal of Personality and Social Psychology, 44,* 807–816.

Salmela-Aro, K. (1992). Struggling with self: The personal projects of students seeking psychological counselling. *Scandinavian Journal of Psychology, 33,* 330–338.

Salthouse, T. A. (1985). *A theory of cognitive aging.* Amsterdam: North Holland.

Schaie, K. W. (1965). A general model for the study of developmental problems. *Psychological Bulletin, 64,* 92–107.

(1989). Individual differences in rate of cognitive change in adulthood. In V. L. Bengtson & K. W. Schaie (Eds.), *The course of later life: Research and reflections* (pp. 65–85). New York: Springer.

Schaie, K. W., & Baltes, P. B. (1975). On sequential strategies in developmental research: Description or explanation? *Human Development, 18,* 384–390.

Schaie, K. W., & Hertzog, C. (1983). Fourteen-year cohort-sequential analyses of adult intellectual development. *Developmental Psychology, 19,* 531–543.

Scheier, M. F., & Carver, C. S. (1992). Effects of optimism on psychological and physical well-being: Theoretical overview and empirical update. *Cognitive Therapy and Research, 16,* 201–228.

Scheier, M. F.; Weintraub, J. K.; & Carver, C. S. (1986). Coping with stress: Divergent strategies of optimists and pessimists. *Journal of Personality and Social Psychology, 51,* 1257–1264.

Schmitz-Scherzer, R., & Thomae, H. (1983). Consistency and change of behavior in old age. Findings from the Bonn longitudinal study of aging. In K. W. Schaie (Ed.), *Longitudinal studies of adult psychological development* (pp. 191–221). New York: Guilford Press.

Schneider, E. L., & Rowe, J. W. (Eds.). (1990). *Handbook of the biology of aging* (3d ed.). San Diego, CA: Academic Press.

Schonfield, D. (1982). Who is stereotyping whom and why? *The Gerontologist, 22,* 267–272.

Schulz, R. (1976). Effects of control and predictability on the physical and psychological well-being of the institutionalized aged. *Journal of Personality and Social Psychology, 33,* 563–573.

(1986). Successful aging: Balancing primary and secondary control. *Adult Development and Aging News, 13,* 2–4.

Schulz, R., & Curnow, C. (1988). Peak performance and age among superathletes: Track and field, swimming, baseball, tennis, and golf. *Journal of Gerontology: Psychological Sciences, 43,* 113–120.

Schulz, R., & Decker, S. (1985). Long-term adjustment to physical disability: The role of social support, perceived control, and self-blame. *Journal of Personality and Social Psychology, 48,* 1162–1172.

Schulz, R., & Fritz, S. (1988). Origins of stereotypes of the elderly: An experimental study of the self–other discrepancy. *Experimental Aging Research, 13,* 189–195.

Schulz, R., & Hanusa, B. H. (1980). Experimental social gerontology: A social psychological perspective. *Journal of Social Issues, 36,* 30–46.

Schulz, R., & Heckhausen, J. (1996). A life-span model of successful aging. *American Psychologist, 51,* 702–714.

    (1997). Emotions and control: A life-span perspective. In M. P. Lawton and K. W. Schaie (Eds.), *Annual Review of Gerontology and Geriatrics,* Vol. 17 (pp. 185–205). New York: Springer.

Schulz, R.; Heckhausen, J.; & Locher, J. (1991). Adult development, control, and adaptive functioning. *Journal of Social Issues, 47,* 177–196.

Schulz, R.; Heckhausen, J.; & O'Brien, A. T. (1994). Control and the disablement process in the elderly. *Journal of Social Behavior and Personality, 9,* 139–152.

Schulz, R.; Musa, J.; Staszewski, J.; & Siegler, R. S. (in press). The relationship between age and major league baseball performance: Implications for development. *Psychology and Aging.*

Schulz, R., & Rau, M. T. (1985). Social support through the life course. In S. Cohen & L. Syme (Eds.), *Social support and health* (pp. 129–149). New York: Academic Press.

Schulz, R.; Tompkins, C. A.; & Rau, M. T. (1988). A longitudinal study of the psychosocial impact of stroke on primary support persons. *Psychology and Aging, 3,* 131–141.

Schwarzer, R. (1992). *Self-efficacy: Thought control of action.* Washington, DC: Hemisphere.

    (1994). Optimistische Kompetenzerwartung: Zur Erfassung einer personellen Bewältigungsreserve [Optimistic competence expectancies: Assessment of personal coping resources]. *Diagnostica, 40,* 105–123.

Seginer, R.; Trommsdorff, G.; & Essau, C. (1993). Adolescent control beliefs: Cross-cultural variations of primary and secondary orientations. *International Journal of Behavioral Development, 16,* 243–260.

Seifert, K. H. (1969). *Grundformen und theoretische Perspektiven psychologischer Kompensation* [Theoretical perspectives on the nature of psychological compensation]. Meisenheim am Gran: Hain.

Seligman, M. E. P. (1975). *Helplessness: On depression, development, and death.* San Francisco, CA: Freeman.

Settersten, R. (1992). *Informal deadlines for family transitions in men's and women's lives.* Paper presented at the Annual Scientific Meeting of the Gerontological Society of America, Washington, DC, September 1992.

Shanan, J., & Kedar, H. S. (1979–1980). Phenomenological structuring of the adult life-span as a function of age and sex. *International Journal of Aging and Human Development, 10,* 343–357.

Sherman, N. C., & Gold, J. A. (1978). Perceptions of ideal and typical middle and old age. *International Journal of Aging and Human Development, 9,* 67–73.

Sherman, N. C.; Gold, J. A.; & Sherman, M. F. (1978). Attribution theory and evaluations of older men among college students, their parents, and grandparents. *Personality and Social Psychology Bulletin, 4,* 440–442.

Silbereisen, R. K.; Eyferth, K.; & Rudinger, G. (Eds.). (1986). *Development as action in context. Problem behavior and normal youth development.* Berlin: Springer.

Simonton, D. K. (1984). *Genius, creativity, and leadership: Historical inquiries.* Cambridge, MA: Harvard University Press.

——— (1988). *Scientific genius: A psychology of science.* Cambridge: Cambridge University Press.

——— (1995). *Greatness.* New York: Guilford Press.

Singh, D. (1970). Preference for bar-pressing to obtain reward over freeloading in rats and children. *Journal of Comparative and Physiological Psychology, 73,* 320–327.

Skinner, E. A. (1985). Action, control judgments, and the structure of control experience. *Psychological Review, 92,* 39–58.

Smith, J.; Woodward, N. J.; Wallston, B. S.; & Wallston, K. A. (1988). Health care implications of desire and expectancy for control in elderly adults. *Journal of Gerontology, 43,* 1–7.

Snyder, M. L.; Stephan, W. G.; & Rosenfield, D. (1978). Attributional egotism. In J. H. Harvey, W. Ickes, & R. F. Kidd (Eds.), *New directions in attribution research,* Vol. 2 (pp. 91–117). Hillsdale, NJ: Erlbaum.

Sofer, C. (1970). *Men in mid-career.* New York: Cambridge University Press.

Sørensen, A. B. (1986). Social structure and mechanisms of life-course processes. In A. B. Sørensen, F. E. Weinert, & L. R. Sherrod (Eds.). *Human development and the life course: Multidisciplinary perspectives* (pp. 177–197). Hillsdale, NJ: Erlbaum.

Sørensen, A. B.; Weinert, F. E.; & Sherrod, L. R. (Eds.). (1986). *Human development and the life course: Multidisciplinary perspectives.* Hillsdale, NJ: Erlbaum.

Statistisches Bundesamt (Ed.). (1993). *Statistisches Jahrbuch für die Bundesrepublik Deutschland* [Statistical yearbook for the Federal Republic of Germany]. Stuttgart: Kohlhammer.

Staudinger, U. M.; Marsiske, M.; & Baltes, P. B. (1993). Resilience and levels of reserve capacity in later adulthood: Perspectives from life-span theory. *Development and Psychopathology, 5,* 541–566.

Suls, J., & Wills, T. A. (1991). *Social comparison: Contemporary theory and research.* Hillsdale, NJ: Erlbaum.

Swan, G. E.; Dame, A.; & Carmelli, D. (1991). Involuntary retirement, Type A behavior, and current functioning in elderly men: 27-year follow-up of the western collaborative group study. *Psychology and Aging, 6,* 384–391.

Taylor, S. E.; Buunk, B. P.; & Aspinwall, L. G. (1990). Social comparison, stress, and coping. *Personality and Social Psychology Bulletin, 16,* 74–89.

Taylor, S. E., & Gollwitzer, P. M. (1995). Effects of mindset on positive illusions. *Journal of Personality and Social Psychology, 69,* 213–226.

Taylor, S. E.; Kemeney, M. E.; & Aspinwall, L. G. (1992). Optimism, coping, psychological distress, and high-risk sexual behavior among men at risk for acquired immunodeficiency syndrome (AIDS). *Journal of Personality and Social Psychology, 63,* 460–473.

Taylor, S. E., & Lobel, M. (1989). Social comparison activity under threat: Downward evaluation and upward contacts. *Psychological Review, 96,* 569–575.

Taylor, S. E.; Wood, J. V.; & Lichtman, R. R. (1984). Attributions, beliefs about control, and adjustment to breast cancer. *Journal of Personality and Social Psychology, 46,* 489–502.

Tesch-Römer, C. (1993). *Coping with hearing loss in old age.* Paper presented at the 46th annual scientific meeting of the Gerontological Society of America, New Orleans, November 1993.

Tetens, J. N. (1777). *Philosophische Versuche über die menschliche Natur und ihre Entwicklung* [Philosophical considerations about human nature and its development]. Leipzig: Weidmanns Erben und Reich.

Thomae, H. (1959). *Handbuch der Psychologie, Vol. 3: Entwicklungspsychologie* [Handbook of Psychology, Vol. 3: Developmental psychology] (2d ed.). Göttingen: Hogrefe.

(1970). Theory of aging and cognitive theory of personality. *Human Development, 12,* 1–16.

(1975). The developmental-task approach to a theory of aging. *Zeitschrift für Gerontologie, 8,* 125–137.

(1979). The concept of development and life-span developmental psychology. In P. B. Baltes & O. G. Brim, Jr. (Eds.), *Life-span development and behavior,* Vol. 2 (pp. 281–312). New York: Academic Press.

(1983). *Alternsstile und Altersschicksale. Ein Beitrag zur Differentiellen Gerontologie* [Styles of aging and fate: A contribution to differential gerontology]. Bern: Huber.

(1988). *Das Individuum und seine Welt. Eine Persönlichkeitstheorie* [The individual and his/her world. A personality theory] (2d ed.). Göttingen: Hogrefe.

(1992). Contributions of longitudinal research to a cognitive theory of adjustment to aging. *European Journal of Personality, 6,* 157–175.

(Ed.). (1976). *Patterns of aging: Findings from the Bonn longitudinal study of aging.* Basel: Karger.

Thomae, H., & Lehr, U. (1986). Stages, crises, conflicts, and life-span development. In A. B. Sørensen, F. E. Weinert, & L. R. Sherrod (Eds.), *Human development and the life course: Multidisciplinary perspectives* (pp. 343–375). Hillsdale, NJ: Erlbaum.

Thomas, E. C., & Yamamoto, K. (1975). Attitudes toward age: An exploration in school-age children. *International Journal of Aging and Human Development, 6,* 117–129.

Thomas, W. C. (1981). The expectation gap and the stereotype of the stereotype: Images of old people. *The Gerontologist, 21,* 402–407.

Thorson, J. A.; Whatley, J. L.; & Hancock, K. A. (1974). Attitudes toward the aged as a function of age and education. *The Gerontologist, 14,* 316–318.

Timko, C., & Moos, R. H. (1990). Determinants of interpersonal support and self-direction in group residential facilities. *Journal of Gerontology, 45,* 184–192.

Tompkins, C. A.; Schulz, R.; & Rau, M. T. (1988). Post-stroke depression in primary support persons. *Journal of Consulting and Clinical Psychology, 56,* 502–508.

Tough, A. (1982). *Intentional changes. A fresh approach to helping people change.* Chicago, IL: Follett.

Trommsdorff, G.; Essau, C.; & Seginer, R. (1994). *Primacy of primary or secondary control in individualistic versus collectivistic cultures.* Paper presented at the 13th Biennial Meeting of the International Society for the Study of Behavioral Development, Amsterdam, Netherlands, June–July 1994.

Tuckman, J., & Lorge, I. (1952). The best years of life: A study in ranking. *Journal of Psychology, 34,* 137–149.

(1954). Old people's appraisal of adjustment over the life span. *Journal of Personality, 22,* 417–422.

Turkheimer, E., & Gottesman, I. I. (1991). Individual differences and the canalization of human behavior. *Developmental Psychology, 27,* 18–22.

Uhlenberg, P. (1974). Cohort variations in family life cycle experiences of U.S. females. *Journal of Marriage and the Family, 36*, 284–292.

Uttal, D. H., & Perlmutter, M. (1989). Toward a broader conceptualization of development: The role of gains and losses across the life span. *Developmental Review, 9*, 101–132.

Van den Daele, L. D. (1974). Infrastructure and transition in developmental analysis. *Human Development, 17*, 1–23.

Verbrugge, L. M., & Jette, A. M. (1994). The disablement process. *Social Science and Medicine, 38*, 1–14.

Vygotsky, L. S. (1978). *Mind in society.* Cambridge, MA: Harvard University Press.

Waddington, C. H. (1957). *The strategy of the genes.* London: Allen & Unwin.

——— (1975). *The evolution of the evolutionist.* Edinburgh: Edinburgh University Press.

Wadsworth, M., & Ford, D. H. (1983). Assessment of personal goal hierarchies. *Journal of Counseling Psychology, 30*, 514–526.

Wahl, H.-W. (1991). Dependence in the elderly from an interactional point of view: Verbal and observational data. *Psychology and Aging, 6*, 238–246.

Walberg, H. J., & Tsai, S.-L. (1983). Matthew effects in education. *American Educational Research Journal, 20*, 359–373.

Watson, J. S. (1966). The development and generalization of 'contingency awareness' in early infancy: Some hypotheses. *Merrill-Palmer Quarterly, 12*, 123–135.

——— (1972). Smiling, cooing, and 'the Game.' *Merrill-Palmer Quarterly, 18*, 323–339.

Weinberger, L. E., & Millham, J. (1975). A multi-dimensional multiple method analysis of attitudes toward the elderly. *Journal of Gerontology, 30*, 343–348.

Weiner, B. (1972). *Theories of motivation.* Chicago, IL: Markham.

Weiner, B.; Frieze, I. H.; Kukla, A.; Reed, L.; Rest, S.; & Rosenbaum, R. M. (1971). *Perceiving the causes of success and failure.* New York: Springer.

Weiner, B.; Heckhausen, H.; Meyer, W.-U.; & Cook, R. E. (1972). Causal ascriptions and achievement behavior: A conceptual analysis of effort and re-analysis of locus of control. *Journal of Personality and Social Psychology, 21*, 239–248.

Weiner, B., & Kukla, A. (1970). An attributional analysis of achievement motivation. *Journal of Personality and Social Psychology, 15*, 1–20.

Weisz, J. R. (1980). Developmental change in perceived control: Recognizing noncontingency in the laboratory and perceiving it in the world. *Developmental Psychology, 16*, 385–390.

——— (1981). Illusory contingency in children at the state fair. *Developmental Psychology, 17*, 481–489.

——— (1983). Can I control it? The pursuit of veridical answers across the life span. In P. B. Baltes & O. G. Brim, Jr. (Eds.), *Life-span development and behavior,* Vol. 3 (pp. 233–300). New York: Academic Press.

Weisz, J. R.; Rothbaum, F. M.; & Blackburn, T. C. (1984). Standing out and standing in: The psychology of control in America and Japan. *American Psychologist, 39*, 955–969.

Weisz, J. R.; Yeates, K. O.; Robertson, D.; & Beckham, J. C. (1982). Perceived contingency of skill and chance events: A developmental analysis. *Developmental Psychology, 18*, 898–905.

Wertlieb, D.; Weigel, C.; & Feldstein, M. (1987). Measuring children's coping. *American Journal of Orthopsychiatry, 57*, 548–560.

Wheeler, L., & Miyake, K. (1992). Social comparison in everyday life. *Journal of Personality and Social Psychology, 62*, 760–773.

White, R. W. (1959). Motivation reconsidered: The concept of competence. *Psychological Review, 66*, 297–333.

Wicklund, R. A., & Gollwitzer, P. M. (1981). Symbolic self-completion, attempted influences, and self-deprecation. *Basic and Applied Social Psychology, 2*, 89–114.

Williams, G. C. (1957). Pleiotropy, natural selection, and the evolution of senescence. *Evolution, 11*, 398–411.

Williamson, G., & Schulz, R. (1992a). Physical illness and symptoms of depression among elderly outpatients. *Psychology and Aging, 7*, 343–351.

  (1992b). Pain, activity restriction, and symptoms of depression among community-residing elderly. *Journal of Gerontology: Psychological Sciences, 47*, 367–372.

Wills, T. A. (1981). Downward comparison principles in social psychology. *Psychological Bulletin, 90*, 245–271.

Wilson, E. O. (1980). *Sociobiology*. Cambridge, MA: Belknap Press of Harvard University Press.

Wood, J. V. (1989). Theory and research concerning social comparison of personal attributes. *Psychological Bulletin, 106*, 231–248.

Wood, J. V., & Taylor, K. L. (1991). Serving self-relevant goals through social comparison. In J. Suls & T. A. Wills (Eds.), *Social comparison: Contemporary theory and research* (pp. 23–49). Hillsdale, NJ: Erlbaum.

Wood, V. (1973). *Role allocation as a function of age*. Paper presented at the 26th annual meeting of the Gerontological Society, Miami Beach, FL.

Wrosch, C. (1994). *Adaptivität sozialer Vergleiche: Der Einfluß interindividueller Unterschiede in primären und sekundären Kontrollstrategien* [Adaptiveness of social comparisons: The influence of interindividual differences in primary and secondary control strategies]. Unpublished master's thesis, Institut für Psychologie, Freie Universität Berlin.

Wrosch, C., & Heckhausen, J. (1996a). Entwicklungsregulation im Partnerschaftsbereich: Primäre und sekundäre Kontrolle bei kürzlich gebundenen und getrennten Personen im mittleren Erwachsenenalter [Developmental regulation in partnership relations: Primary and secondary control in recently committed and separated adults in mid-life]. Paper presented at the 40th Congress of the Deutsche Gesellschaft für Psychologie, Munich, September 1996.

  (1996b). Adaptivität sozialer Vergleiche: Entwicklungsregulation durch primäre und sekundäre Kontrolle [Adaptiveness of social comparisons: Developmental regulation via primary and secondary control]. *Zeitschrift für Entwicklungspsychologie und Pädagogische Psychologie, 28*, 126–147.

  (in press). Being on-time or off-time: Developmental deadlines for regulating one's own development. To appear in: A. N. Peret-Clermont, J. M. Barrelet, A. Flammer, D. Miéville, J. F. Perret, & W. Perrig (Eds.), *Mind and time*. Göttingen: Hogrefe.

Wundt, W. (1874). *Grundzüge der physiologischen Psychologie* [Foundations of physiological psychology]. Leipzig: Engelmann.

Yates, E., & Benton, L. A. (1995). Biological senescence: Loss of integration and resilience. *Canadian Journal on Aging, 14*, 106–120.

Zepelin, H.; Sills, R. A.; & Heath, M. W. (1986–7). Is age becoming irrelevant? An exploratory study of perceived age norms. *International Journal of Aging and Human Development, 24*, 241–256.

Zirkel, S. A. (1992). Developing independence in a life transition: Investing the self in the concerns of the day. *Journal of Personality and Social Psychology, 62,* 506–521.

Zirkel, S., & Cantor, N. (1990). Personal construal of life tasks: Those who struggle for independence. *Journal of Personality and Social Psychology, 58,* 172–185.

Name Index

Subject Index